THE CONSTITUTION OF MYANMAR

This timely and accessible book is the first to provide a thorough analysis of the 2008 Constitution of Myanmar (Burma) in its historical, political and social context. The book identifies and articulates the principles of the Constitution through an in-depth analysis of legal and political processes and practices, particularly since the 1990s. The core argument of this book is that the 2008 Constitution is crucial to the establishment and maintenance of the military-state. The military-state promotes the leadership role of the military in governance based on a set of ideological commitments and a centralised form of organisation based on the concept of the Union. The book develops this argument by demonstrating how the process of constitution-making and the substance of the 2008 Constitution contribute to its lack of credibility and fuel demands for reform. The vision offered by the 2008 Constitution and its associated institutions has been the subject of fierce contestation, not least, for example, due to concerns over the militarisation of the state. This book is animated by debates over fundamental ideas such as the nature of democracy, the possibility of peace and federalism, the relationship between the executive and the legislature, relations between the Union government and sub-national governments, debates over judicial independence and the oversized role of the Tatmadaw (armed forces). Central to the future of the Constitution and the military-state is the role of the Tatmadaw, which will be a key determinant in any potential shift from the present highly centralised, partly-democratic Union to a federal or decentralised democratic system of governance.

T0315825

Pictorial Narrative

Myanmar 2008: The Cyclone Nargis Constitution

Two images predominate to form the foundations of this composition. Cyclone Nargis devastated the Irrawaddy delta region of lower Myanmar in May 2008: an estimated 200,000 people were killed, while 2.5 million suffered serious disruption. In the same month, notwithstanding this tragedy, the armed forces (Tatmadaw) held a referendum to endorse the 2008 Constitution. On the top right-hand side we find the vortex of the cyclone, with the year 2008 emblazoned in its wake. The upper lighter orange pyramid contains the deconstructed emblems of each of the armed forces (star, wings and anchor) signifying the ever-present and all-powerful military-state. A deeper orange central pyramid represents Naypyidaw, Myanmar's seat for the administration of the Union (portrayed here by deconstructed architectural features). In the top left, a purple triangle containing the image of army officers represents British colonialism, which ended in 1947. Immediately below (taken from a contemporary propaganda poster) a trio of individuals (construction worker, farmer and solider) stand for the 'Burmese way to socialism' and General Ne Win's dictatorial and brutal socialist programme in the 1960s–80s. This is counterbalanced by a peacock denoting the National League for Democracy, the pro-democratic political party, the Konbaung monarchy and the anti-colonial movement. An assembly of ethnic groups fronted by General Aung San are shown signing the Panglong Agreement in 1947 to acknowledge the autonomy for the Chin, Kachin and Shan peoples within a united Burma. The congregation continuing across the foreground also demonstrates Myanmar's social diversity. Rudyard Kipling on the far right personifies a 19th century romantic view of Burma.

Putachad
Artist

Constitutional Systems of the World
General Editors: Benjamin L Berger, Rosalind Dixon,
Andrew Harding, Heinz Klug, and Peter Leyland

In the era of globalisation, issues of constitutional law and good governance are being seen increasingly as vital issues in all types of society. Since the end of the Cold War, there have been dramatic developments in democratic and legal reform, and post-conflict societies are also in the throes of reconstructing their governance systems. Even societies already firmly based on constitutional governance and the rule of law have undergone constitutional change and experimentation with new forms of governance; and their constitutional systems are increasingly subjected to comparative analysis and transplantation. Constitutional texts for practically every country in the world are now easily available on the internet. However, texts which enable one to understand the true context, purposes, interpretation and incidents of a constitutional system are much harder to locate, and are often extremely detailed and descriptive. This series seeks to provide scholars and students with accessible introductions to the constitutional systems of the world, supplying both a road map for the novice and, at the same time, a deeper understanding of the key historical, political and legal events which have shaped the constitutional landscape of each country. Each book in this series deals with a single country, or a group of countries with a common constitutional history, and each author is an expert in their field.

Published volumes

The Constitution of the United Kingdom; The Constitution of the United States; The Constitution of Vietnam; The Constitution of South Africa; The Constitution of Japan; The Constitution of Germany; The Constitution of Finland; The Constitution of Australia; The Constitution of the Republic of Austria; The Constitution of the Russian Federation; The Constitutional System of Thailand; The Constitution of Malaysia; The Constitution of China; The Constitution of Indonesia; The Constitution of France; The Constitution of Spain; The Constitution of Mexico; The Constitution of Israel; The Constitutional Systems of the Commonwealth Caribbean; The Constitution of Canada; The Constitution of Singapore; The Constitution of Belgium; The Constitution of Taiwan; The Constitution of Romania; The Constitutional Systems of the Independent Central Asian States; The Constitution of India; The Constitution of Pakistan; The Constitution of Ireland; The Constitution of Brazil; The Constitution of Myanmar

Link to series website

www.bloomsburyprofessional.com/uk/series/
constitutional-systems-of-the-world

The Constitution of Myanmar

A Contextual Analysis

Melissa Crouch

·HART·

OXFORD · LONDON · NEW YORK · NEW DELHI · SYDNEY

Hart Publishing
Bloomsbury Publishing Plc
Kemp House, Chawley Park, Cumnor Hill, Oxford, OX2 9PH, UK

HART PUBLISHING, the Hart/Stag logo, BLOOMSBURY and the Diana logo are
trademarks of Bloomsbury Publishing Plc

First published in Great Britain 2019
First published in hardback, 2019
Paperback edition, 2020

A catalogue record for this book is available from the British Library.

Library of Congress Cataloging-in-Publication data

Names: Crouch, Melissa, author.
Title: The Constitution of Myanmar: a contextual analysis / Melissa Crouch.
Description: Oxford [UK]; Chicago, Illinois: Hart Publishing, 2019. | Series: Constitutional
systems of the world | Includes bibliographical references and index.
Identifiers: LCCN 2019021086 (print) | LCCN 2019021903 (ebook) |
ISBN 9781509927364 (EPub) | ISBN 9781509927357 (hardback)
Subjects: LCSH: Constitutional law—Burma. | Constitutions—Burma.
Classification: LCC KNL1750 (ebook) | LCC KNL1750 .C76 2019 (print) | DDC 342.59102—dc23
LC record available at https://lccn.loc.gov/2019021086

ISBN: HB: 978-1-50992-735-7
PB: 978-1-50993-314-3
ePDF: 978-1-50992-737-1
ePub: 978-1-50992-736-4

Typeset by Compuscript Ltd, Shannon

Preface

THIS BOOK IS the postscript to the past decades of military rule without a Constitution. I consider the workings of the 2008 Constitution and explore how it operates in practice. In keeping with the series, the purpose of this book is to provide an accessible analysis and overview of the 2008 Constitution in its socio-legal context. Unlike many other books in the series, I do not have the luxury of drawing on and synthesising a large body of secondary monographs on the subject (either in Burmese or English). I have sought to balance the need to write for a comparative constitutional law audience with the importance of explaining the Constitution on its own terms and in a way that speaks to the local context. I have attempted as best I know how to navigate the challenge of writing about a Constitution drafted under a military regime. While avoiding either sanctioning the Constitution or critiquing it from a top-down international perspective, I do suggest that the military-state has its own internal logic (although not based on liberal democratic ideals).

References in this book are kept to a minimum, consistent with the style of the series, although it is important to briefly explain the scope of materials drawn upon. The book is based on parliamentary records, court decisions past and present, and media analysis. Many sources referred to in this book are in Burmese only. All legislative records cited are in Burmese. Most citations to court decisions post-1962 are also all in Burmese. This is except for a handful of Constitutional Tribunal decisions, where some English translations are available, or Supreme Court decisions pre-1962 that were published in English. I have given Constitutional Tribunal cases names for ease of reference. All laws and regulations cited are in Burmese, although some are also available in English.

This is the first book to draw on records of the new Pyidaungsu Hluttaw. I would like to express my appreciation to the National Library of Australia, including Sophie Viravong and Chenwilai Hodgins, who oversee the Burmese collection, for access to the legislative records since 2011. In the footnotes, legislative records have been cited by abbreviations: PH stands for Pyithu Hluttaw; PDH stands for Pyidaungsu Hluttaw and AH stands for Amyotha Hluttaw. Abbreviated citations identify the house, year, session and day, and where relevant page number, of the legislative records.

This book primarily considers the 2008 Constitution across three political eras: direct military rule (1988–2010); the Thein Sein Government (2011–2016); and the NLD Government (2016–2021).

Finally, on terminology, I use the term 'Myanmar' to refer to the country post-1989 and the term 'Burma' prior to that date (see Chapter 6 for more on the importance of naming and territory). I generally refer to the armed forces as the 'Tatmadaw' given its particular connotations in Myanmar (though I note that the government often uses the English term 'Defence Services'). I use the term 'Advocate' for lawyer, as this is the term used for people who have undertaken chambers, passed as a Higher Grade Pleader and gone on to be admitted as an Advocate. I use the term 'legislature' (Hluttaw) to distinguish this branch of government from parliamentary systems.[1] Other terms I clarify throughout the text. I have used Burmese font in this book selectively to explain key concepts that have a specific meaning in Myanmar. A word of caution is also necessary to anyone relying on the English translation of the Constitution, which is neither a consistent nor accurate translation of the official Burmese version. This book emphasises the need to understand the provisions of the Constitution in their social and historical context.

---

[1] In using the term 'legislature', I follow Myint Zan, who noted the lack of similarities with parliamentary systems and the more fitting use of the term 'legislature': Myint Zan (2014) 'The New Supreme Court and Constitutional Tribunal' in Nick Cheesman et al (eds) *Myanmar's Transition*. Singapore: ISEAS. p 265.

Acknowledgements

THIS BOOK is informed by numerous archive and library visits, workshops, interviews and observations over the last ten years. This project required deep and sustained engagement in Myanmar as well as with the Burmese diaspora. There are many colleagues and friends to thank, although some who need to remain anonymous. From Myanmar, I particularly want to acknowledge U Kyaw San, Daw Khin Khin Oo, Daw Yin Myo Su, and Kyaw Min San. A special note of acknowledgement also goes to the late U Ko Ni (d. 2017), the Saya (teacher) who taught me more than anyone else about the 2008 Constitution and the cost of trying to change it.

This book took me across the breadth and depth of the field of comparative constitutional law in search of points of comparison that would illuminate the workings of the Constitution in Myanmar. In challenging my own repertoire of comparative examples, the process of writing the book helped me to appreciate the possibilities of new perspectives for comparative constitutional law. I am grateful for the intellectual guidance, comparative expertise and generosity of Theunis Roux. I am grateful for the wisdom and civil passions of Martin Krygier and for shared opportunities to puzzle over the rule of law as the door in the field in Myanmar. I also thank my other co-collaborators in the Australia-Myanmar Constitutional Democracy Project – Catherine Renshaw, Wojciech Sadurski and Adam Czarnota – whose collective wisdom on human rights, constitutional courts and transitional justice I have learnt from. I am indebted to many other colleagues at UNSW Law and I count it a real privilege to call such a vibrant and engaged academic community home. I want to particularly thank Rosalind Dixon for her comparative expertise and guidance, and generous support for this volume.

This book has emerged from countless workshops over the past few years. I am indebted to the many participants who came from all walks of life – former communist insurgents, ethnic armed leaders, judges, lawyers, activists, former prisoners, legislators and civil servants. You have helped me to refine certain ideas while affirming others. It is a privilege to be a part of this unusual nexus of teaching, advocacy and research at a critical point in time. I also want to thank Sai Myint Aung for his outstanding research assistance and for our many conversations over the nuances of law and legal practice in Myanmar.

At an institutional level, it is my pleasure to thank the Dean of the Law Faculty of UNSW, first David Dixon and now George Williams, for their support and for faculty funding for this project. As an early career scholar, it has been a privilege to find myself at such a supportive institution as UNSW Law. I deeply appreciate the intellectual vision of the faculty and its commitments to justice through its role as an engaged community of scholars. Several other institutions also funded aspects of this project. This project was supported by an Australian Research Council Discovery Project (DP 180100772). The UNSW Institute for Global Development Myanmar Seed Funds supported a conference on peace processes. In 2018, I was grateful to spend time at Melbourne Law School as a Kathleen Fitzpatrick Fellow hosted by Adrianne Stone; and at the American Bar Foundation and Northwestern Law School in Chicago hosted by Jothie Rajah.

I am grateful to Nick Cheesman for sharing his expertise on Myanmar and for his insightful comments on previous drafts. The military and its various forces present a particular difficulty to understand and I would like to thank Andrew Selth, John Buchanan, Nick Cheesman and Maung Aung Myoe for their suggestions and clarifications. I would also like to thank all those who generously contributed their comparative expertise, time and thoughts to the book manuscript review session in 2018: Will Partlett, Cheryl Saunders, Jeremy Webber, Ben Schonthal, Theunis Roux, Martin Krygier, Nick Cheesman and Rosalind Dixon. It was a privilege to have feedback from scholars from fields as diverse as Buddhist studies, socialist legality, rule of law, federalism and comparative constitutional law, and this is testimony to some of the different ideas that inform constitutional practice in Myanmar. I am also grateful for comments on parts of the manuscript from Gabrielle Appleby, Sean Turnell, Melinda Tun, Tarun Khaitun, Janelle Saffin, Myint Zan and Michael Lidauer. Finally, I wish to convey my sincere thanks to the editors Benjamin Berger, Rosalind Dixon, Andrew Harding, Heinz Klug and Peter Leyland for their generous editorial guidance and for the opportunity to publish in this series, *The Constitutions of the World.*

Table of Contents

Abbreviations

ABSDF	All Burma Students Democratic Front
AFPFL	Anti-Fascist People's Freedom League
AH	Amyotha Hluttaw
ALP	Arakan Liberation Party
ANP	Arakan National Party
ARSA	Arakan Rohingya Salvation Army
ASEAN	Association of Southeast Asian Nations
BGF	Border Guard Force
BSPP	Burma Socialist Programme Party
CDF	Constituency Development Fund
CNF	Chin National Front
CPB	Communist Party of Burma
DACU	Development Assistance Coordination Unit
DKBA-5	Democratic Karen Buddhist Army-5
EAO	Ethnic Armed Organisations
FPNCC	Federal Peace Negotiation Central Committee
GAD	General Administration Department
ICESCR	International Covenant on Economic, Social and Cultural Rights
KIA	Kachin Independence Army
KIO	Kachin Independence Organisation
KNU	Karen National Union
KNU/KNLA	Karen National Union/Karen National Liberation Army
KNPP	Karenni National Progressive Party
MEC	Myanmar Economic Corporation

MNDAA	Myanmar National Democratic Alliance Army
MPC	Myanmar Peace Centre
NCA	National Ceasefire Agreement
NDAA	National Democratic Alliance Army
NDF	National Democratic Front
NDA-K	New Democratic Army-Kachin
NDSC	National Defence and Security Council
NLD	National League for Democracy
NMSP	New Mon State Party
PDH	Pyidaungsu Hluttaw
PH	Pyithu Hluttaw
PNLO	Pa-O National Liberation Organisation
PNO	Pa-O National Party
PSLA	Palaung State Liberation Army
PSLP	Palaung State Liberation Party
RCSS	Restoration Council of Shan State
RNDP	Rakhine National Democratic Party
SLORC	State Law and Order Restoration Council
SPDC	State Peace and Development Council
SSPP	Shan State Progress Party
TNLA	Ta'ang National Liberation Army
UAGO	Union Attorney General's Office
UCSB	Union Civil Service Board
ULO	Union Level Organisation
UMEHL	Union of Myanmar Economic Holdings Limited
UNFC	United Nationalities Federal Council
USDP	Union Solidarity and Development Party
UWSA	United Wa State Army

States and Regions of Myanmar[1]

Ayeyarwaddy Region – formerly known as Irrawaddy
Bago Region – formerly known as Pegu
Chin State
Kachin State
Kayah State – formerly known as Karenni State
Kayin State – formerly known as Karen State
Magway Region
Mandalay Region
Mon State
Rakhine State – formerly known as Arakan State
Sagaing Region
Shan State
Tanintharyi Region – formerly known as Tenasserim
Yangon Region – formerly known as Rangoon

[1] Prior to 2011, 'Regions' were known as 'Divisions'. The changes to the names of States/Divisions occurred in 1989.

Table of Cases

Supreme Court Decisions (တရားလွှတ်တော်ချုပ် တရားစီရင်ထုံးများ)

Constitutional Tribunal Decisions and Advisory Decisions
(နိုင်ငံတော်ဖွဲ့စည်းပုံအခြေခံဥပဒေဆိုင်ရာခုံရုံး ဆုံးဖြတ်ချက်များ)[1]

---

[1] Cases in Burmese are simply titled 'Constitutional Tribunal (case year and number). I have created case names for ease of reference and because occasionally the numbers are misleading.

xx   *Table of Cases*

Table of Legislation

Legislation[1] (ဥပဒေများ)

---

[1] I have listed legislation alphabetically, with the exception of amendments. Amendments are not combined with the original law in Myanmar, but for ease of reference I have noted any amendments to the original law in brackets.

Legislative Records

Amyotha Hluttaw [အမျိုးသားလွှတ်တော် အစည်းအဝေးမှတ်တမ်းများ][2]

---

[2] Reference to the 'First Amyotha Hluttaw' and so on refers to the Thein Sein term
(2011–2016), while reference to the 'Second Amyotha Hluttaw' refers to the NLD term
(2016–2021)

Pyidaungsu Hluttaw [ပြည်ထောင်စုလွှတ်တော် အစည်းအဝေးမှတ်တမ်းများ]

Pyithu Hluttaw [ပြည်သူ့လွှတ်တော် အစည်းအဝေးမှတ်တမ်းများ]

1

Introducing Myanmar's 2008 Constitution

Cyclone Nargis – Social, Geographic and Economic Context – Constitutional Codification – The Military-state

THE OPULENT DEFENCE Services Museum in the capital Naypyidaw praises the military's response to natural disasters such as Cyclone Nargis. In one section, the display features pictures of the military delivering aid to cyclone-affected communities. Yet Myanmar's 2008 Constitution is haunted by the humanitarian tragedy, regime obstinance, and political defiance surrounding Cyclone Nargis. On 2 May 2008, the most dangerous and destructive cyclone in the history of Myanmar hit the Irrawaddy delta region of lower Myanmar. Part of the tragedy is that there is no credible acknowledgment of the victims. Conservative estimates suggest 130,000 people died, while other sources claim that the human life toll was as high as 200,000.[1] In addition, over 2.5 million people were seriously affected by the cyclone, many injured, without shelter, their rice paddies ruined just before harvest, communities irreparably affected.[2] Part of the tragedy lies in the fact that the scale of the human impact could have been reduced. The international community expressed deep frustration at the Tatmadaw's (armed forces) initial refusal to accept humanitarian aid and disaster assistance. Ten long days after the cyclone first hit, on 12 May 2008, the United Nations Secretary-General Ban Ki-moon expressed his grave concerns for victims of the cyclone and denounced the military regime for its unacceptable response to the suffering of its people in this crisis.

---

[1] TNI, *Beyond Panglong: Myanmar's National Peace and Reform Dilemma 2017.* Myanmar Policy Briefing No 21 (The Netherlands, 2017) www.tni.org.
[2] See International Crisis Group, *Burma/Myanmar After Nargis: Time to Normalise Aid Relations* (Brussels, 2008). www.icg.org.

Even once the Tatmadaw began distributing aid, there were reports of less than a quarter of the actual need being met, and serious allegations of the misuse of aid materials, such as selling on the black market. Meanwhile, parallel to the cyclone crisis, the carefully planned constitutional referendum, part of the general's roadmap to democracy, went ahead on 10 May in areas not affected by the cyclone, and on 24 May in areas that had been affected. Humanitarian imperatives caused by the worst cyclone in Myanmar's recent history would not deter or derail the Tatmadaw's plans to approve the Constitution, a text that at the time few had even seen or read.

Ten years after the constitutional referendum, the dubious circumstances of the referendum are just one of many reasons why the 2008 Constitution faces a credibility deficit. Both the process of constitution-making and the substance of the Constitution are contested. The validity of the 2008 Constitution of the Republic of the Union of Myanmar ('the Constitution') is questioned because of the authoritarian circumstances of its drafting during some of the darkest years of military rule (1993–2007). The process was controlled by the military regime and participation was highly circumscribed. The Constitution is criticised for the way it privileges the Tatmadaw, such as the qualified system of democracy it establishes, with some legislative seats reserved for the Tatmadaw.

In this book, I explain why the constitution-making process, its substance and implementation are the reason many local actors discredit the Constitution. The debate over the legitimacy of the Constitution was originally so polarised that in 2010 the National League for Democracy (NLD), the primary pro-democratic political party, boycotted the first elections under the new Constitution. While the NLD later agreed to enter the new political and constitutional system by running in the by-elections of 2012, there remains reluctance on the part of pro-democratic actors to attribute any validity to the Constitution.

In this book, I emphasise that the Constitution is not new, but rather many of its key features were part of military propaganda published in books and State-run newspapers as early as the 1990s. In this regard, I measure the age of the Constitution from the 1990s, rather than since formal enactment in 2011. This reperiodisation of constitutional law emphasises the origins of the core principles and structure of the Constitution and how the substance of the Constitution is seen as closely related to the former military regime. The foundations of the Constitution were articulated, enacted and embodied through military rule since this time. For example, as I will show, in the 1990s the Tatmadaw began its propaganda campaign of the Three Main National Causes, which function as the three meta-principles of the military-state (Chapter 3). To a local audience, these principles are not new and did not first appear in the Constitution. Instead society has been socialised in these principles for several decades and there is a strong association between these three meta-principles and direct military rule. Since 2011, the political structures of the Constitution have come to life, although these institutions are animated and held in place by the foundations laid by the previous regime.

Many aspects of the Constitution remain highly contested. There is significant debate over the meaning and nuance of key ideas such as democracy, federalism and the military. What precisely is 'disciplined' democracy? How can 'genuine' federalism be achieved? Different interest groups use the semantic debate over 'democratic federalism' or 'a federal democratic system' as tactical manoeuvres in the process of constitution-making. The most frequent questions that arise relate to whether the Constitution is federal in nature, whether the Constitution can actually be amended and the role of the Tatmadaw.

The crisis of credibility and the contestation over constitutional principles reoccur throughout the course of this book. In the chapters that follow, I explain key ideas articulated in the Constitution and illustrated in practice. I begin by setting the social, economic and cultural context in which the Constitution governs. The Constitution is important because it is a key part of the establishment and maintenance of the military-state in Myanmar. I briefly introduce the contours of the military-state, which include the leadership role of the military in governance, its military ideology, and the principle of coercive centralism.

I. CONSTITUTIONAL CONTEXT

The place known today as Myanmar has long captured and captivated the attention of the international community. The country has been the subject of famous poems and novels, from Rudyard Kipling's *Mandalay*,[3] an iconic ode to the beauty of the place and its people, to George Orwell's novel *Burmese Days*,[4] a scathing critique of the colonial enterprise of

---

[3] For the history of how the poem inspired a song, see Andrew Selth, *Burma, Kipling and Western Music: The Riff from Mandalay* (London, Routledge, 2017).

[4] George Orwell, *Burmese Days: A Novel* (London, Secker & Warburg, 1951).

which Orwell was a part. These writings express the beauty and distinctiveness of the cultures and peoples of Myanmar, and its complex history, even if these traditions and ways of life are at times idealised and romanticised in the western imagination. Many human rights advocates admired and were, at least until 2017, attracted to Aung San Suu Kyi, Nobel Laureate winner, former political prisoner and author of *Freedom from Fear*.[5]

Yet there are another parallel set of writings that document decades of atrocities and flagrant abuses of individual and collective rights in Myanmar. There are a persistent series of reports both from local civil society groups and international advocacy organisations documenting forced labour, armed conflict, mass displacement, the use of landmines, the illegal drug trade, torture, disappearances, corruption, arbitrary detention, and the jailing of political dissidents. During the northern Rakhine State conflict that began in 2016, Suu Kyi was implicated in the alleged genocide of the Rohingya, blurring the lines between black and white for human rights advocates.[6] Myanmar's Constitution is required to govern over this captivating landscape and people in an environment where armed conflict and violence are normalised.

Three features of the social, economic and geographic environment combine to offer a challenging environment for constitutional rule. These features include the country's socio-cultural diversity with a mix of religions, peoples and traditions; a disparate and difficult geographic terrain to govern; and serious socio-economic concerns including severe poverty, displacement, and significant education gaps.

The Constitution operates within a highly diverse social environment, although does not cater to a vision of a multicultural society, but rather offers a crude categorisation of the population. These categories have a homogenising effect and oversimplify issues of ethnic, religious and cultural identity. A clear majority of the population, 89 per cent, identify as Buddhist according to the 2014 census. Buddhists in Myanmar adhere to Theravada Buddhism, like its neighbours – Thailand, Cambodia, Sri Lanka and Laos. This population count needs to be viewed with some caveats. Over one million Rohingya were not permitted to participate in the census, so the claim that 2.3 per cent of the population are Muslim

---

[5] Aung San Suu Kyi, *Freedom From Fear and Other Writings*. (England, Penguin Books, 2010, 3rd ed). Since 2017, Suu Kyi has lost much of her status as a human rights and democracy advocate due to allegations of genocide against the Rohingya.

[6] See Melissa Crouch (2019) 'States of Legal Denial: How the Rohingya Lost the Right to Vote and the Role of Legal Denial in Myanmar' *Journal of Contemporary Asia*.

is a conservative figure. The remainder of the population includes 6.3 per cent Christian, 0.5 per cent Hindu and 0.8 per cent animist. The people are also extremely diverse ethnically, although the census is primarily concerned with maintaining the government's radicalised divisions rather than reflecting or fostering actual diversity. Most of the population are ethnic Burman, with other major ethnic groups including the Shan, Karen, Kachin, Kayah, Mon, Rakhine and Chin (see Chapter 7). The government recognises 135 ethnic groups, although many people do not fit into these categories and it is not uncommon for identity cards to show hyphenated identities (for example, 'Bamar-Shan'). The official language of the Constitution and the courts is Burmese, although an estimated 100 languages are spoken in Myanmar.[7] Many aspects of the Constitution and the makeup of the government indicate the dominance of ethnic Burman Buddhists over other people groups in Myanmar. These features of social diversity, and persistent concerns of 'Burmanisation' of minority groups are a challenge to address in future constitutional reform.

The land mass that is now known as the country of Myanmar is a broad, rich and yet challenging terrain to govern. The country has a relatively large land mass in proportion to its population of 52 million, and is dwarfed by its two most populous neighbours, China and India. The country is edged by mountainous borderlands married to the flat plains of the dry centre that extend to tropical coastal areas. The most important and largest river is the Irrawaddy, running north to south. The rivers are a source of life and livelihood for many, although also pose a threat in the monsoon season. Flooding has been the cause of periodic humanitarian crises, such as the displacement in 2017 of 100,000 people. Rivers, as well as forests, brim with rare wildlife that are stalked by poachers and sold on the regional and global black market.

Myanmar shares a long expanse of borders with multiple countries, which means that issues from conflict and displacement to environmental degradation overlap with the concerns of its neighbours, including Bangladesh, Thailand, Laos and Cambodia. Not least among these neighbours are China and India, and certain pressures come with living between two rapidly growing economies and a burgeoning middle-class with increasing demands of consumption.[8] Under years of military rule,

---

[7] David Bradley, 'Languages', in I Halliday et al (eds) *Routledge Handbook on Contemporary Myanmar* (London, Routledge, 2018).

[8] Bertil Linter, *Great Game East* (Yale University Press, 2015); Thant Myint U, *Where China meets India* (New York, Farrar, Straus and Giroux, 2011).

Myanmar's borders have been sites of significant illegal border trade, such as the annual black market in jade worth an estimated US$31 billion.[9] Access to mountainous areas contribute to the difficultly of governing and have also provided cover to many insurgent groups. The highlands are sparsely populated and are home to many of the country's ethnic minorities. The agency of these upland people groups and their relationship to central state power is encapsulated in James C Scott's seminal exploration of upland resistance as the 'art of not being governed'.[10] The Constitution faces the challenges of attempting to rule these arbitrary borders and unruly landscape. The Constitution also reorients the country geographically and centralises power in a new capital centre: Naypyidaw (see Chapter 3).

The third contextual feature that presents a challenge for any government serving under the Constitution is the vulnerable nature of Myanmar's contemporary socio-economic environment. Myanmar's economy officially hit rock bottom in 1987, when the country was infamously designated Least Developed Country status. One reason why this label was such a source of shame is because this economic crisis came after the golden era of the early 1900s when Burma was known as the rice bowl of Asia for the scale of its exports to the region. This is no longer the case, and on any measure of economic status, health,[11] education or quality of life, Myanmar is found close to the bottom. Despite its poverty, the one global ranking Myanmar tops is in generosity.[12]

Inequality has become a major issue. Across the country, 33 per cent of people live below the poverty line. There are over one million internally displaced people.[13] The levels of government spending on health are the lowest of any country in the world.[14] Myanmar has the lowest life expectancy in all of the Association of Southeast Asian Nations (ASEAN), at just 66 years of age.[15] The country has a high youth population and

---

[9] Global Witness, *Jade: Myanmar's Big State Secret* (London, 2015).

[10] James C Scott, *The Art of Not Being Governed: An Anarchist History of Upland Southeast Asia* (Yale University Press, 2010).

[11] Céline Coderey, 'Health', in Ian Halliday et al (eds) *Routledge Handbook on Contemporary Myanmar* (London, Routledge, 2018).

[12] As ranked in the World Generosity Index, British Charities Aid Foundation, www.cafonline.org.

[13] TNI, *Beyond Panglong: Myanmar's National Peace and Reform Dilemma 2017.* Policy Briefing No 21. (The Netherlands, 2017).

[14] Save the Children, *Lives on Loan: Extreme Poverty in Yangon* (Yangon, 2016).

[15] Ibid.

an emerging middle class. Child labour is high: of children aged 10–17, one-in-five are working instead of getting an education.[16] Urban poverty is more severe than levels of poverty in rural areas. More than 35 per cent of children in Yangon are stunted in their growth.[17] Many people survive on less than USD 0.86 per day. Agriculture is the main source of livelihood for up to 70 per cent of the population and most farmers have no access to credit. Land tenure security is a major concern. The past military regime placed significant pressure on farmers to plant certain crops deemed national priorities.[18] Work for many is season dependent, and often there is no work available in the monsoon season (May to August). The Constitution does contain some significant aspirational provisions on socio-economic concerns – such as free primary education, reducing unemployment and conserving the environment.[19] Yet as I discuss in Chapter 8, constitutional duties take priority and constitutional protections are difficult to enforce.

These chronic levels of poverty are in contrast with the accumulation of mass wealth by a handful of military officers, crony businessmen and ethnic warlords. This disproportionate concentration of wealth is a phenomenon that has primarily occurred over the last three decades. The Tatmadaw elite has both formal and informal means of income generation. Wealth has primarily accumulated in the top ranks of the Tatmadaw. In 2006, leaked footage of the wedding of General Than Shwe's daughter generated outrage over the sheer extravagance of the wedding, his daughter's bejewelled dress and wedding gifts estimated at over USD 50 million. From the 1990s onwards, the Tatmadaw's offer of ceasefire deals ushered in an era of the super-rich ethnic warlords and cronies. Some have been involved in the new institutions of government, such as the leader of the People's Militia in Northern Shan State, U T Khun Myat, who was a member of the legislature from 2011–2016 (see Chapter 3).

It is important to bear in mind the challenges that this context presents when understanding Myanmar's Constitution and the limits of what it can and cannot achieve.

---

[16] The Union Report: Occupation and Industry. Department of Population, 2016 cited in Save the Children (2016).

[17] Save the Children, *Lives on Loan* above n 14.

[18] Mary Callahan, 'Of Kyay-su and Kyet-su: The Military in 2006' in Monique Skidmore and Trevor Wilson (eds) *Myanmar: The State, Community and the Environment* (Canberra, ANU Press, 2007).

[19] See 2008 Constitution, ss 28(c)–(d), 31 and 45 respectively.

II. CONSTITUTIONAL CODIFICATION
AND THE CONSTITUTIONAL TRIBUNAL

Myanmar's Constitution is a document that leaves few details to the imagination or future negotiation. The Constitution creates new structures, procedures and processes for political and legal practice. The Constitution is systematic, and its level of detail suggests a codified understanding of constitutional law. A codified approach to constitutional law means that many matters of governance that would be deferred in many other constitutions around the world, or delegated to the executive or legislature to fill in the details, are instead mapped out carefully in the Constitution. The Constitution aims to be the final and complete word on political organisation. The Constitution is comprehensive and systematic. It unites a system of law that was fragmented and piecemeal under military rule. It is an act of national consolidation. The Constitution was intended to be clear, because the function of judges in Myanmar is limited and they do not have power to fill in the gaps of the law.[20] Yet at the same time the Constitution is drafted at a level of generality intrinsic to legal codes and grants wide discretionary power to certain elite actors. This is constitutional law by codification.

The Constitution seeks to establish a supreme and permanent order. The Constitution's claim to completeness and universality is evident in its 457 lengthy provisions, structured and divided into 15 chapters. The order of the Constitution is important, with the military's governance agenda given priority in the chapters on Basic Principles (Ch I), followed by the branches of government (Chs II–VI) and the military as a fourth branch (Ch VII). Only after these sections do we come across the duties and rights of citizens (Ch VIII), the electoral process (Chs IV–X), and other matters such as the process of formal amendment (Chs XI–XV). This level of detail makes the Constitution a highly prescriptive document. It rivals the notoriously lengthy Indian Constitution.

The official name of the country is 'The Republic of the Union of Myanmar'. As a Union, the Constitution articulates and details the unitary nature of the State. There are seven States and seven Regions at the sub-national level, and then self-administered areas with some

---

[20] See John Henry Merryman and Rogelio Perez-Perdomo, *The Civil Law Tradition: An Introduction to the Legal Systems of Europe and Latin America* (Stanford University Press, 3rd ed, 2007), pp 27–30. In this way there are broader similarities with the German approach to codification, which is to codify existing principles rather than abolish the past law and replace it with a new one; the French approach to codification of clarifying the law so citizens could understand their rights has little relevance.

autonomy below this. The legislature is tricameral in structure with the Constitution granting significant powers to the Pyidaungsu Hluttaw, the joint sitting of the two houses, the Pyithu Hluttaw and Amyotha Hluttaw (see Chapter 5). According to the Constitution, the executive and legislature are marked by a formal separation of powers and institutions. The President is the leader of the executive branch alongside two vice-presidents, and neither they nor any minister can hold legislative seats concurrently. The legislature at the subnational level is unicameral and structurally adheres to a Westminster-style fusion of the executive and legislative branch, although has limited law-making powers.

The Constitutional Tribunal deals with questions about the scope and delineation of political powers, or other matters of interpretation arising from the Constitution. My examination of constitutional debates in this book suggests that the meaning of the Constitution in Myanmar has been significantly determined by the legislature. The legislature has made claims to the meaning of the Constitution and legislative debates have been a key part of this process of constitutional meaning-making. In contrast, the Constitutional Tribunal is not widely regarded as having power to authoritatively determine the meaning of the Constitution in practice. In this book, I draw on a wide range of examples to demonstrate that it is often the legislature, rather than the Constitutional Tribunal, that features as a site of constitutional debate. Nevertheless, I also take every opportunity to demonstrate how, or to what extent, decisions of the Constitutional Tribunal inform political and legal practice.

I acknowledge and discuss constitutional matters that the Constitutional Tribunal has decided in its decisions and several advisory opinions.[21] However, the broader problem of the Constitution's legitimacy, and the legislature's flagrant disregard for decisions of the Tribunal, means we cannot take the Tribunal's authority and its decisions as settled law. The side-lining of the Constitutional Tribunal is based on discontent with its design. These criticisms also stem from an understanding of the judiciary as fulfilling an administrative role, rather than as a check on the administration. The legislature keeps a check on the executive and the courts, while the Tatmadaw oversees these three branches. Further, the Tribunal

---

[21] Final decisions of the Constitutional Tribunal are known as အပြီးသတ်ဆုံးဖြတ်ချက်, while advisory decisions are ကနဦးဆုံးဖြတ်ချက်. The later means 'preliminary' or 'interim' decision, but I avoid using these terms as it suggests another decision will follow, which is not necessarily the case. Advisory decisions do not involve court hearings, the matter is dealt with in writing, and the decision is not binding on other branches of government.

has taken different approaches to deciding cases over time. A common or shared approach to constitutional interpretation has yet to emerge.

The Constitution is an amalgamation of both continuity and change, reconciling old and new debates (though primarily domestic debates) in constitutional law in Myanmar. The field of constitutional law is in part wholly new in Myanmar, emerging in 2011 as an area of practice, teaching, advocacy and discourse after decades of military rule. In this sense, constitutional law is an exciting but also highly contentious and turbulent field. There is at the same time a sense of the renaissance of constitutional law. Constitutional law, at least for the senior generation of lawyers, is part of the past that has returned to life. The period of parliamentary democracy from 1947–1962 was an intense time of debate over core constitutional principles, with several major constitutional amendments, and both constitutional and administrative review cases being heard in the Supreme Court. From 1974–1988, the socialist regime nominally operated under a Constitution. The ensuing military era without a constitution was a period when the Tatmadaw was preoccupied with constitution-making for the best part of 20 years (see Chapter 2). The challenge in Myanmar now is how to make sense of the new and the old in constitutional law to forge a common constitutional discourse. The 2008 Constitution is a patchwork of ideas from the 1947 Constitution, the 1974 Constitution, and military ideology leftover from periods of direct military rule. In this light, the Constitution is best understood as a hybrid constitutional system consisting of various overlapping layers of development.[22]

Most constitutional provisions in this patchwork Constitution have not been the subject of constitutional adjudication. There are very few Constitutional Tribunal decisions, access to the court is highly restricted and the protection of constitutional rights via the writs petition in the Supreme Court is highly circumscribed.[23]

The Constitution seeks to be exhaustive, but also includes loopholes to allow for discretion. Constitutional loopholes are provisions that allow for broad exercise of discretion, but that have a hidden meaning and potentially broad scope for misuse for undemocratic or illiberal means. Many critics believe that the ambiguities and inconsistencies in the Constitution are a constitutional design strategy used to the

---

[22] Melissa Crouch, 'The Layers of Legal Development in Myanmar' in Melissa Crouch and Tim Lindsey (eds) *Law, Society and Transition in Myanmar* (Oxford, Hart Publishing, 2014).

[23] See Melissa Crouch, 'The Prerogative Writs as Constitutional Transfer' (2018) *Oxford Journal of Legal Studies* 1–23.

Tatmadaw's advantage. In the case of Myanmar, these loopholes are the prerogative of the Tatmadaw. While in theory other groups, such as the NLD, may seek to take advantage of these loopholes, there are unspoken limits on democratic power.

III. THE CONSTITUTION IN A MILITARY-STATE

The 2008 Constitution institutionalises a military-state in Myanmar.[24] I use the term 'military-state' in a manner distinct from direct military rule. The military-state is a way of explaining the co-existence of both military and civilian authorities. The 2008 Constitution is used to distribute and limit power in Myanmar's military-state. The military-state in Myanmar has three key features: enabling the role of the military in governance; sanctioning the constitutional ideology of the military-state; and the organisation of institutions based on the principle of coercive centralism. Similar to other kinds of authoritarian regimes, the control of political leadership, state ideology and the organisational basis of the state furthers authoritarian ends. These concepts share broad resemblance to the 'party-state' of socialist regimes, with the leading role of the party, an ideological commitment to socialism and the idea of democratic centralism. Myanmar's military-state is a type of authoritarian regime. I introduce these three features here and then provide further illustrations throughout the book.

The first element of the military-state, as I am using the term, is that the Tatmadaw has a 'leading role' in governance, or what is referred to in Myanmar as 'national politics' (as opposed to 'party politics') (see Chapter 3). This distinction means that the Tatmadaw claims to independently oversee the political system though does not technically have its own political party. In many respects this mirrors the monopoly of power that the party was given in socialist systems. The terminology of a 'leading role' is a means to facilitate the military's monopoly on power, similar to the party's monopoly of power in socialist regimes.[25] The Constitution is permissive and enables the involvement of the Tatmadaw in the leadership of the state.[26]

---

[24] I elaborate on the concept of the military-state in Melissa Crouch (under review) 'Constitutional Legacies in Authoritarian Regimes: How the Military uses the Constitution to Rule Myanmar'.

[25] Archie Brown (2009) *The Rise and Fall of Communism*. Great Britain, Random House, p 2.

[26] 2008 Constitution, s 6(f).

In the military-state, the military has both explicit and implicit structural advantages. By the military's 'explicit structural advantages', I mean the constitutional provisions, laws and rules that give the Tatmadaw officially sanctioned advantages. The classic example is the constitutional amendment rule that requires the support of Tatmadaw members due to the approval threshold of more than 75 per cent. 'Indirect structural advantages' include the informal capture of institutions and individual loyalty, which enables the Tatmadaw to shape political practice. The key example is the Tatmadaw's practice of transferring officers into the civilian administration, both in high levels of leadership as well as in the lower ranks. The loyalty of former officers allows the Tatmadaw to informally monitor and subordinate civilian institutions (see Chapter 3).

The second element of Myanmar's military-state is an ideology that supports the role of the military in governance. I refer to this ideology as the three meta-principles of the military-state. These three meta-principles are repeated in multiple provisions of the Constitution. In English translations by the government, these three principles are distilled as: non-disintegration of the Union; non-disintegration of national solidarity; and, the perpetuation of sovereignty. The Constitution is one means the Tatmadaw uses to command loyalty and maintain control. Loyalty to these constitutional principles is required by the people, political parties, Tatmadaw officers, the administration, the judiciary and legislators. In short, all branches of government, as well as citizens individually and collectively, are bound by these three principles. These principles not only limit the power of the state, but also restrict the demands of citizens. I explain this ideology and its importance to constitutional law in further detail in Chapter 3.

The third element and organising principle of Myanmar's military-state is 'coercive centralism'.[27] Coercive centralism describes the relationship between the branches of government, and between the Union and the sub-national units. In a party-state, democratic centralism in its actually existing form allowed the party to control the decision-making process and elections were held but usually with sole candidates chosen by the party. I emphasise the strong culture of coercive cooperation and collaboration among the institutions of the military-state.

---

[27] Similarly, Callahan has observed that the military built a 'coercion intensive state': Mary P Callahan, *Making Enemies: War and State Building in Burma* (NUS Press, 2004) p 222.

The Tatmadaw demands a strong sense of loyalty and discipline to the military-state. The Tatmadaw holds uncontested seats in the legislature. Governance in Myanmar is highly centralised in the Union Government. Among the branches of government there is expected to be a high degree of cooperation, rather than conflict and competition. The Constitution is replete with references and exhortations to loyalty to the Union and implies an absence of disagreement. Section 11(a) of the Constitution is the earliest reference in the text to the three branches of government and a division of powers. The dominant conception of the relationship between the judicial, legislative and executive branch is of centralised collaboration and coordination. Taken in light of the Constitution as a whole, these three branches are subordinated to a fourth branch, the Tatmadaw. There are no checks on the power of the Tatmadaw.

Coercive centralism describes the way that the Constitution contains and controls democracy through a multi-party system that is 'disciplined'.[28] The branches of government are coerced into cooperation. The Constitution is also based on the idea of 'the Union' (နိုင်ငံတော်) and conceives of the country as a united entity. There has been significant debate over if, or to what extent, the Constitution allows for a limited form of federalism. The use of the term 'Union' is a *deliberate* choice and excludes the term 'federalism'.[29] Crucial to coercive centralism is that the Union still controls most appointment processes and lines of accountability of the States/Regions. Coercive centralism means that there is no genuine horizontal separation of powers between branches. It also means there is no vertical separation between different levels of government. Instead, the sub-national governments derive their existence from the Union Government and are subordinate to the Union Government.

IV. ORGANISATION OF THE BOOK

It has become commonplace to argue that the exercise of power in Myanmar is highly personalised.[30] My book demonstrates that legal institutions and rules also matter. This does not mean that the

---

[28] 2008 Constitution, ss 6(d), 7. Walton argues that the concept of discipline-flourishing democracy is 'firmly rooted in Burmese Buddhist views of human nature', see *Buddhism, Politics and Political Thought in Myanmar* (CUP 2017), p 136.

[29] Eg, see Minye Kaungbon, 1994, p 180.

[30] See Renaud Egreteau, *Caretaking Democratization: The Military and Political Change in Myanmar* (Hurst & Co Publishers, 2016) pp 119–122.

Constitution matters in all places and times, but it has a tangible presence and influences political developments.

In Chapter 2, I explain the importance of history to understanding the origins and content of the 2008 Constitution. I contrast the Panglong Agreement with the ensuing 1947 independence Constitution. After a period of direct socialist rule in the 1960s, this was followed by a socialist-inspired Constitution of 1974. The extent of continuity and change in the 2008 Constitution can only be understood considering this history. I emphasise that the essence of the draft Constitution emerged in the early 1990s, validating an approach to the Constitution starting from this date. The Constitution presents a hybrid model that mixes presidentialism at the national level with a parliamentary-style system at the State/Region level; a system in which citizens duties and obligations take priority over rights; a system that qualifies the language of democracy and carves out exceptions to allow the perpetuation of military governance.

My approach to understanding the branches of government – by which I mean the executive, the legislature, the judiciary and the military – is to distinguish between institutions and power. I use the term 'institutions' to mean the organisations and bodies that are considered to be part of the relevant branch: such as the President's Office, the Cabinet and government ministries, particularly the General Administration Department, as the core of the executive institutions; the Pyidaungsu Hluttaw and the State/Region Hluttaw as the primary legislative bodies; and the courts as the key judicial institutions. I use the term 'power' to mean the ability to exercise executive, legislative or judicial authority. The reason for distinguishing between institutions and powers is that often certain institutions exercise more than one type of power, or some institutions that are considered to be part of one branch in fact exercise power of another branch. For example, the Supreme Court can prepare draft laws, which is an example of a judicial institution contributing to the law-making process. The Tatmadaw exercises executive, legislative and judicial power. The courts can be conceptualised as a subordinate administrative agency.

In Chapter 3, I explain how the Constitution enables military involvement in governance. The military is a fourth branch of government, exercising executive, legislative and judicial power. It also has indirect influence over all major executive, legislative and judicial institutions. The next three chapters focus on the two core branches of the Union Government where civilian actors mix with

Tatmadaw officers: in Chapter 4, I consider how the Constitution regulates and constrains political participation, and in Chapter 5, I focus on legislative power and the role of the legislature. In Chapter 6, I deal with the scope of executive power, and the institutions and actors that make up the executive.

In Chapter 7, I consider three features of the Constitution that offer ethnic recognition but that deliberately avoid mention of federalism and self-determination: the designation of seven States and seven Regions; the appointment of Ministers for National Races Affairs; and the Self-Administered Areas. The concept of the Union in Myanmar emphasises the responsibility of these levels of government or positions to the centralised Union Government. I emphasis the way State/Region leaders and governments are appointed by, accountable to and dependent on the Union Government. Many claims to ethnic and cultural recognition are not recognised by the Constitution and calls persist for a 'federal Union'.

The following two chapters concern the courts. In Chapter 8, I consider the nature of judicial power and the judicial institutions in Myanmar, with a focus on the Supreme Court, High Courts and Constitutional Tribunal. In Chapter 9, I emphasise the preoccupation with citizens' duties and the conditional and limited nature of rights protection. This includes the lack of rights claims in the Constitutional Tribunal and writ proceedings in the Supreme Court. The courts occupy a subordinate position in the military-state, subject to executive, legislative and military influence.

In Chapter 10, I focus on the parallel processes of formal constitutional amendment and the national peace process. I show how the breakdown of ceasefire agreements from the 1990s necessitated a new peace process initiated by the executive, although not anticipated by the Constitution. I question the constitutionality of this process although argue that despite the questionable constitutional status of the National Ceasefire Agreement, the main contribution of the peace process has been to disconnect discussions of federalism from secession. The power of the Tatmadaw comes from its combination of implicit and explicit advantages. My overview of key debates for constitutional reform brings together issues raised throughout the book on the demands and limits of reform.

In Chapter 11, I restate my theory of the military-state in Myanmar and identify implications for comparative constitutional inquiry. What will become evident is that the shadow of the Tatmadaw looms large over the Constitution. In all chapters of the Constitution, the Tatmadaw is above civilian authorities and the people. To maintain this supremacy the Tatmadaw insists on faithfulness to the Constitution. It is true that the Tatmadaw now permits debate over ideas such as democracy and federalism in a way that was not possible in the past. Yet if these debates are perceived by the Tatmadaw to threaten its core role in governance, it could lead to a nation-wide emergency, or at worst another coup.

2

The Origins and Content of the 2008 Constitution: An Overview

Preamble – Panglong Agreement – Parliamentary Democracy – Socialist-Military Rule – Unconstitutional Rule – Constitution-Drafting – National Convention – Basic Principles

YANMAR'S LEGAL SYSTEM consists of multiple layers of different legal traditions[1] and the Constitution is no different. Myanmar's constitutional history is often used as a point of contrast to the 2008 Constitution. I show how constitutional history helps us to understand the origins, content and operation of the 2008 Constitution. Burma was colonised by the British and under the authority of British India until 1937 when the Government of Burma Act came into force, although independence was not far off. The Panglong Agreement was an important precursor to independence and to the 1947 Constitution as a voluntary commitment by some ethnic leaders to be part of the Union. One of the reasons the 1947 Constitution is criticised is because of the perceived departure from the Panglong Agreement and its promises of autonomy and self-determination. The country has had two major periods of unconstitutional rule (1962–1974, 1988–2010), but in the middle experienced the socialist 1974 Constitution under General Ne Win. This history informs our understand of the 2008 Constitution, which borrows from the text of many of these past documents.

Myanmar's history and the circumstances in which its constitutions were drafted are highly contentious and subject to competing narratives.

[1] Melissa Crouch, 'The Layers of Legal Development in Myanmar' in Melissa Crouch and Tim Lindsey (eds) *Law, Society and Transition in Myanmar* (Oxford: Hart Publishing, 2014) pp 33–58.

One partisan narrative is contained in the preamble to the 2008 Constitution that tells a short history of constitutional law in Myanmar. The preamble is a starting point to unpack the selective history offered by the Tatmadaw as a written justification for the military-state. The preamble is deliberate in its omissions, papering over the history of conflict, insurgency and failed ceasefires since independence as well as ignoring prominent and persistent calls for federalism. I take the preamble as my point of departure to show how the unresolved issues of federalism and democracy that emerged both in the process of drafting the 2008 Constitution and in its substance affect its credibility.

I. PARLIAMENTARY DEMOCRACY AND THE 1947 CONSTITUTION

Myanmar's (then Burma's) first post-colonial independence constitution, the 1947 Constitution, was a key document articulating the new Union that had emerged among various highland ethnic groups and the majority lowland Burman population. The 1947 Constitution set out a complex arrangement for recognition of ethnic claims, though one that failed to satisfy ethnic demands. The idea of federalism – including self-determination and autonomy – was a persistent demand in this era of parliamentary democracy.

The independence Constitution of Burma was heavily influenced by the draft Indian Constitution and sentiments of democratic socialism. Formally, there was a clear break with the British when Burma rejected the invitation to become part of the Commonwealth. Burma was only one of two colonies (the other being Aden), that declined to become part of the Commonwealth. This is one indication of the desire for independence in political life and suggests the Burmese Constitution should not necessarily be read like Westminster constitutions. The 1947 Constitution, like constitutions in other post-colonial contexts, departed from the British example by being a written constitution and embodied nationalist reactions against illiberal colonial rule.

There were two constitutional templates that preceded the independence Constitution of 1947 – the Government of Burma Act 1935 and the Constitution imposed under Japanese occupation – although neither are given significant weight in Myanmar. The country was annexed to British India in three stages (from 1825 to 1885), with areas of both direct rule in Ministerial Burma or Burma Proper, and indirect rule in the Scheduled or Excluded Frontier Areas. Up until 1937, the constitution of the British empire was the Government of India Act.[2] In 1937, Burma Proper became an independent colony under the Government of Burma Act 1935. This constitutional document had a short lifespan, being in operation just five years prior to World War II and three years after the war. Under the 1935 Act, the Governor as head of the executive had immense power, the franchise was limited, and the legislative body had circumscribed powers. The only right included was the right to property. During the period of occupation from 1942–1945, the Japanese imposed a new constitution, though this is given little mention in the legal history of Burma.

Some ethnic groups agreed to fight with the British against the Japanese during World War II based on offers of future recognition that were never realised. As part of the political negotiations towards independence that took place in the late 1940s, the Anti-Fascist People's Freedom League (AFPFL) held discussions with some ethnic groups. Emerging from these discussions was the Panglong Agreement, which recognised the need for separate governance arrangements. The 1947 conference at Panglong in Shan State was a meeting between General Aung San, leader of the independence movement, and father of current State Counsellor Aung San Suu Kyi, with representatives of the Shan, Kachin and Chin ethnic groups. The conference resulted in the signing of the Panglong Agreement that was a crucial step towards Burma's independence from colonial rule and national unity, and a significant textual precursor to the 1947 Constitution. One of the key aspects of the agreement was the recognition of the 'full autonomy' of these ethnic groups in the administration of their internal affairs. The Panglong Agreement remains a symbolic political pact between the majority Burmans and minority groups,[3] and is used by some as evidence of the claim to self-determination. The Panglong Agreement was not a ceasefire or peace deal, as there was no insurgency at this time. It constituted an agreement by some ethnic areas to join the Union and retain full autonomy, internal administration and a share of national wealth. It is common for ethnic groups today to still quote General Aung San who reportedly said that 'If Burma gets one kyat, you will get one kyat'. This is taken as an unfulfilled promise for economic redistribution and control

---

[2] For the history of this act see Arun Thiruvengadam, *The Constitution of India: A Contextual Analysis* (Hart Publishing, 2017).

[3] Matthew Walton, 'Ethnicity, Conflict, and History in Burma: The Myths of Panglong' (2008) 48:6 *Asian Survey* 889–910.

over natural resources. There is debate about whether the Panglong Agreement has legal effect today.[4]

Several months after the signing of the Panglong Agreement, General Aung San's political party, the AFPFL, met to put together a preliminary draft Constitution. In April 1947, a Constituent Assembly was then elected to draft a constitution, according to the terms of elections under the Government of Burma Act 1935. Dissent began to emerge, with two major organisations, the Communist Party of Burma and the Karen National Union, boycotting the elections.[5] From June to September 1947, the 111-member Constituent Assembly met to draft the 1947 Constitution. The draft AFPFL constitution was submitted to the Constituent Assembly for discussion, debate and revision. In July, the assassination of General Aung San and other members of the cabinet disrupted the process of constitution-making, and changes to the draft constitution were made after his death. On 10 December 1947, the Parliament of the United Kingdom passed the Burma Independence Act to acknowledge the independence of Burma as a sovereign state, which came into effect the following January. The Constituent Assembly became the provisional Parliament until the first elections were held.

The 1947 Constitution was a constitution that promoted a social democracy. The executive was led by the Prime Minister and the Cabinet. The government functioned according to the conventions familiar to the British cabinet and parliamentary democracy. The structure of the Constitution was considered to be a semi-unitary state instead of a federal state. Aung San had placed significant emphasis on the distinction between a Union and a unitary state, and the draft AFPFL Constitution offered substantive forms of subnational recognition. In contrast, the 1947 Constitution is perceived to be a Union in name only. Some ethnic groups point to the later admission of Chief Justice U Chan Htun who held that while the Constitution was in theory federal, in operation it was unitary. Others complained about the inconsistencies in the kinds of recognition given to different ethnic groups.

In its final form, the 1947 Constitution recognised special arrangements for certain ethnic groups. Shan State and Karenni State were created with a right to secession after ten years. The Kachin relinquished the

---

[4] Discussed further in Melissa Crouch (forthcoming) 'Reconciling the Past and Present in Peace Processes and Constitution-making: Constitutional Touchstones in the Debate on Federalism in Myanmar' *International Journal of Constitutional Law*.

[5] See Ardeth Maung Thawnghmung, *The Other Karen in Myanmar* (Lexington Books, 2012) pp 41–42.

right to secession in favour of incorporation of two major districts into Kachin State. Kawthulay (Karen) Region was a provisional arrangement, in anticipation that a future commission would consider the creation of a Karen State. In 1951, after recommendations from the Regional Inquiry Committee, an amendment to the Constitution granted the Karen the full status of a state, but less than a quarter of Karens lived within its borders and the right to secession for Karen was removed. The Constitution also established Chin Division. Despite these forms of recognition, some ethnic groups criticised the 1947 Constitution because it differed from the broad promises of the Panglong Agreement in ways that they felt compromised aspirations for a truly federal system. In 1948–49, the Arakan, Karen, Karenni and Mon fought against the government, as well as communist insurgents. By 1958, U Nu offered an 'Arms for Democracy' initiative that included extending an offer of amnesty to rebel groups. However new rebellions broke out in Shan State (1959) and Kachin State (1961), prolonging the internal instability.

Also in 1958, the governing party, the AFPFL, split in two, and a caretaker military government was invited to take control from 1959–1960. This was the military's first direct experience at leading the entire country. The period of parliamentary democracy (1948–1962) was marked by the 'confederate' nature of the dominant political parties[6] and their subsequent splintering. Political factionalism in Burma was partly attributed to the fact that the constituent groups within each political party were permitted to set and maintain their own separate goals and organisation.[7] This situation is relevant to the contemporary commitment to a 'multi-party' system under the 2008 Constitution (see Chapters 3 and 4). The military as guardian of this system claims to sit above political factionalism.

Some of the constitutional provisions concerning ethnic groups were later abolished through constitutional amendments based on negotiations and deals made with ethnic leaders. In March 1961, other ethnic groups that were not yet included in the Constitution were given some recognition through the appointment of the Mon Affairs Minister and Arakan Affairs Minister.[8] After part of Shan State was subject to military administration from 1952, negotiations took place between

[6] Josef Silverstein, 'The Burma Socialist Party Programme and its Rivals: A One-Plus Party System' (1967) 8(1) *Journal of Southeast Asian History* 8–18.

[7] Ibid, p 17.

[8] Kyaw Yin, *The Foundations of Public Administration in Burma: A Study in Social and Historical Perspectives* (University Microfilms, 1958), p 299.

the government and Shan State leaders.[9] Subsequently, the system of feudalism that had existed and the rights of Shan chiefs and their representation in the Chamber of Nationalities were annulled through constitutional amendment.[10]

In the 1960s, aspirations for a federal system gained renewed momentum among minority groups. In February 1961, a major national conference on federalism and constitutional reform took place. Attended by 226 representatives, the conference led to the ratification of a document known as the Federal Proposal.[11] The proposal acknowledged the principles in the draft AFPFL Constitution regarding various territorial and symbolic arrangements for ethnic groups including the Union State, Autonomous States and National Areas. Proposed reforms included rearranging the division of legislative power between the Union and the States to give the States greater power. Another proposal was to restructure the Chamber of Nationalities so that each state had equal (rather than proportional) representation. The Report of the Government Advisory Committee largely rejected the suggestions of this movement.[12] On 1 March 1962, a Constitutional Reform Conference was scheduled to be held in Taunggyi, Southern Shan State. The main agenda was the 'federal principle' – that is the proposal that Burma Proper (the lowland, Burman-majority areas) become a state alongside seven other ethnic states (including recognition of the new states of Arakan and Mon). On 2 March 1962, a coup led by General Ne Win was carried out, partly in reaction to concerns over federal aspirations and fears of secession. Many key members of the elected government and ethnic leaders involved in the federal proposal were arrested and detained. These unresolved debates remain part of the constitutional landscape.

II. NE WIN'S 'BURMESE' SOCIALISM AND THE 1974 CONSTITUTION

The federalist movement became the pretext for General Ne Win's coup. The period from 1962 to 1988 started with 12 years of direct military

---

[9] Sai Aung Tun, *History of the Shan State: From its Origins to 1962.* (Bangkok, Silkworm Books, 2009) pp 317, 338.

[10] The Constitution Amendment Act 1959 (second) repealed s 154(2).

[11] *The Shan Federal Proposal: Document Containing Proposals for the Revision of the Constitution of the Union of Burma Submitted by the Shan State* (translated by Sao Singha, 1961) Rangoon: Dotawun Press, Ministry of Information.

[12] Report of the Government Advisory Committee on the Amendment of the Constitution as proposed by the Shan State and its People 1962. 8 January 1965. Rangoon.

rule without a constitution followed by another 14 years under the 1974 Constitution. This period was marked by various conflicts and insurgencies, as well as negotiations and ceasefires.

In 1962, many elites, from the President to the Chief Justice, members of Parliament, ethnic leaders, businesspersons, and high-level civil servants, were detained. A Leninist-inspired political system with a centralised command and control structure was introduced. At the centre of this system was the Revolutionary Council, occupied by military generals who oversaw the centrally administered Security and Administrative Councils. The Revolutionary Council set up the Burma Socialist Programme Party (BSPP) and propagated an ideology of *The Burmese Way to Socialism*,[13] a document that rejected key tenets of parliamentary democracy and was used to indoctrinate new recruits to the BSPP. The BSPP party members in the early years were a mix of both military and civilian recruits,[14] although the military held the top positions.[15] In 1964, key leaders of the Revolutionary Council travelled to Switzerland, Yugoslavia, Czechoslovakia and East Germany. From this trip, they borrowed the concept of the 'People's War' that is used to justify the establishment of various people's militia and the role of the military in politics.[16] Rapid nationalisation led to the virtual elimination of the private sector and the devastation of the economy. The Revolutionary Council took control of all banks, and all imports and exports.[17]

In April 1963, Ne Win made minimal efforts to negotiate with communist insurgents and ethnic armed organisations (although not with political leaders detained since 1962). The offer of a temporary amnesty was conditioned on acceptance of the Burmese way to socialism. Between June and November that year, leaders of almost every underground group came to Rangoon. These negotiations fared poorly, and by mid-November negotiations collapsed and the Revolutionary Council continued with mass arrests. While these early attempts at ceasefires and

---

[13] The Burmese Way to Socialism is included in *The System of Correlation of Man and His Environment and The Constitution of the BSPP* (1963).

[14] Josef Silverstein, 'The Burma Socialist Party Programme and its Rivals: A One-Plus Party System' (1967) 8(1) *Journal of Southeast Asian History* 8–18.

[15] Maitrii Aung-Thwin, 'The State', in Ian Halliday et al (eds) *Routledge Handbook on Contemporary Myanmar* (London, Routledge, 2018) p 17.

[16] Maung Aung Myoe, *Building the Tatmadaw: Myanmar Armed Forces Since 1948* (Singapore: ISEAS, 2009).

[17] Josef Silverstein. 'First Steps on the Way to Burmese Socialism' (1964) 4(2) *Asian Survey* 716.

amnesty failed, the regime persisted with its efforts to entrench its rule via a new constitution. Several years later, in November 1969, General Ne Win convened a group of 33 former politicians, including former leaders who had been released from detention such as Prime Minister U Nu, to participate in an Internal Unity Advisory Board. The Board had six months to consult the public and provide advice on the drafting of a new constitution. There was disagreement among the Board, and Ne Win did not agree with the federal draft proposed, and so instead initiated his own constitution-making process.

The process of drafting the 1974 Constitution was characterised by an emphasis on form over substance in terms of participation by the people and took place within a restrictive environment. The 1974 Constitution was drafted over a period of three years. In June 1971, the First BSPP Party Congress was convened, and six principles for constitutional reform were set out. The Central Committee of the BSPP formed a 97-member Commission to draft a constitution. The Constitution Drafting Commission was chaired by General San Yu, who later became the chairperson of the Council of State and president, the most powerful person in Burma second only to Ne Win. The government formally invited submissions, although some individuals were arrested for their suggestions, particularly where they advocated for a federalist system.[18] In August 1973, the final draft was presented to the BSPP Central Committee. In December 1973, a national referendum was held to vote on the Constitution. This was the first time a referendum had been held to approve a constitution in Burma although it was a form of mass participation along coercive socialist lines. The process was also corrupt. Ballots cast into a black box marked 'no' to vote against the proposed constitution were in some cases transferred by officials into the white box marked 'yes'. The alleged approval rate was 90.19 per cent, although in some of the ethnic states it was lower, with just 69 per cent in Kachin State, 66 per cent in Shan State, and 71 per cent in Kayah State.[19]

On 3 January 1974, the Constitution was enacted. It constitutionalised a single party system with the BSPP as the sole political party. It established a unicameral legislature as the most powerful state organ. The Council of State was formed from the members of the unicameral legislature and remained responsible to it. The unicameral legislature

---

[18] Christina Fink, *Living in Silence in Burma: Surviving Under Military Rule* (Silkworm, 2009) p 31.

[19] David Steinberg, *Burma's Road Toward Development* (Westview Press, 1982), p 65.

elected all major bodies including the Council of Ministers, the Council of People's Justices, the Council of People's Attorneys and the Council of People's Inspectors. Members of the Pyithu Hluttaw were in theory directly elected, and elections were to be held every four years. Elections were held in 1974, 1978, 1981 and 1985. These elections, however, usually only had one candidate for each seat.[20] In some areas where independent candidates were proposed for election, these candidates were put under arrest without trial.[21] The unicameral legislature, rather than the courts, had the power to interpret the law and the Constitution. In this way, the 1974 Constitution signalled the overt rejection of the separation of powers. The judicial role of the Council of People's Justices was subordinate to the legislature and to the socialist system, which it was required to uphold.

The 1974 Constitution introduced a new formula for constitutional recognition of ethnic claims. Seven States and Seven Divisions were formalised, putting the eight major ethnic groups on an ostensibly equal plane. The new flag represented this division with 14 stars. These regions did not have independent sovereignty nor a right to self-determination, and there was no longer a right to secession. The ethnic groups previously given some forms of special recognition in the 1947 Constitution were formally promoted to the status of States (Kayah State, Karen State, Chin State, Kachin State, Shan State), along with the addition of Mon State and Arakan State. The seven States were on the same administrative level as the seven Divisions, and roughly covered what British authorities previously termed 'the excluded areas'.[22] At this time, the States and Divisions had few substantive powers, because it was the central unicameral Hluttaw that retained all legislative power for the entire country.

Burma's socialist constitutional system did not last. The collapse of the economy and drastic, unanticipated demonetisation measures by the regime were the tipping point for widespread social unrest. In 1988, student protests calling for democracy led to the collapse of the socialist regime. Rather than a transition to democratic rule, the socialist regime was replaced by direct military rule.

---

[20] Albert D Moscotti, *Burma's Constitution and the Elections of 1974* (ISEAS 1977) p 157.

[21] Steinberg, above n 19, p 70, giving the example of a township in Sagaing Division.

[22] Mary Callahan, *Political Authority in Burma's Ethnic Minority States* (Washington, East-West Center, 2007) p 12.

III. THE MILITARY AND CONSTITUTION-MAKING:
1990s–2000s

Some scholars have argued that the 2008 Constitution merely had 'contested beginnings',[23] implying that it is no longer contested. Yet it is precisely this contested drafting process that *continues* to animate debates on constitutional reform. This debate focuses on the grievances of representatives in the 1990 elections who were denied office; the increasing hostility between the regime, pro-democratic actors and ethnic groups; and the staged and controlled National Convention process, resulting in the 2008 constitutional referendum shortly after Cyclone Nargis. This process of constitution-making deeply undermines the legitimacy of the 2008 Constitution.

After the military took over in 1988, it set about preparing for national elections. In the May 1990 elections, the National League for Democracy (NLD) won by a significant margin due to a first-past-the-post voting system. This was an unexpected shock and humiliating defeat for the military. Two months after the May 1990 elections, in July, the State Law and Order Restoration Council (SLORC) decided it would not convene the legislature, but rather mandate that a new constitution be drafted. General Khin Nyunt publicly announced that a National Convention would have the sole task of drafting a new constitution, which was expected to take five to ten years. This set off two decades of dispute with the NLD and other parties who demanded that the military honour the results of the election by allowing them to form Parliament. In the 1990s, a government in exile was set up of elected members who had been denied office, known as the National Coalition Government of the Union of Burma. As late as 2010, the 1990 election results were declared to be legally invalid.[24]

During this period of unconstitutional rule, a new set of constitutional principles were formulated and propagated. From 1993 to 1996, state-controlled media issued a series of basic principles as reported at the National Convention. Coverage in The New Light of Myanmar suggests that the Tatmadaw had already determined the core of the new political structure. The National Convention process broke down in 1996, with several NLD and minority members expelled from proceedings and the Convention was suspended. It was not until 2003,

---

[23] Maitrii Aung-Thwin, 'The State', in I Halliday et al (eds) *Routledge Handbook on Contemporary Myanmar* (Routledge, 2018) p 15.

[24] Pyithu Hluttaw Electoral Law No 3/2010, s 91(b).

after General Khin Nyunt articulated a seven-step roadmap, that the National Convention was reconvened. This time the venue was moved from Yangon to a remote, purpose-built location, isolating constitution-makers and constitutional debate. This process occurred in the era before wide internet coverage in Myanmar and so local actors had recourse to limited, historical materials and hardcopies of constitutions of other countries. The Convention was to be followed by the introduction of a disciplined democracy; finalisation of the draft Constitution; endorsement of the Constitution via a referendum; elections; the convening of the legislature; and the establishment of a modern democratic state. During the National Convention, some ethnic groups made submissions calling for federalism. For example, the Kachin Independence Organisation submitted a 19-point proposal that included recognition of official second languages and of customary law.[25] These proposals were ignored. The restrictive nature of the constitution-making process did not escape the international community and in 2005, the National Convention was criticised by the UN Commission on Human Rights.[26]

Several other important developments took place parallel to the National Convention. One was the emphasis on national reconciliation, which included both ceasefires with ethnic armed organisations, and negotiations with the National League for Democracy and Aung San Suu Kyi.[27] The extensive ceasefires of the 1990s led to the inclusion of these groups in the National Convention and the designation of a Self-Administered Area for four ceasefire groups (see Chapter 7). These ceasefires were relatively simple, allowing ethnic armed organisations to retain their arms and their territory. The 1990s–2000s also saw the militarisation of governance, with the military exercising executive, legislative and judicial power and expanding in size, scale and scope. The military became a powerful entity not only politically and ideologically, but also commercially. Opposition groups, such as the NLD, were harassed, detained and silenced.

The 2008 Constitution was drafted in one of the longest constitution-making exercises in the world. The conditions under which the Constitution was adopted were severely strained and revealed the

---

[25] Lian H Sakhong, *In Defence of Identity: The Ethnic Nationalities' Struggle for Democracy, Human Rights, and Federalism in Burma* (Bangkok: Orchid Press, 2010). pp 137–142.

[26] Ashley South, *Ethnic Politics in Burma* (London: Routledge, 2008). pp 129–133.

[27] Maung Aung Myoe, 'National Reconciliation Process in Myanmar' (2002) 24(2) *Contemporary Southeast Asia* 371–384.

regimes' indifference to humanitarian concerns. In May 2008, Cyclone Nargis tore through parts of lower Myanmar and the delta region. The effect of the cyclone was made worse by the delays and bureaucratic barriers to the delivery of humanitarian aid. The scheduled referendum to vote on the Constitution was only postponed in cyclone-affected areas by a few days. Given restrictions on the provision of aid, parts of the country hit by the cyclone were in no state to be voting on a referendum.[28]

One reason the Constitution Committee and the National Convention remain significant is because some constitution-drafters are active members in the legislature and the executive post-2011. One way to measure the first period of a constitution is by whether the original constitution-makers are still involved in politics.[29] There are both high and low-profile participants from the National Convention from the military, the USDP, ethnic groups and the NLD who remain influential in government. This includes high-level elites such as president Thein Sein (2011–2016); the Chief Justice of the Supreme Court; and the former Speaker and chair of the Legal Affairs and Special Cases Assessment Commission, Shwe Mann. It also includes former representatives of national races at the National Convention, some of whom are now Ministers for National Races Affairs, and high-level elites such as U T Khun Myat, appointed Speaker of the Pyithu Hluttaw in 2018 and former member of the constitution-drafting committee and constitutional referendum commission.[30] One NLD member who was elected in 1990 and was involved in the National Convention is U Win Myint, who in 2018 was appointed by the NLD Government as president. Other actors who were involved in the constitution-drafting process are retired but remain present behind the scenes, including U Tun Shin (former Attorney General and chairperson of the National Convention from 2004); U Tin Aung Aye, former member of the Constitutional Tribunal (2011–2012); and U Aung Toe, former Chief Justice and key figure at the National Convention. In this regard, the first period of the Constitution continues under the influence of the constitution-drafters. It is in this atmosphere that the Basic Principles of the Constitution were formulated as the vision for the military-state.

---

[28] Andrew Selth, 'Even Paranoids Have Enemies: Cyclone Nargis and Myanmar's Fears of Invasion' (2008) 30(3) *Contemporary Southeast Asia* 379–402.

[29] Tom Ginsburg and Aziz Huq, *Implementing New Constitutions* (CUP forthcoming 2019).

[30] Moe Myint, 'From Militia Leader to House Speaker', *The Irrawaddy*, 24 May 2018, www.irrawaddy.com/news/analysis-militia-leader-house-speaker.html.

IV. THE PREAMBLE AND THE BASIC PRINCIPLES
OF THE CONSTITUTION

Printed copies of the Constitution begin with a series of notifications that come before the preamble. These notifications confirm the 2010 constitutional referendum results and bear the official ratification of the most powerful military officer at the time, General Than Shwe. Although now in retirement and not holding any official position since 2011, 'Number One', as Than Shwe is known, is still considered to have a significant influence over the entire political system.

The history of debates over federalism, democracy and public participation in constitution-making and political life contrasts with the history told in the preamble to the 2008 Constitution. The 2008 Constitution begins with 1885 as a dark moment when British claims to empire were complete. The preamble then jumps forward 60 years to mark 4 January 1948 as the culmination of the anti-colonial struggle and the beginning of independence as a modern state. The preamble omits reference to the most important pre-independence document, the Panglong Agreement, because of its association with General Aung San and claims to self-determination, autonomy and federalism. The reasons the preamble offers about national races being divided and weak fit with the Tatmadaw's narrative of its role in leadership of the country, though are insufficient to explain why Burma fell to British rule. The preamble to the 2008 Constitution speaks little of socialist and military rule for fear of implicating those who were part of it. The preamble to the 2008 Constitution blames the short, three month drafting process of the 1947 Constitution and the lack of democratic consolidation as the reason for the shift to a socialist regime. It omits mention of the undemocratic coup that paved the way for the socialist era. The preamble acknowledges that the 1974 Constitution instituted a one-party state, although claims this system received endorsement from the people in a national referendum. Neither the gross economic and political failures of the socialist regime, nor the period of unconstitutional rule from 1962–1974, are mentioned.

The preamble of the 2008 Constitution does acknowledge the role of the State Peace and Development Council (SPDC),[31] depicting the Tatmadaw ruling body as central to the emergence of the

---

[31] The Constitution refers to SPDC as the name of the regime since 1997. From 1988 to 1997 the regime was known as the State Law and Order Restoration Council, and the reference to SPDC here presumably includes the full period from 1988–2010.

2008 Constitution. The Constitution attributes to the SPDC the turn to competitive elections and the shift to a market economy. The preamble suggests that experts from a range of sectors came together to contribute to the alleged success of the National Convention held to draft the Constitution. In vague terms, the preamble does hint at the difficulties that plagued the National Convention from 1992 to 2007 but does not acknowledge that 1988–2010 was a period of unconstitutional rule. The preamble concludes with an exhortation to national races, compelling them to adhere to the Three Main National Causes as the ideology of the military-state (see Chapter 3). The preamble to the 2008 Constitution does not acknowledge the history of the struggle for federalism, nor the inability of the government under parliamentary democracy to meet these demands.

The substance of the 2008 Constitution bear traces of this constitutional history. The constitutional design of the Basic Principles in Chapter I of the Constitution mixes ideas from the former 1947 and 1974 Constitutions.[32] The Basic Principles Chapter I contain abstract principles of the State, statements of State structure, citizens' duties and rights, and obligations of the State. Chapter II of the 1947 Constitution concerned fundamental rights, while Chapter IV contained directive principles. The 1974 Constitution swapped the order of these chapters, prioritising the Basic Principles of the socialist order and relegating rights to a later chapter. Retaining this order of priority, the 2008 Constitution uses the Basic Principles to entrench the Tatmadaw in the governance of the country. The provisions in Chapter I are a guide for the legislature and for the courts.[33] The Basic Principles inform the legislature in its legislative responsibilities and guide the courts in the interpretation of law.[34]

The principles of the state affirms a centralised government featuring a leading role for the Tatmadaw in the governance of the country. The Tatmadaw is given prime position in the political system and is central to the objectives of protecting national unity, maintaining territorial unity and guaranteeing the sovereignty of the nation.[35] I refer to these ideological commitments as the three meta-principles of the military-state (see Chapter 3), which are a feature of the Constitution that has been overlooked in analyses of Myanmar's Constitution. The Basic Principles

[32] This was based on the example of Directive Principles in the constitutions of India and Ireland.
[33] 2008 Constitution, s 451.
[34] Ibid, s 48.
[35] Ibid, s 6(a)–(c).

uphold a range of other principles of the state, such as the independence and sovereignty of the state, a commitment to a Union Republic, and a division of powers among the executive, legislature and judiciary. It also specifies adherence to a competitive political system that is disciplined; articulates a principle of non-secession; requires the Defence Services to play a guiding role in national governance including through guaranteed seats in the legislature; and mandates a foreign policy that is marked by a stance of non-alignment and non-aggression.[36] These principles are not uncontested in Myanmar. Economically, there is a commitment to a market economy; a principle of non-nationalisation of the economy and non-demonetisation (see Chapter 6).[37] The principle of non-secession and self-determination remain a point of controversy for ethnic armed organisations, and the role of the Tatmadaw in governance is the main point of contestation for pro-democratic actors.

The Basic Principles also contain statements of state structure that identify the design of the political and legal system and specify which institutions exercise power. The state is a Union that consists of seven Regions and Seven States, six Self-Administered Areas and one Union territory (Naypyidaw, the capital). There are many indications that this is a highly centralised system with the sub-units remaining dependent and subordinate to the central government. For example, the flag includes one big star,[38] representing unity. This contrasts with the 1974 flag that featured 14 stars representing the States/Regions, a small acknowledgement of diversity. The Union legislature consists of the Pyithu Hluttaw (lower house) and the Amyotha Hluttaw (upper house), and when sitting jointly these houses are known as the Pyidaungsu Hluttaw (see Chapter 5). The bulk of legislative power is held at the Union level, as is all residual power, with a nominal list of legislative powers given to the unicameral State/Region Hluttaw and the Self-Administered Areas. Both Union and sub-national Hluttaw include Tatmadaw members, and State/Region Hluttaw may include Ministers for National Races Affairs. The scope of executive power is concurrent with legislative power. Tatmadaw personnel have specific mandates over key defence and security matters. In terms of judicial institutions, the Basic Principles confirm that there is a Supreme Court, High Courts in each State and Region, and lower courts. A Constitutional Tribunal also exists for the resolution of constitutional disputes. The Commander-in-Chief is recognised as the head

[36] Ibid, ss 2, 8, 6(d), 7, 10, 11, 6(f), 14, 35, 41–42.
[37] Ibid, ss 36 (d) and (e).
[38] Ibid, s 437.

of all armed forces, which in Myanmar is a reference not only to the army, but also to People's Militia, Border Guard Forces, and other forces (see Chapter 3).

The Basic Principles features the duties of citizens and some rights. This includes the positive rights of equality, liberty and justice; freedom of conscience, freedom of religion; the right to vote and to be elected; and the right to recall legislators.[39] The Union must also allow citizens the right to private property and inheritance. It also includes negative rights to ensure citizens are not detained for more than 24 hours; criminal sanctions are not applied retrospectively, and punishment does not infringe upon human dignity.[40] While the rule against retrospectivity may be an important principle, some suggest it is just one of many loopholes in the Constitution intended to protect the Tatmadaw from prosecution of past crimes. Constitutional rights as directive principles are unenforceable, and so have no possibility of being upheld in court. However, some of these rights are repeated or elaborated further in Chapter VIII of the Constitution, where they are also heavily qualified. All citizens are deemed responsible for maintaining stability, order and public peace.[41] The citizens' rights and duties contained in the Basic Principles are an important indication of the relationship between the people and the military-state. Unlike in countries such as India, there is no possibility that the court would read the directive principles into Chapter VIII. Some argue that the citizens' rights in the Basic Principles should be amended to be made justiciable. Another omission and point of contention is that national races have no right to self-determination. Instead the Basic Principles navigate around this issue by offering a compromise in the form of weak, qualified cultural rights of citizens, and unenforceable obligations on the Union, in the Basic Principles.[42]

Finally, there are Basic Principles that are framed as state duties and responsibilities. These obligations are not mandatory and are often cast in terms of 'assisting', 'permitting' or 'fostering'. These state duties are heavily qualified by the phrase 'to the extent possible'. Some of these principles can be considered aspirational, however other principles simply bind the sub-national units or the people to the Union. Many of the provisions are specifically directed to national races in terms of promoting their languages, culture and traditions, as well as aspiring to support

---

[39] Ibid, ss 21(a), 34, 38.
[40] Ibid, ss 21(b), 43, 44.
[41] Ibid, s 21(c).
[42] Ibid, s 22, 27.

key socio-economic goals such as education and health.[43] The existence of these principles implicitly acknowledges that the seven ethnic-based States, particularly ones such as Chin State or Rakhine State, are far less developed and have higher levels of poverty than other Regions. The principles also implore the Union to protect and support a range of other people groups beside national races. These groups include peasants, workers, academics, civil servants, mothers, children, orphans of deceased defence service personnel, and injured defence personnel.[44] The Constitution exhorts the Union to support young people in achieving the Burmese Buddhist ideals of the five noble strengths:[45] faith, knowledge, perseverance, stability and prudence. This is the only reference to Buddhist principles in the entire Constitution. Like citizens' rights, these state duties are also unenforceable.

The Basic Principles include a mandate for the state to provide certain goods and services, such as free primary education, a modern education system, materials to support mechanised agriculture, foster industries, and the provision of jobs (and reduce unemployment).[46] There is also a vaguely expressed state responsibility to protect the environment. The state has responsibilities in a time of emergency to exercise its powers to prevent territorial disintegration, social breakdown or interference with national sovereignty. The Basic Principles articulate key elements of the military-state and offer a lens through which the 2008 Constitution was designed to be read.

V. CONCLUSION

The preamble of a constitution often tells a narrative of the history of that country. This narrative is always partial and quarantines off certain events or readings of a country's past. This history reveals something of the identity the constitution-makers imagine for their country and its people. A preamble makes deliberate claims about the authenticity of the Constitution and omits details that undermine these claims. Myanmar's 2008 Constitution is no different. The preamble marks key dates in the history of Myanmar and yet in omitting much of the socialist and military era, obscures much more than it reveals.

---

[43] Ibid, s 22, 28(b).
[44] Ibid, ss 23–26, 32, 33.
[45] Ibid, s 33.
[46] Ibid, ss 28(c) and (d), 29, 30, 31.

The history of constitutions in Myanmar is contested. Central to these debates have been demands for a federal system and calls for greater democratic representation and participation. Many past developments, including features of past constitutions as well as past failed proposals such as the federal proposal of 1961, emerge in contemporary discussions of the Constitution. The lack of regard and credibility with which the 2008 Constitution is viewed stems from its failure to resolve past debates on federalism and democracy, both in terms of the circumstances under which it was drafted and in its substance of a highly centralised political system. The preamble is one example of how certain constitutional milestones and unresolved debates have been removed from official versions of history.

The Basic Principles of the Constitution offer an articulation of the military-state, with priority given to the Tatmadaw as the leader and guardian of national governance. I turn to explain the centrality of these principles in detail in the following chapter.

FURTHER READING

Michael Charney, *A History of Modern Burma* (CUP, 2009).

Melissa Crouch, 'The Layers of Legal Development in Myanmar' in Melissa Crouch and Tim Lindsey (eds) *Law, Society and Transition in Myanmar* (Oxford, Hart Publishing, 2014).

Yoshihiro Nakanishi, *Strong Soldiers, Failed Revolution: The State and the Military in Burma* 1962–88 (NUS Press, 2013).

Martin Smith, *Burma: Insurgency and the Politics of Ethnicity*, 2nd ed. (White Lotus, 1991).

Robert Taylor, *The State of Myanmar* (2nd edition, NUS Press, 2009).

Matthew Walton, *Buddhism, Politics and Political Thought in Myanmar* (CUP, 2017).

3

The Military: The Pre-eminence of the Tatmadaw in Governance

Commander-in-Chief – Armed Forces – The Legislative, Executive and Judicial Power of the Tatmadaw – Tatmadaw as the Superior Branch

AT THE ENTRANCE to Myanmar's Defence Services Academy in Pyin Oo Lwin, several hours drive from Mandalay, a large sign in gold lettering reads 'The Triumphant Elite of the Future' (in Burmese and English). The message is clear – the Tatmadaw (တပ်မတော်), the armed forces, sees itself as the future elite class of Myanmar. The Constitution cannot be fully appreciated without first understanding the power of the Tatmadaw and the role of its personnel in the creation and operation of the Constitution. Since 1988, the Tatmadaw has morphed from a relatively small force of 180,000, to an estimated force of over 400,000.[1] Over time, the Tatmadaw has come to view its own people as the enemy.[2] The line between civilian and military interests has blurred as active and retired military officers take up positions in government or business. The increase in the size and scale of the Tatmadaw is evident across the country. Large areas of land were confiscated for military garrisons, which reach into areas of Myanmar where the government administration is absent. Because of the ceasefires of the 1990s (explained in Chapter 6), Tatmadaw personnel took on an expanded role in both the formal and informal economy – overseeing and running plantations and industries; manning road tolls and checkpoints; and coordinating and coercing local villagers in the construction of major infrastructure projects such as roads and bridges, as well as oil

---

[1] Maung Aung Myoe, 'Partnership in Politics: The Tatmadaw and the NLD in Myanmar', in Gerard McCarthy, Justine Chambers and Nicholas Farrelly (eds) *Myanmar Transformed: People, Places and Politics* (ISEAS, 2018).
[2] Mary P Callahan, *Making Enemies: War and State Building in Burma* (NUS Press 2004) p 5.

pipelines and dams. The expansion of the Tatmadaw also includes the establishment of a set of services and privileges for Tatmadaw personnel and their families that run parallel to state services – from housing to health care and education.[3]

It is against this backdrop of institutional strength that Chapter VII of the Constitution is devoted to the Tatmadaw (often referred to in English as 'the Defence Services'). The Constitution confers certain structural advantages on the Tatmadaw and permits it wide institutional autonomy. The Tatmadaw's personnel are primarily Burman Buddhists. In this regard the structural advantages do not simply privilege the armed forces, it privileges a dominant ethnic and religious group. In addition to formal structural advantages, the Tatmadaw also enjoys indirect influence over many key institutions in society and in this way has captured key elements across all branches of government. The three meta-principles of the military-state have morphed from Tatmadaw doctrine into constitutional ideology. The Constitution acknowledges the Commander-in-Chief but does not limit his role in any way. The constitutional role of the Tatmadaw members of the legislature, who make up 25 per cent of seats, is one of 'watchmen' over their civilian counterparts. The response of the Tatmadaw on legislative proposals can often be taken as a barometer reading of political tensions.

The National Defence and Security Council ('the Defence Council') is one means for the Tatmadaw to have direct power and influence over the State. The Defence Council's powers to take over during a state of emergency if there is a threat to the Basic Principles of the Constitution cast a shadow over the reform era. The General Administration Department is a key aspect of the executive branch under the control of the Ministry of Home Affairs, who is selected by the Commander-in-Chief. The courts martial are the formal institution through which the Tatmadaw exercises judicial power. In this way, the Tatmadaw is the fourth and unaccountable branch of government in Myanmar.

I. THE THREE MAIN NATIONAL CAUSES

The Constitution contains a set of three principles that form the ideological basis of Myanmar's military-state. As I explained in Chapter 1,

---

[3] Mary Callahan, 'Of Kyay-su and kyet-su: the Military in 2006' in Monique Skidmore and Trevor Wilson (eds) *Myanmar: The State, Community and the Environment* (ANU Press, 2007) p 47.

I use the term 'military-state' to describe the co-existence of civilian and military authorities. This arrangement is animated by three principles that are included as explicit written provisions in the Constitution. These principles were originally known as 'Our Three Main National Causes', capitalised in English translations.[4] In the 1990s, these principles were announced through military orders.[5] In 1993, the Union Solidarity Development Association (the precursor to the political party known as the Union Solidarity and Development Party), was formed to promote and preserve the Three Main National Causes. In official English translations by the government, these three principles are distilled as:

> non-disintegration of the Union;
> non-disintegration of national solidarity;
> the perpetuation of sovereignty.

These principles are living artefacts of direct military rule. By emphasising that these are 'Our' causes, the Tatmadaw co-opts the people into its cause. The principles claim priority in terms of their status as the 'Main' or preeminent principles of the state. The principles claim an intimate connection to the state as '*National* Causes', even though it was the Tatmadaw at the time running the apparatus of the state. These principles appear on nine separate occasions in the Constitution.

The Constitution is one means by which Tatmadaw directives command the loyalty of the people, political parties, Tatmadaw officers, the administration, the judiciary and legislators. In short, all branches of government, as well as the people individually and collectively, are bound by these principles. These are deeply conservative principles and profess to maintain the status quo. This was a deliberate drafting strategy and aspect of constitutional design.

The first element, *non-disintegration of the Union*, embodies the territorial unity of the military-state. This principle represents the rejection and denial of the secessionist and separatist demands of ethnic groups. The Tatmadaw has long rallied against groups that oppose the government or take up arms, whether it be communist insurgents, pro-democracy activists or ethnic armed organisations. Independent Burma struggled to contain and control insurgency by the Communist Party of Burma and the armed struggles of armed ethnic organisations for

---

[4] One example of Burmese publications on this topic is Minye Kaungbon, *Our Three Main National Causes* (Yangon, News and Periodical Enterprise, 1994).

[5] See, eg, SLORC Declaration No. 1/90, 27 July 1990; SLORC Order 13/1992, 2 October 1992.

territory and recognition (see Chapter 2). The unusual constitutional option of secession for certain ethnic groups after ten years in the 1947 Constitution was never realised, and this became a rallying point for ethnic grievances. The principle of non-disintegration is a reference to the territorial integrity of the country and is anti-secessionist. The principle seeks to combat the perceived risk of anarchy, disunity and chaos with an exhortation to resist and prevent state fragmentation or collapse. The potential fragmentation of the state is designed to invoke fears of crisis and chaos. The use of the negative form implies that the Union is already fully integrated and so all that is needed is to maintain this state of affairs.

The second element, the *disintegration of national solidarity*, overlaps with the first principle but also hints at the idea that there is a certain people or nation that is the subject of the Constitution. This is also cast in the negative and presumes that national solidarity has already been achieved. In Myanmar, the Constitution conceives of 'the people' in limited terms as national races (တိုင်းရင်းသား). The state recognises 135 ethnic races, although Burmans are the dominant group (see Chapter 1, for more detail see Chapter 7). The Constitution insists these national races must stand in unity, and this discourse on unity has been shared by both the military and pro-democratic actors.[6] Recognition as a national race confers legitimacy and inclusion in the state. The absence of recognition as a national race leads to exclusion and marginalisation and, at worse, statelessness. Cheesman suggests that the concept of national races has overtaken and become a precondition for citizenship.[7] National races are based on an arbitrary race matrix. According to this principle, no national race should attempt to secede from the military-state.

Third, the perpetuation of sovereignty is a reference to the integrity of the state. The need to defend state sovereignty against the risk of foreign interference was a constant source of paranoia for the military regime. This fear of foreignness had multiple manifestations but includes resistance to colonial rule, fear of communist insurgents, fear of the West and of the international community as embodied in the United Nations, and fear of its populous and powerful neighbours, China and India. One reason (among others) for the relocation and building of a new capital in Naypyidaw was to reduce the risk of invasion by foreign powers.

---

[6] Callahan, above n 2, p 227.
[7] Nick Cheesman, 'How in Myanmar "National Races" Came to Surpass Citizenship and Exclude Rohingya', (2017) 47:3 *Journal of Contemporary Asia* 461–483.

The principle of the consolidation and longevity of sovereignty is related to the continuity of the state and its main political actors, that is, the role of the Tatmadaw in protecting national sovereignty.

The first two principles imply that the goal of national solidarity and integration of the Union has *already* been achieved, and that all that is left to do now is to ensure that it does not fall apart. Like the first two, the third principle presumes that sovereignty has been attained. All that is left to do is for the Tatmadaw to ensure the maintenance and longevity of this sovereignty.

The Tatmadaw has created a historical narrative to justify these three principles. In the Tatmadaw mindset, the need for these principles arises from the tragedy of colonial rule.[8] The Tatmadaw depicts Burma during the period of colonial conquest (1823–1885) as weak and divided. The official narrative goes that Burma lost control of its territory and forfeited its national sovereignty because of its divided and disorganised nature. All blame is placed on British colonisers for suspicions, divisions and antagonisms between different national races. They also blame the British for exploiting natural resources,[9] but in doing so the Tatmadaw's narrative glosses over the economic and political devastation wrought by the socialist regime and the decades of rampant resource exploitation by cronies. The Tatmadaw rallies against British 'imperialists' and Japanese 'fascists',[10] but never acknowledges the decades of exploitative Tatmadaw rule. The purpose of this re-telling of national history is to cast all blame on a group other than the Tatmadaw and to paint over the complicity of the socialist and military regimes in the demise of the state.

The three meta-principles of the military-state link to and reinforce the role of the Tatmadaw as leading the country: in silencing secessionist claims and brokering ceasefire deals; in building and promoting a fixed and exclusive idea of national races; and in holding the line against any unwanted interference by foreign powers. These principles are repeated consistently and regularly throughout the Constitution. The principles first appear in the preamble and Chapter I on the Basic Principles of the Constitution. The principles are listed as a core responsibility of the Tatmadaw.[11] Citizens also have the responsibility

---

[8] Minye Kaungbon, *Our Three Main National Causes* (Yangon. News and Periodical Enterprise, 1994) pp 10, 15.

[9] Ibid, pp 115, 122.

[10] Ibid, p 151.

[11] 2008 Constitution, ss 6, 20(e).

to uphold and protect these principles.[12] In addition, the principles are contained in the oath sworn by the president and vice-presidents, the oath for all legislators, as a constitutional obligation of all citizens, and as a constitutional requirement that all political parties include these principles in their objectives.[13] The principles are also given a prominent place in legislation, particularly in the laws of 2010 that were drafted by the prior military regime in preparation for the implementation of the Constitution.

These principles embody the constitutionalisation of the Tatmadaw's vision of the state. This vision was developed over several decades of direct military rule. The principles emanated from every orifice of the state: over the radio, in schools and printed in newspapers. In 1999, the first defence policy issued by the Tatmadaw included reference to the Three Main National Causes.[14] The principles were required to be printed on the inside cover of every book and publication under the censorship regime enforced by military rule. The principles were listed in the Tatmadaw's defence policy of the State Law and Order Restoration Council (SLORC).[15] The Tatmadaw remains an active proponent and promoter of this doctrine. Even today, the Tatmadaw still refers to 'Our Three Main National Causes' along with exhortations to protect the Constitution, in line with section 20(f) of the Constitution.

These constitutional principles not only limit state institutions, but place limits on other actors – ethnic groups, civil society, political parties, elite political actors, individuals – and calibrate their relationship to the Tatmadaw. The principles do not of themselves constitute a limit on the power of the strongest institution, the Tatmadaw. Although the idea of a constitution as placing limits on public power is prominent globally, there is also recognition in the academic literature that many aspects of a constitution are enabling and facilitate the use of power. These principles justify and facilitate the role of the Tatmadaw as the leading body. The Three Main National Causes condition the lived experiences of people in Myanmar's military-state. There is little public space to debate whether these principles are ideas that the people of Myanmar want as the foundation and basis of their future society.

---

[12] Ibid, s 283.

[13] Ibid, ss 65, 404 and Sch 4.

[14] Maung Aung Myoe, *Military Doctrine and Strategy in Myanmar: A Historical Perspective* (Working Paper No 339. Strategic and Defence Studies, ANU, 1999).

[15] Maung Aung Myoe, *Building the Tatmadaw: Myanmar Armed Forces Since 1948* (Singapore: ISEAS, 2009) p 1, 34.

II. THE COMMANDER-IN-CHIEF

The Basic Principles in the Constitution set out a series of pronounce-
ments on the role of the Commander-in-Chief and the Tatmadaw in
relation to the Constitution.[16] The Commander is the head and leader
of the armed forces. The Commander-in-Chief promotes and protects
the meta-principles of the military-state. The Commander-in-Chief also
has full control over all aspects of the internal administration of the
Tatmadaw.

There is controversy over the appointment and tenure of the
Commander-in-Chief. Formally, the Commander-in-Chief is appointed
by the president on the approval of the Defence Council. The
Commander-in-Chief is not subordinate to the executive branch. He
is the only high-level political position that is not limited to a five-year
term. There has been controversy over the lack of details about the
Commander-in-Chief's length of service and whether this role is limited
by a mandatory retirement age for civil servants. In 2011, under the Thein
Sein Government, Senior General Min Aung Hlaing was appointed as
Commander-in-Chief. In 2016, Min Aung Hlaing was approaching
61 years of age, but the rules governing civil servants require retirement at 60. Concerns were raised that the Commander-in-Chief was
not subject to any age limitation, although in Myanmar high ranking government officials can be granted exemptions to this rule. The
Tatmadaw confirmed that a 1973 directive allowed a military officer
to remain in service beyond the age limit if necessary.[17] However it was
reported that the Defences Services Act had been amended in January
2014 to set the age limit for the Commander-in-Chief at 65 years old.
Reports surfaced that the Tatmadaw amended this law using section 291
of the Constitution as justification, which allows for military laws to
regulate its role. This suggests that the Tatmadaw also has legislative
power, for example, to amend sections of the Defence Services Act.[18]
The legislature has amended other laws relating to the Tatmadaw.[19]

The Commander-in-Chief is the head of the Tatmadaw as the leading
body of the military-state. His role as the public face of the Tatmadaw
is to promote the ideology of the military-state and maintain adherence

---

[16] 2008 Constitution, s 20(a)–(f).
[17] Ei Ei Thu, 'Commander-in-Chief retirement age set at 65', *The Myanmar Times*,
21 July 2016, www.mmtimes.com/national-news/21491-commander-in-chief-retirement-
age-set-at-65.html.
[18] Defence Services Act 1959.
[19] Eg, the Law Amending the Law on Military Ranks No 42/2014.

to the disciplined and centralised system of governance. Senior General Min Aung Hlaing's public appearances and speeches reinforce the role of the Tatmadaw in overseeing governance and ensuring the security and unity of the country. For example, on the 71st commemoration of Armed Forces Day (27 March), Min Aung Hlaing rallied the Tatmadaw around 'Our Three Main National Causes', that is, sections 6(a)–(c) of the Constitution.[20] His public speeches uphold the leading role for the military and promote adherence to the three meta-principles of the military-state.

In addition, because of the Commander-in-Chief's role in upholding these principles, any remarks perceived to be derogatory towards him are not taken lightly. For example, in July 2017, the Yangon Chief Minister and NLD member was reprimanded by the Tatmadaw for suggesting that the position of the Commander-in-Chief is the same as a director general level administrator, implying it is a low-level office compared to other positions of political leadership. This comment was made while the Chief Minister was at a workshop run by an international organisation in Yangon, suggesting that military intelligence, known as the Special Branch, may have been present at this workshop. The Tatmadaw released several public statements in response, claiming these remarks were an insult to the Commander-in-Chief. The Chief Minister submitted a written letter of apology to the Commander-in-Chief, and the NLD also publicly noted that they had reprimanded the Chief Minister as an NLD member.[21] This incident is one indication of the deference that even the NLD shows to Tatmadaw officials and is an implicit acknowledgment of the Tatmadaw's leading role in governance.

The Commander-in-Chief has the power to make key appointments. The Basic Principles give the Commander-in-Chief the power to nominate Tatmadaw personnel who will be responsible for the exercise of executive power in relation to matters of defence, national security and border administration.[22] The most important and influential areas of government administration – Home Affairs, Defence, Border Affairs – report regularly to the Commander-in-Chief. Although these ministers are appointed by the Commander-in-Chief through a process in which

[20] Ministry of Information, 'Here to Stay: Commander in Chief addresses 71st Armed Forces Day Parade, 28 March 2016, www.moi.gov.mm/moi:eng/?q=news/28/03/2016/id-6779.

[21] San Yamin Aung, 'Yangon Chief Minister Apologies to Military Chief', 17 July 2017, *The Irrawaddy*, www.irrawaddy.com/news/burma/yangon-chief-minister-apologizes-military-chief.html.

[22] 2008 Constitution, s 17(b).

the Commander-in-Chief refers names to the president, a president has not yet rejected a recommended candidate. These ministerial positions are important because the Ministry of Home Affairs includes the police force of 80,000 officers.[23] The head of the police is a serving Lieutenant General, ensuring that the Tatmadaw and police remain deeply intertwined. Up until December 2018, the General Administration Department sat under the Ministry of Home Affairs, forming the core of the government administration at the State/Region level. On 28 December 2018, it was announced that the General Administration Department will be moved to the Ministry for the Office of the Union Government, which is an intentional effort to place it under civilian control. The Ministry of Border Affairs has historically been used to control and contain areas on the territorial periphery of the country that have experienced ethnic armed insurgencies. This border containment and control function is crucial to the principle of non-disintegration. Aside from the Ministry of Border Affairs, Home Affairs and Defence, there are other ministries that the Tatmadaw has de facto influence over, such as the Ministry of Immigration. This became clear in January 2016 when efforts were made in the legislature to pass a law to allow the Commander-in-Chief to appoint the Minister for Immigration. While the proposal failed to gain support, the Tatmadaw clearly wanted to formalise its influence over immigration as part of its core role in the face of the uncertainty of the incoming NLD Government.

The Commander-in-Chief oversees the powerful role that the Constitution imagines for the Tatmadaw. Its oversized role is due to the number of its officers, the size of its weaponry, and the size of its budget.[24] One possible constitutional limit on the role of the Tatmadaw is the prohibition on the Union going to war with a foreign power.[25] However, the Constitution allows for a convenient loophole and measure of protection against external threats of aggression: no foreign troops are allowed in the country.[26] The Commander-in-Chief must also maintain internal cohesion of the Tatmadaw and often exhorts officers to abide by the military code of conduct, a set of 60 principles.[27]

---

[23] Andrew Selth, 'Police Reform and the Civilianisation of the Security in Myanmar', in Melissa Crouch and Tim Lindsey (Eds) *Law, Society and Transition in Myanmar.* (Hart Publishing, 2014) p 274.

[24] 2008 Constitution, s 20(a).

[25] Ibid, s 42(a).

[26] Ibid, s 42(b).

[27] Military Code of Conduct, 60 principles, on file with the author (in Burmese).

The Commander-in-Chief leads the Tatmadaw in responding to disasters,[28] and this power is included in the Constitution. Implicitly, this power is in response to the controversy over the role of the Tatmadaw in Cyclone Nargis in 2008. Further, military conscription is mandated by the Constitution, although this has never been enforced.[29] In terms of officers below the Commander-in-Chief, some are designated as serving under military law.[30] This means that issues such as retirement age, promotion, suspension, commendation or censure fall under military law.

III. FORCES AFFILIATED WITH THE TATMADAW

In January 2016, at the first Union Peace conference, the Commander-in-Chief articulated a vision of the Tatmadaw as a 'standard army'.[31] The Commander-in-Chief regularly makes references in his speeches to building a 'Standard Army'. The use of this phrase is understood to be distinct from 'professional army' (which has negative connotations) and from the proposal for a 'federal army' which is the demand of ethnic armed organisations. The Tatmadaw is a broad umbrella and includes not only the army, navy and air force, but also a range of other security forces[32] – including the police, Border Guard Forces, paramilitary forces, auxiliary forces and gangs. These forces are said to be authorised by section 128 in the Code of Criminal Procedure, which permits the police to obtain the assistance of civilians to disperse public assemblies and arrest and confine participants.[33] In March 2015, the President's Office referred to article 128 as a justification to crack down on student protests in Yangon, while NLD ministers and Chief Ministers have also referred to the legitimacy of the police obtaining civilian support to disperse unauthorised gatherings.[34]

---

[28] 2008 Constitution, s 341.

[29] Ibid, s 386.

[30] Ibid, s 291.

[31] See, eg, Ko Zan (2018) *Mingalarba Tatmadaw*. n.p.; Yangon; Tin Maung Maung Than, 'Burma: The New Professionalism of the Tatmadaw', in Muthiah Alagappa (ed) *Military Professionalism in Asia*. (East West Centre 2001).

[32] 2008 Constitution, s 338.

[33] Code of Criminal Procedure, ss 127–128.

[34] Asian Human Rights Commission 'Attack gangs and falsification against the orders of the day' 11 March 2015, www.humanrights.asia/news/ahrc-news/AHRC-STM-039-2015/.

The Constitution is silent on the role and position of the police, with the exception of section 292, which mentions that members of the police force who are also civil servants are to be regulated by a specific law.[35] Section 338 of the Constitution implies that the police, who also bear arms, are under the control of the Tatmadaw. The police sit under the Ministry of Home Affairs and the Commander-in Chief is authorised to submit a candidate to the President for the position of Minister for Home Affairs.[36] In practice, the Minister for Home Affairs is seen as a military-appointed position. The close relationship between the Tatmadaw and police is confirmed in the 2015 Defence White Paper. In a section on 'National Defence', the role of the army, navy and air force is followed by a section on reserves and the police as part of the reserve force.[37] The White Paper also includes a separate paragraph on the police who are to focus on internal security and law enforcement. The paragraph immediately following the police notes that the above forces are insufficient and a People's War strategy with People's Militia is necessary. Like other institutions of the military-state, the police also have a mandate to fulfil the Three Main National Causes.[38] There has not yet been efforts to separate the police from the Tatmadaw, although there have been calls from ethnic armed organisations for separate state-based police forces.

Aside from the police, the Constitution explicitly refers to other forces and militia.[39] One such force is known as the People's Militia. The People's Militia first emerged as part of counter-insurgency operations in the 1960s and the emphasis on the 'People's War'.[40] The Tatmadaw still refers to the 'People's War', such as in its 2015 Defence White Paper. People's Militia were used against political opponents and to counter the efforts of armed organisations who are perceived to be hostile to the Tatmadaw.[41] The use of the term 'People's Militia' has changed over

---

[35] See Myanmar Police Force Maintenance of Discipline Law 1995; Police Manual Vols 1–3, 2000, 2001.

[36] 2008 Constitution, s 232(b)(ii). The candidate is then put to the legislature for final approval, but the Pyiduangsu Hluttaw has no power to refuse an eligible candidate. See also Andrew Selth, 'Myanmar's Police Forces: Coercion, Continuity and Change' (2012) 34(1) *Contemporary Southeast Asia* 53–79.

[37] The Republic of the Union of Myanmar, *Defence White Paper*, Naypyidaw, December 2015, paras 57–58.

[38] Andrew Selth 'Myanmar's Coercive Apparatus', in David Steinburg (eds) *Myanmar: The Dynamics of an Evolving Polity* (London: Lynne Rienner Publishers, 2015). p 33.

[39] 2008 Constitution, s 340.

[40] Maung Aung Myoe, above n 15, p 27.

[41] Jane M Ferguson, 'Sovereignty in the Shan State' in Nick Cheesman et al (eds) *Ruling Myanmar in Transition* (ISEAS, 2010) p 54.

time, although the term is still used in the English version of the Defence White Paper.[42]

Other militia are ethnic armed organisations that are allowed to retain their arms and given certain concessions in return for their service, such as the right to traffic opium and heroin. From the mid-2000s, the Tatmadaw invested heavily in the training of militia.[43] Leaders of ethnic militia have gained influence in the reform era, such as by becoming legislators (see Chapter 5).

Another force affiliated with the Tatmadaw are known as Swunashin (စွမ်းအားရှင်), although the meaning, use and interpretation of this term varies.[44] Cheesman suggests these groups are different in nature and kind from past People's Militia. He instead depicts them as an ambiguous form of gang and a proxy for the Tatmadaw or police, rather than an auxiliary force.[45] Swunashin are said to have played a role in the 2007 Saffron Revolution by targeting monks involved in the protests, some of whom were killed, and many hundreds arrested and detained.[46] While the government claims that Swunashin no longer exist, unidentified armed gangs continue to use the same methods and techniques against civilians to support the police and other authorities, such as breaking up peaceful protests.[47]

There is also the Border Guard Force, although this is only hinted at in the Constitution. In 2009, the SPDC regime ordered ethnic armed organisations to transform into Border Guard Forces. The intention of this order was that ethnic armed organisations would eventually be disestablished and relegated to the role of Border Guard Forces subordinate to the Tatmadaw. In 2009, when the Tatmadaw introduced this change it was met with strong opposition from several armed organisations, including the Kachin Independence Organisation, the Kokang Myanmar National Democratic Alliance Army (MNDAA), the New Mon State Party (NMSP) and the United Wa State Army. A total of 23 Border Guard Forces were formed from some smaller ethnic armed organisations.

[42] The Republic of the Union of Myanmar, *Defence White Paper*, Naypyidaw, December 2015, ss 57, 59–60.
[43] See John Buchanan, *Militia in Myanmar* (The Asia Foundation, 2016) for a typology of people's militia, though noting that the Burmese terms are often used inconsistently.
[44] See Nick Cheesman, *Opposing the Rule of Law: How Myanmar's Courts Make Law and Order* (CUP 2015), pp 205–2010, noting that Swunashin is often conflated by people in Myanmar with agencies like the fire brigade.
[45] Ibid, p 205.
[46] *Preliminary Report of the Ad Hoc Commission on Depayin Massacre* (Bangkok: Burma Lawyers Council and the National Council of the Union of Burma, 2004).
[47] Asian Human Rights Commission 'Attack gangs and falsification against the orders of the day' 11 March 2015, www.humanrights.asia/news/ahrc-news/AHRC-STM-039-2015/.

Ethnic armed organisations who resisted becoming Border Guard Forces object to section 338 of the Constitution, which states that all armed forces are under the control of the Commander-in-Chief and is taken to include ethnic armed organisations.[48] Some leaders of the Border Guard Force have entered the Union legislature (see Chapter 4).

In addition to the above forces, organisations like the fire brigade and the Myanmar War Veterans Association are considered to be auxiliary forces of the Tatmadaw.[49] The Tatmadaw exerts its influence through these multiple and varied security forces and militia, although the name, nature and organisation of many of these militia groups is contested and changes over time.

IV. THE NATIONAL DEFENCE AND SECURITY COUNCIL

The National Defence and Security Council ('the Defence Council') is an example of a constitutional structure that facilitates Tatmadaw intervention in governance. The Defence Council includes the highest Tatmadaw, executive and legislative actors. The Defence Council has powers to take over during a state of emergency if there is a threat to the Basic Principles of the Constitution. There have been efforts to propose a law on the Defence Council, because there are no constitutional or legal procedures that set out how it operates or the scope of its powers. In December 2015, a Bill was circulated, though it was not formally proposed to the legislature.[50] One of the proposals in the Bill was that the president would only sit as chairperson of the Defence Council and only vote if the Defence Council was split. The Bill would have strengthened the Tatmadaw and reduced the power of the president on the Defence Council, although the Bill was never tabled in the legislature.

Under the Thein Sein Government, the Defence Council met regularly, up to three times a week. Since 2016, the NLD Government has refused to convene a meeting of the Defence Council,[51] which reflects the lack

---

[48] Renaud Egreteau, *Caretaking Democratization* (Hurst & Co Publishers, 2016), p 101.

[49] Maung Aung Myoe, *Building the Tatmadaw: Myanmar Armed Forces Since 1948* (Singapore: ISEAS, 2009:40).

[50] *The Myanmar Times*, 'New Bill would strengthen military hold over powerful security council, 24 December 2015, www.mmtimes.com/national-news/nay-pyi-taw/18288-new-bill-would-strengthen-military-hold-over-powerful-security-council.html.

[51] *The Irrawaddy*, 'Lower House Votes Down ANP Proposal to Tighten Security Rakhine', 13 July 2017, www.irrawaddy.com/news/burma/lower-house-votes-anp-proposal-tighten-security-rakhine.html.

of trust between the NLD and the Tatmadaw. The NLD is concerned that the Defence Council will concede power to the Tatmadaw and to the Commander-in-Chief, such as by declaring a state of emergency and allowing the Commander-in-Chief to take charge. Given the inaction of the Defence Council, there have been proposals in the legislature for greater Tatmadaw intervention. In November 2016, there were calls from the USDP and 12 other political parties for the Defence Council to meet and discuss how to respond to the conflict in Rakhine State. Again, in August 2017, the Pyithu Hluttaw received a proposal from a representative of the Arakan National Party (ANP) to increase security measures in northern Rakhine State. This was supported by Tatmadaw legislative members, but did not receive the support of the NLD in a vote. This proposal was controversial because just after this vote, on 25 August, coordinated attacks occurred by the Arakan Rohingya Salvation Army (ARSA) against 30 police stations in northern Rakhine State. Those in favour of the failed Tatmadaw motion suggest that these events proved the need for the Defence Council to meet.

V. STATES OF EMERGENCY

A constitutional state of emergency is provided for in the Basic Principles of the Constitution.[52] A state of emergency is understood as a response to any threat to the three meta-principles of the military-state.[53] There is confusion over section 40(c) of the Constitution that provides the Commander-in-Chief can take over in a state of emergency. Some pro-Tatmadaw commentators suggest that this means the Commander-in-Chief can legally take over power at any time. However, this overlooks the fact that section 40(c) is in the Basic Principles chapter. If read with Chapter XI on Emergency Powers, it may instead be the case that the president must first declare a state of emergency before the Commander-in-Chief can then be invited to take over.

How and when emergency powers can be exercised, and by who, remains highly relevant because of Myanmar's conflict-ridden history. The country has been plagued with various insurgencies, communist resistance and ethnic armed rebellions since independence.

---

[52] 2008 Constitution, s 40(a)–(c). See Melissa Crouch, 'The Everyday Emergency', in Andrew Harding (ed) *Constitutionalism and Legal Change in Myanmar* (Hart Publishing, 2017) pp 157–172.

[53] 2008 Constitution, s 40(c).

Successive governments have engaged in armed conflict, as well as tried to broker peace agreements and ceasefires. There remains ongoing conflict in parts of Shan State, Kachin State and Rakhine State, as well as intermittent communal violence.

The scope of power during a state of emergency is extensive and unlimited, and many have raised concerns that these powers are open to abuse. Constitutional powers are often dependent on existing administrative practices, namely the use of section 144 orders under the Code of Criminal Procedure. The use of emergency powers also illustrates the difference between the Thein Sein Government's relationship with the Tatmadaw, and the NLD Government's relationship with the Tatmadaw. The constitutional states of emergency declared under Thein Sein show the close trust and working cooperation between the USDP and the Tatmadaw. I contrast this with the refusal of the NLD Government to declare a state of emergency, despite persistent and serious conflict in several parts of the country but most acutely in northern Rakhine State.

A. Constitutional Emergency Powers

Textually, the constitutional emergency powers are broad in scale and scope. Emergency powers are connected to the breach of the three meta-principles of the military-state. In practice, the power remains dependent on the willingness of the government administration. The lengthy constitutional provisions on emergency provide for three categories of emergency. In all three types, the president is vested with the power to declare a state of emergency, although only after he confers with the National Defence and Security Council. This is understood to mean that the Defence Council could decide a state of emergence is necessary even if the president disagrees. As mentioned above, a majority of the Defence Council's eleven members are Tatmadaw officers, according to the Constitution. The president has exercised his wide powers to declare a state of emergency three times since the Constitution came into effect in 2011.

In a category-one emergency, an emergency is declared when a local administrative body at the State/Region or Self-Administered Zone level is unable to fulfil its administrative duties.[54] This type of emergency allows the Union Government wide discretion to take control in any situation

---

[54] Ibid, ss 40(a), 410.

where a local authority lacks capacity to meet its duties. It allows the president to exercise the executive and legislative powers of the State/Region, essentially overriding the powers of sub-national governments.[55] There is no guarantee for human rights in a state of emergency, as the president has ultimate power to limit or suspend any rights.[56] The constitutional writs are suspended during an emergency, even habeas corpus.[57] The president sets the duration, although the default is 60 days because any declaration requires the approval of the Hluttaw within this time. The Constitution prohibits legal action being taken against any authorised decisions or actions made during an emergency.[58] A category-one emergency under the 2008 Constitution has not yet been exercised in Myanmar.

A category-two emergency covers any situation that threatens public safety or property, or places lives or property at risk, with two levels of severity.[59] In the first stage, the Tatmadaw can be called upon to assist local administrative bodies. This arrangement anticipates the Tatmadaw working together with local agencies. In the second and more serious stage, the president can declare a military administrative order, which confers all executive and judicial power on the Commander-in-Chief.[60] This allows the Tatmadaw to completely take over from the local authorities. Category two emergencies share some similarities with category one: human rights can also be restricted, and the president specifies the time limit. The main use of this emergency power has been in response to communal conflict in Rakhine State and other parts of Myanmar. This included the conflicts against the Rohingya in Rakhine State in June 2012. In July 2012, the issue was put to the legislature, where most of those who contributed to the debate, from the USDP or Rakhine political party, spoke in favour of extending the state of emergency.[61] In March 2013, a state of emergency was declared in Meiktila District.[62] In May, the legislature approved a motion, introduced by the Minister for Religious Affairs on behalf of the president, to extend the emergency.[63] In February 2015, this power was again exercised in the Kokang

---

[55] Ibid, s 411.
[56] Ibid, s 414(b).
[57] Ibid, ss 296(b), 381(c).
[58] Ibid, s 432.
[59] Ibid, ss 40(b), 412, 413(a).
[60] Ibid, s 413.
[61] See PDH2012-4:2.
[62] Ordinance No 1/2013 on a Declaration of a State of Emergency, 22 March 2013.
[63] See PDH2013.

Self-Administered Zone in Shan State, bordering China.[64] These actions were perceived to be necessary and appropriate by the government, although the minority groups it affected would disagree.

A category-three emergency is where the state is at risk of collapse or the sovereignty of the state is under threat.[65] In this situation, the Commander-in-Chief is given complete control with all powers conferred directly on him.[66] This includes the suspension of the legislature, and the dismissal of all legislators. The Commander-in-Chief, rather than the president as in the two former categories, has the power to restrict any individual rights.[67] Type-three is clearly the most serious form of emergency, as it automatically lasts for one year, although this power has not been used to date.

These three kinds of constitutional states of emergency exist in relationship to section 144 of the Code of Criminal Procedure, allowing the Tatmadaw, via the General Administration Department, to impose emergency-like conditions even without approval of the courts, the legislature or the president.

B. The General Administration Department: Controlling Local Governance

The Code of Criminal Procedure grants a judge the power to issue a section 144 order in response to a threat to public order. This is a judicial power and an order is intended to be temporary. A judge can require a person to stop a certain act or compel them to undertake action if it will prevent any risk of injury or threat to human life or public order. Such an order may be against one individual or applicable to the public generally. The judge must give the person an opportunity for a hearing to explain their behaviour. An order made under this section is only valid for up to 60 days, unless it is a situation that presents 'danger to human life, health or safety, or a likelihood of a riot or an affray', in which case the president can extend the order beyond 60 days. Stretching from the colonial era through to the period of military rule, the executive has not hesitated to appropriate this power. Section 144 orders have been issued in response to student protestors in 1974, pro-democracy protestors in 1988, and protests by monks in 2007.

---

[64] Order 1/2015, Declaration of Emergency, 17 February 2015.
[65] 2008 Constitution, s 40(c).
[66] Ibid, s 417.
[67] Ibid, ss 414(b) and 420 respectively.

In the post-2011 environment, it is the General Administration Department (GAD) that issues section 144 orders. The GAD was formed by the State Law and Order Restoration Council as a division of the Ministry of Home Affairs. It provides the administrative backbone for the country and exists at many levels of government. It is based on a similar design to that of the Security and Administrative Councils during the Ne Win era (1962–1988). Since 2011, it forms the nucleus of the State/Region government offices, yet up until 2018 it remained under the control of the Ministry of Home Affairs. Through the Minister for Home Affairs (who is appointed by the Commander-in-Chief), the GAD is linked to the Tatmadaw. The NLD has initiated an effort to transfer the GAD to the Ministry of the Union Government, though it is too early to know if this will bring the GAD effectively under civilian control. The GAD's reach is pervasive, and it takes responsibility for an incredibly broad range of issues. Among its roles are the enforcement of laws, licensing and control over permit schemes, land registration, taxation, and other local general administration matters.[68] The GAD works with all government departments, and with the police and the courts. The office of the GAD is usually located near the courts, and it has a self-proclaimed 'judicial role'.

One aspect of this judicial role is the authority to declare a curfew and restrictions on freedom of movement under section 144. This is evident in the response of the GAD to the anti-Muslim riots since 2012. Between May and October 2012, a serious outbreak of violence occurred in Rakhine State primarily committed by Buddhists against Muslims. It is estimated that hundreds of people were killed, and tens of thousands of people were displaced; most of these were the Rohingya in northern Rakhine State. A section 144 order by the GAD imposed curfews, and banned gatherings, particularly at mosques, in Maungdaw, Buthedaung and Sittwe.[69] This practice continued in 2013, with section 144 orders following anti-Muslim violence in Meiktila, Maubin Township, Ayeyarwaddy Region; Bago Region; in Lashio, Shan State; Okkan Township, Yangon Region; and Thandwe Township, Rakhine State.[70] There are no shortage of other examples: in 2014 in Mandalay, in 2015 in the Kokang region, and in 2016–2017 in response to the alleged terrorist threat in northern

[68] Kyi Pyar Chit Saw and Matthew Arnold, *Administering the State: An Overview of the General Administration Department* (Asia Foundation and MDRI, 2014).

[69] Maungdaw Township General Administration Department, Code of Criminal Procedure Section 144, Curfew Order No 1/2012, 8 June 2012.

[70] Burma News International, *Deciphering Myanmar's Peace Process* (2014), available at: www.bnionline.net.

Rakhine State. Township administrators wield section 144 orders as an immediate means of exercising executive power and limiting individual freedoms. Section 144 is part of the chain of authority that runs from the GAD at the township level to the Ministry of Home Affairs at the Union level, to the Tatmadaw. control).

The present use of constitutional emergency powers has been conditioned by the expansion of the military administrative apparatus. The GAD has appropriated judicial power for itself, subverting the courts. Section 144 is a necessary precondition for a full constitutional state of emergency to be declared. This demonstrates a connection between the use of the Code of Criminal Procedure as an administrative power and the exercise of the constitutional powers of emergency. The Tatmadaw has co-opted section 144 orders and this power *precedes* any exercise of constitutional power. This suggests that the Tatmadaw has open to it avenues of power that do not rely solely on the Constitution, and poses a challenge to the authority of the Constitution itself.

VI. TATMADAW WATCHMEN IN THE LEGISLATURE

The very existence of the legislature is conditional on the presence of the Tatmadaw. The Basic Principles mandate that there must be Tatmadaw members in both the Union and sub-national legislature.[71] Tatmadaw members are not elected, but rather are selected by the Commander-in-Chief. This is one way the leading role of the Tatmadaw is embodied in political structures. The Tatmadaw contribute to the broader functions of the legislature in terms of its role in law-making, as a check on the judiciary and its complaints handling function (see Chapter 5). The relationship between Tatmadaw members and the executive is more complex. When the USDP was in government, there was generally agreement between the president and the Tatmadaw, though the tension between the president and the Speaker of the Pyithu Hluttaw, Shwe Mann, meant that there was division within the USDP. The Tatmadaw members have not consistently sided with the USDP nor necessarily voted as a block. Since 2016, the Tatmadaw have begun to act as an opposition block against the NLD-led Government.[72]

---

[71] 2008 Constitution, s 14.

[72] Walton offers an extended discussion of the various Burmese Buddhist interpretations of party politics and national politics: Walton, *Buddhism, Politics and Political Thought in Myanmar*, pp 65–95.

The main role of the Tatmadaw members of the legislature is as *watchmen* of the constitutional and political system of government. This surveillance role as watchmen is not a passive function but rather involves active engagement in all activities of the legislature. The Tatmadaw remains vigilant in protecting this conception of the military-state. Opposition by Tatmadaw legislators can be taken as a barometer of political tensions between civilian and military authorities in Myanmar.

The Tatmadaw has developed justifications for its role in governance. For example, the Tatmadaw emphasises the distinction in Burmese between 'party politics' ပါတီနိုင်ငံရေး and 'national politics' အမျိုးသားနိုင်ငံရေး.[73] According to the Tatmadaw, it cannot be involved in party politics, that is, it cannot have an official military political party. There is no Tatmadaw political party, although the USDP is perceived to be a proxy party for the military. At the same time, the history of Myanmar is used to suggest that political parties are subject to infighting and cannot be trusted to protect the integrity and unity of the country. This is where the Tatmadaw's role in governance fits in, as the guardian of 'national politics', that is, the territorial integrity and sovereignty of the country, above and beyond mere party politics.[74] The Tatmadaw designates to its members a special role distinct from other members of the legislature. The Constitution clearly demarcates those who are central to national governance, but above or removed from party politics. Those who are required to be free from 'party politics' also include the judiciary and members of the executive.[75] The Tatmadaw is committed to a formal separation between the legislature and executive, and between the executive and judiciary at the Union level. The Tatmadaw does not insist on separation between itself and other branches of government.

The Tatmadaw seats in the legislature allow the Tatmadaw to maintain a direct influence over legislative policy without necessarily having to rely on the USDP.[76] On one level, Tatmadaw legislators have all the special privileges and immunities of civilian members (see Chapter 5). However, the accountability measures only apply to elected members, so Tatmadaw members cannot be the subject of the constitutional right to recall. The Tatmadaw has adopted a deliberate practice of rotating

---

[73] See Tin Maung Maung Than, *State Dominance in Myanmar* (Singapore, ISEAS, 2007) p 393.

[74] For one explanation see Mya Win, *Tatmadaw's Traditional Role in National Politics* (Yangon, News and Periodicals Enterprise, Ministry of Information, 1992) pp 77–78.

[75] 2008 Constitution, ss 26(a), 64, 232(k), 237(h), 242(g), 285(g), 300(a), 301(f), 309(a), 310(f), 330(c), 333(e), 398(7).

[76] See Egreteau, above n 48, pp 90–96.

officers so that they are not in the legislature long enough to build connections or form allegiances with other political actors, such as the NLD or ethnic political parties. The NLD has protested this practice, arguing that at the very least Tatmadaw officers appointed to the legislature should be required to serve the full five-year term, rather than being subject to constant rotations.

The reservation of 25 per cent of legislative seats does *not* enable the Tatmadaw to block legislative proposals, as proponents of the system often emphasise. The reserved seating system does ensure that the Tatmadaw members can infiltrate and monitor democratically elected members of the legislature, as well as participate in various high-level appointments. For example, the Tatmadaw members, along with the Amyotha Hluttaw and Pyithu Hluttaw, each appoint a candidate for the positions of president and two vice-presidents. This means that, at the very least, the Tatmadaw appoints a vice-president. In addition, the constitutional amendment clause requires more than 75 per cent approval in the legislature, thus giving the Tatmadaw veto power over any future constitutional amendment proposal (see Chapter 10). In addition to Tatmadaw members in the legislature, the USDP members are often seen as military officers who have simply exchanged their military uniforms for civilian guise. Most USDP members are retired military officers. Under the NLD Government, USDP members in the legislature have often supported the position of military members. In this respect, other political parties perceive the USDP as a proxy for the Tatmadaw.

The role of the Tatmadaw as watchmen in the legislature is not just a reactive function but also a proactive function. Some Tatmadaw officers, or military appointed ministers, have initiated proposals in the legislature. One prominent example in late 2016 concerns the fighting that occurred in northern Shan State. On 20 November 2016, a group calling itself the Northern Alliance (a coalition supported by the Kachin, Talaung, Arakan and Kokang ethnic armed organisations) initiated an attack on the police and Tatmadaw outposts. Several days later, on 3 December, the Minister for Defence (a Tatmadaw appointee) proposed to the Pyithu Hluttaw that it should pass a resolution declaring the Northern Alliance as a 'terrorist organisation'. This proposal was not successful at the Union level, but it was then raised by Tatmadaw members sitting in the Shan State Hluttaw. With the additional support of the USDP, the proposal passed 61 to 45. This declaration of the Northern Alliance as a terrorist organisation was highly controversial. This is not only because it was initiated at the state level, but also because in the past these groups have simply been referred to in Myanmar as 'ethnic armed organisations', rather than terrorists.[77] The Anti-Terrorism Law confers power on the Anti-Terrorism Committee to declare an organisation a 'terrorist' organisation, not on the State Hluttaw. This resolution is also a demonstration of the way the Tatmadaw are willing to use legislative processes, in addition to force, to advance their agenda.

Under an NLD-dominated Pyidaungsu Hluttaw since 2016, the Tatmadaw have also been vocal in its opposition to a range of measures proposed and ultimately passed by the NLD. One critical example is the Law on the State Counsellor, as the first Bill proposed by the NLD Government (see Chapter 6). There remains little public space for constitutional amendment to abolish or phase out the role of the Tatmadaw in the legislature.

VII. COURTS MARTIAL

The courts martial are a separate and independent judicial body with absolute jurisdiction over Tatmadaw personnel.[78] The courts martial are established under the Defence Services Act and Regulations.[79] The officers of the courts martial come from the Judges' Advocates General of the Ministry of Defence. There are occasional cases of soldiers being prosecuted in the civilian court system, rather than the courts martial. For example, in 2014, the courts martial transferred the case of a soldier accused of kidnap and rape to a civilian court in Shan State.[80] Courts martial can transfer a case to a civilian court if a soldier is accused of breaching the Penal Code. In 2016, courts martial found seven soldiers guilty of the murder of five people from a village in northern Shan State. More often, civil society groups have tried but failed to secure information on cases heard or pending in the courts martial. In January 2018, the courts martial found six soldiers guilty of killing three people in Kachin State and sentenced them to ten years in jail.[81] In February 2018, courts

[77] *The Irrawaddy*, 'Shan State Parliament Approves Branding of Northern Alliance as Terrorists', 7 December 2016, www.irrawaddy.com/news/burma/shan-state-parliament-approves-branding-of-northern-alliance-as-terrorists.html.

[78] 2008 Constitution, s 343.

[79] Defence Services Act 1959 and Defence Service Regulations.

[80] Aileen Thomson, 'Civilian justice trumps military impunity in Myanmar' 11 December 2014, www.opendemocracy.net/opensecurity/aileen-thomson/civilian-justice-trumps-military-impunity-in-myanmar.

[81] *Network Media Group*, 'Court martial sentences Tatmadaw soldiers for killing villagers' 22 January 2018, www.bnionline.net/en/news/court-martial-sentences-tatmadaw-soldiers-killing-villagers.

martial tried seven soldiers for killing 10 Rohingya in northern Rakhine State.[82] In 2015, the NLD proposed to amend the Constitution so that the courts martial would be subordinate to the Supreme Court, but this proposal was not included in the draft Bill to the legislature. There is no right of appeal from a decision of the courts martial to the general court system.

VIII. CONCLUSION

The operation of the 2008 Constitution is conditioned by the future role the Tatmadaw has carved out for itself. For people in Myanmar, the inclusion of the ideological commitment to the Three National Causes in the Constitution is a reminder of the former period of direct military rule. While these principles were once mere Tatmadaw slogans, they manifest in many aspects of cultural life, such as the teaching of a subject on 'military law' that is compulsory for all law students at university. This ideological commitment is a link between direct military rule and the present military-state. The Commander-in-Chief is the main public spokesperson and advocate of the Three Main National Causes and its centrality to the military-state.

The growth in the size of the Tatmadaw in the 1990s–2000s adds force to constitutional provisions on the military. Spanning military and civilian institutions, the difficulty of separating military from civilian affairs is compounded by the fact that many non-active, discharged or retired military officers now occupy positions in the civilian institutions of the state. The Tatmadaw is an elite institution that is predominantly filled with ethnic Burmans. Despite this, there are cracks in the unity of the Tatmadaw, evident from tensions within and between the USDP and the Tatmadaw under Thein Sein. The Tatmadaw is not one force but many and I have highlighted the constitutional role of various kinds of forces and Border Guard Force. The police also remain connected to the Tatmadaw through the Ministry of Home Affairs. In the legislature, the non-elected Tatmadaw members play an active 'watchman' role, supervising the civilian members. The surveillance function of Tatmadaw members has become more pronounced under the NLD-led Government. The negative reaction of Tatmadaw members on certain matters

---

[82] *The Myanmar Times*, 'Tatmadaw investigates 16 people suspected in Inn Dinn Massacre, 12 February 2018, www.mmtimes.com/news/tatmadaw-investigates-16-people-suspected-inn-din-massacre.html.

of policy – such as the creation of the Office of State Counsellor – can be taken as a barometer reading of political tension in Myanmar.

The National Defence and Security Council is an important body on matters of national security, including states of emergency. In the absence of a constitutional emergency, the ability of the Tatmadaw to work through the General Administration Department and its section 144 powers is an example of its indirect structural advantages. In the following chapters I show that the combined force of formal and informal advantages ensures the leading role of the Tatmadaw in national governance.

FURTHER READING

Kyi Pyar Chit Saw and M Arnold, *Administering the State: An Overview of the General Administration Department* (Asia Foundation and MDRI, 2014).

Mary P Callahan, *Making Enemies: War and State Building in Burma.* (Singapore NUS Press, 2004).

Maung Aung Myoe, *Building the Tatmadaw: Myanmar Armed Forces Since 1948* (Singapore: ISEAS, 2009).

Andrew Selth, *Burma's Armed Forces: Power Without Glory* (EastBridge, Norwalk, 2002).

Andrew Selth, *Transforming the Tatmadaw: The Burmese Armed Forces Since 1988.* Strategic and Defence Studies Centre (ANU, Canberra, 1996).

4

The Electoral System and Limits on Political Participation

Political Participation – The Right to Vote – Debating Proportional Representation – Electoral Regulation – Electoral Disputes – The Right to Recall

IN 1988, AFTER several decades of one-party rule, the military regime made clear that its plans were to hold multi-party elections.[1] Another issue central to the validity of the Constitution is the credibility of the electoral system it installs. There are two chapters of the Constitution that address elections: Chapter X on political parties and Chapter IX on the electoral process and the Union Election Commission. The Basic Principles also contain several key provisions on elections and requires the Union to pass a law on political parties to enable this party system.[2] The Constitution mandates a symmetrical legislature, with the entire Union Government, as well as the State/Region government, at stake in elections every five years. The first elections for 20 years were held in 2010, although conditions were not considered to be free and fair. The election was ostensibly held according to the procedures and rules set out in the 2008 Constitution, although there was pervasive manipulation of the 2010 election results.[3]

The Constitution reintroduces a multi-party system. This comes after decades of socialist rule, when all parties except the Burma Social-ist Program Party (BSPP) were banned, and after the failure to honour

---

[1] See, eg, Announcement No 1/88 of the State Law and Order Restoration Council, 18 September 1988.

[2] 2008 Constitution, ss 6(d), 7, 39.

[3] Michael Lidauer and Gilles Saphy, 'Elections and the Reform Agenda', in Melissa Crouch and Tim Lindsey (eds) *Law, Society and Transition in Myanmar* (Hart Publishing, 2014), at 203, 211.

the results of the 1990 elections. One of the controversies with the concept of democracy as articulated in the Constitution is that it is to be 'disciplined'. This term sits uncomfortably in the Constitution because it follows from the proclamation that this is a 'genuine' democracy. Disciplined democracy is taken to mean that democracy is qualified, it is something less than full democracy. The legislature includes Tatmadaw officers and so is only partially democratically elected. In this chapter I explain the importance of the constitutional provisions on elections. The Constitution offers a break from a one-party state and from direct military rule without a constitution. The Constitution has facilitated a return to competitive elections, permitting the existence of political parties.

There are limitations and conditions placed on acceptable forms of political participation. The Constitution regulates political parties to fit within the Union and disciplined democracy. The Constitutional Tribunal has addressed two issues related to elections. The first is the question of who can vote and run for political office, which is tied to the issue of citizenship. The second is the constitutionality of proportional representation. I also explain the role of the Union Election Commission in the administration of elections and electoral disputes. An unusual feature of the Election Commission's role is to receive complaints to recall an elected member of the legislature, based on a low threshold of just one per cent of a constituency. This constitutional right to recall is open to abuse against political opponents.

I. POLITICAL PARTIES AND CANDIDATES

The Constitution regulates the form and process of political participation in Myanmar. In the past, political participation has been highly contested. After the demise of the socialist regime, the Tatmadaw promised to hold elections and it was presumed that these elections were to appoint a new legislature. In the May 1990 elections, the National League for Democracy (NLD) won by a significant margin. However, on 27 July 1990, General Khin Nyunt claimed that a National Convention would be established (rather than a legislature) and the Convention would have the sole task of drafting a new constitution. In effect, SLORC decided it would *not* convene the legislature, but rather mandate that a new constitution be drafted as a prior condition to convening the legislature. The Tatmadaw warned that the process may take five to ten years.[4] In response, the NLD demanded that the legislature should be formed by September 1990. The Tatmadaw ignored this demand and refused to step down. No one who was elected was permitted to take office, and many were arrested and put in prison.[5] The 2008 Constitution by its silence refuses to acknowledge the 1990 elections and the results of the 1990 elections were officially abrogated prior to 2011.

Against this historical background, political parties and their candidates approached the 2010 and the 2015 elections with some scepticism and caution. Candidates compete for positions in the Pyithu Hluttaw, Amyotha Hluttaw and State/Region Hluttaw every five years, and the process is further regulated by law.[6] Candidates for the Pyithu Hluttaw run in single member constituencies. For the Amyotha Hluttaw, candidates compete for one of 12 seats per State/Region. Political parties are closely regulated and monitored under the Constitution and by law. Political parties have so far been vehicles for advancing ideological positions or personal agendas rather than policy platforms. These ideological positions can be identified broadly in three main way: the nationalist Tatmadaw ideology of the USDP; the democratic (though pro-Bamar) ideology of the NLD and other smaller parties such as the National Democratic Front (a splinter of the NLD); and the ethno-nationalist, autonomy-seeking ideology of ethnic-based political parties.

The internal organisation of political parties must comply with the three meta-principles of the military-state[7] which, for example, means that parties cannot advocate for secession. The threshold requirement to form a political party is low and requires just 15 people. There are various restrictions on who can form a political party. Specifically, the law prohibits a member of a group that has been classified by the government as an insurgent group from establishing a political party.[8] This means ethnic armed organisations that have not signed the National Ceasefire Agreement and remain on the blacklist under the Unlawful Associations Act (see Chapter 10), cannot establish a political party. The requirements are much more stringent once the party is registered. Within 90 days, the

---

[4] Bertil Linter, *Outrage: Burma's Struggle for Democracy* (Review Publishing, 1989).

[5] One record of the criminal charges against NLD elected representatives is found in: All Burma Students Democratic Front, *Situation of the Elected MPs from the National League for Democracy, May 1990* (Documentation and Research Centre, ABSDF, 1996).

[6] Law No 3/2010 on the Pyithu Hluttaw Election; Law No 4/2010 on the Amyotha Hluttaw Election; Law No 5/2010 on the Region/State Hluttaw Law.

[7] Law on Political Party Registration No 2/2010, s 6(a–c).

[8] Ibid, s 4(f).

political party needs to attract a minimum of 1,000 members if the party has applied to be a national political party or 500 members if it is only seeking registration in one State/Region.

There are restrictions on who is prohibited from voting. Constitutional restrictions rule out religious leaders, which includes the country's vast monastic order but also leaders of other religions.[9] This reflects a formal concept of the separation between religion and politics in Myanmar.[10] This is not unusual, with similar restrictions in other countries in the region, such as in Thailand. It also does not mean that religious orders have no political influence. In fact, throughout Myanmar's history, the Buddhist monastic order has played a significant informal role in political change.[11] The Constitution also prohibits religion from being abused for political gain,[12] although this is not enforced. There have been many incidents in recent years that could be characterised as breaching this provision, particularly the use of anti-Muslim rhetoric as a technique of political campaigns. Rather, these rules reflect the Tatmadaw's concern that Buddhist monastic authority is a rival centre of power that needs to be contained in the military-state.

In terms of the regulation of campaign finance, there is a constitutional prohibition on political parties or candidates receiving funding from a religious association or from a foreign government or person.[13] This protects two further elements of the military-state: that there would be a formal separation between religion and politics so that the power of religious authority cannot rival the power of the Tatmadaw, and that the Constitution would protect the sovereignty of the country. Candidates are required to lodge a campaign finance form to the electoral sub-commission where they were registered. For the 2015 elections, many candidates failed to meet this requirement, and so ad hoc tribunals were formed in response. The tribunals did not hesitate to disqualify many of these candidates, although those who attended the hearings often reported misunderstandings of the requirement, or practical impediments such as illness or travel commitments.[14] Campaign finance is likely to become an issue in future elections.

---

[9] 2008 Constitution, s 392(a).
[10] For one perspective on how Buddhism has influenced political thought in Myanmar, see Matthew Walton, *Buddhism, Politics and Political Thought in Myanmar* (CUP 2013).
[11] For an historical perspective, see Alicia Turner, *Saving Buddhism: The Impermanence of Religion in Colonial Burma* (University of Hawaii Press, 2014).
[12] 2008 Constitution, s 364; Law on Political Party Registration No 2/2010, s 6(e).
[13] 2008 Constitution, s 407.
[14] Carter Centre Report, *Observing Myanmar's 2015 General Elections: Final Report* (Atlanta, 2015) p 66.

While political parties compete in elections every five years, the Constitution also provides for by-elections. By-elections are necessary because the political system at the Union level requires appointed ministers to vacate legislative seats, so there are always vacancies as soon as executive positions are filled. The absence of a constitutional time limit within which to hold by-elections led to concerns that the Thein Sein Government was delaying holding a by-election for fear that the USDP would lose seats to the NLD. The by-election was held over a year after the formation of government. The by-election was the first time the NLD agreed to participate, and it won 43 of 44 seats, a victory some saw as a vindication of the 1990 results. In 2016, the law was amended to require the government to hold a by-election within one year of the first term of the legislature, and in years two to four of its term, to hold a by-election within six months of notification of the vacancy of a seat.[15] Under the NLD, by-elections have been held in April 2017 and November 2018. The NLD won only nine of the 19 available seats, in part because many of these seats were in ethnic areas where NLD support is weaker. The role of the legislature in amending the law to clarify the by-election time frame is an example of how the legislature often fills in the details not included in the Constitution, rather than leaving it to regulation by the administration.

Aside from the constitutional regulation of political parties and their candidates, a second key issue of concern has been the right to vote and run for electoral office, which I turn to next.

II. THE RIGHT TO VOTE AND RUN FOR OFFICE

Given the centrality of the legislature and the emphasis on elections, the right to vote and run for political office has become a subject of contestation.[16] The criteria to be eligible to run as a member for the legislature is set out clearly in sections 120–121 of the Constitution.[17] There are four eligibility criteria: a minimum age requirement (25 years old for the Pyithu Hluttaw; 30 years old for the Amyotha Hluttaw); full citizenship (that is, both parents must also be citizens); a minimum in-country residency of ten years; and any other criteria required by electoral laws.[18]

---

[15] Law 30/2016 amending the Pyithu Hluttaw Election Law.

[16] 2008 Constitution, ss 391–393.

[17] Candidates for all other high-level executive, legislative and judicial appointments must also comply with these requirements.

[18] 2008 Constitution, s 120.

The latter category leaves a significant amount of discretion to the legislature to regulate the right to run for political office.

There are 12 constitutional grounds that disqualify a person from running for the legislature,[19] which I group into three categories. First are disqualifications based on a criminal conviction, which includes being sentenced to jail, being declared insolvent, or having committed an offence under relevant electoral laws. While these categories appear to be a low bar because they do not depend on the severity of the crime, in practice this requirement is flexible. For example, in 2011, the legislature amended the Political Parties Registration Law to allow a person who is convicted of a crime to vote.[20] This amendment appears to allow former political prisoners, such as NLD members, to run and serve in political office, even though it contradicts the Constitution.[21] The second category relates to the health of the candidate, that is, whether they are of sound mind. The third category aims at ensuring an eligible candidate does not have any ties that will compromise their role in the legislature. The prohibition against owing allegiance, or enjoying the privileges of, a foreign country is about ensuring that the loyalty of legislators are with the Union and not a foreign country. The disqualification from being a member of the civil service, or receiving government funds, aims to maintain the separation between the administration and the legislature. The disqualification of a person from a religious order, or who receives religious funds, is designed to neutralise religious authority and institutions in the political sphere, as discussed above.

Aside from the right to run for office, there are also restrictions on the right to vote. In 2015, the legislature, executive and judiciary further restricted the right to vote. The Constitutional Tribunal contributed to the decreasing political space for temporary registration card holders (known as 'white cards'), most of whom are Rohingya. Among the Buddhist-majority country, the 2014 census recorded Muslims as four per cent of the population. An additional one million Rohingya Muslims were not recorded in the census. Myanmar has a history of Muslim political participation.[22] In 2010 and 2012, temporary registration card holders were permitted to vote and to run in the elections. Muslim candidates were permitted to run for office and some won

---

[19] Ibid, s 121.
[20] Political Parties Registration Law No 2/2010, amended by Law 11/2011.
[21] 2008 Constitution, s 121(a).
[22] Nicholas Farrelly, 'Muslim Political Participation in Myanmar' in Melissa Crouch (ed) *Islam and the State in Myanmar* (OUP, 2016).

seats in elections during this period. Political parties run by Muslims in Myanmar have never been based on an Islamist ideology and do not advocate for the institutionalisation of Islamic law, unlike Islamist political parties in the region.[23] Since 2012, public space for Muslims has declined as mass violence specifically targeting Rohingya and Muslims more broadly became an issue. In the lead-up to the 2015 elections, this led to overt anti-Muslim campaigns and attempts to discredit the NLD as 'pro-Muslim'.

In August 2013, Aye Maung, the chairperson of the ethnic Rakhine Buddhist Rakhine National Development Party (RNDP) proposed amendments to the Political Parties Registration Law[24] in the Amyotha Hluttaw.[25] The Bill proposed to remove the right of naturalised and associate citizens, as well as temporary registration card holders (white cards) to be members of a political party or to vote. In September 2014, the amendment was passed so that only citizens or associate or naturalised citizens have the right to run for political office.[26]

In November 2014, a separate Bill was submitted for the holding of a referendum on amendments to the 2008 Constitution in anticipation of a constitutional referendum in 2015 (although this never eventuated). This Bill would initially have *allowed* white card holders to vote in a constitutional referendum. Due to opposition by the RNDP, the provision was removed.[27] The Bill was sent to the President's Office for approval. On 9 February 2015, the president returned the Bill to Pyidaungsu Hluttaw, which he has the constitutional power to do (see Chapter 6), on the basis that white card holders *should* be allowed to vote because they voted in the referendum for the 2008 Constitution. Due to a separate legislative motion that white card holders should be abolished completely, on 11 February 2015, the President's Office announced that from 31 May, white cards were no longer valid. On the same day, the Speaker of the Pyidaungsu Hluttaw requested an opinion from the Constitutional Tribunal on the matter of citizenship and the right to vote.[28]

---

[23] Melissa Crouch, 'Myanmar's Muslim Mosaic and the Politics of Belonging', in Melissa Crouch (ed) *Islam and the State in Myanmar* (OUP, 2016).
[24] Law on Political Parties Registration No 2/2010, s 10(a).
[25] See AH2013-7:26.
[26] Yen Saning, 'President Signs Amended Law Barring Non-Citizens From Politics', 3 October 2014, *The Irrawaddy*, www.irrawaddy.com/news/burma/president-signs-amended-law-barring-non-citizens-politics.html.
[27] see Ei Ei Toe Lwin, 'White card holders cut from voting in national referendum', 24 Nov 2014, *The Myanmar Times*, www.mmtimes.com/national-news/12372-white-card-holders-cut-from-voting-in-referendum.html.
[28] See PDH2015-12:14, pp 448–449.

In February 2015, the Referendum Law was passed in the legislature to set out the process for a referendum on constitutional amendment, and it did allow white card holders to vote. As a result, an application was brought to the Constitutional Tribunal challenging this provision on the basis that allowing white card holders to vote in a referendum was unconstitutional. The provision in question was section 11(a) of the Referendum Law.[29] The Pyidaungsu Hluttaw sought clarification of the constitutional provisions concerning the right to vote, which mention that not only citizens but other persons may have this right.[30]

On 16 February 2015, the Constitutional Tribunal responded in a written opinion to the Pyidaungsu Hluttaw, which is recorded in the legislative minutes. The Advisory Opinion of the Tribunal is short and was only signed by the chairperson (not all nine members). The Tribunal referred to three provisions of the Basic Principles in the Constitution to hold that white card holders cannot vote. The Tribunal noted that its approach to interpretation must be guided by the provisions in the Basic Principles, namely that sovereign power comes from 'citizens' and that *only* citizens have the right to vote and to be elected.[31] The Tribunal determined that 'persons who have the right to vote' was only intended to mean other qualified citizens (such as associate citizens), but not white card holders. The Tribunal declared section 11(a) of the Referendum Law inconsistent with the Constitution. Questions were then raised about whether the Tribunal's Advisory Decision was final and binding. Some members of Parliament were unsatisfied with this Advisory Decision and applied for a full decision to the Tribunal.

Meanwhile, on 20 March 2015, the Union Election Commission issued an order that required every political party to expel white card holders and associate citizens.[32] This was an effective purge of white card holders from the political system. The order also sought to undermine political parties that consisted primarily of white card holders. Even the NLD reportedly had to expel 8,000 members from its party, although the NLD claimed it would help expelled members try to gain citizenship.

In the meantime, an application seeking a decision of the Constitutional Tribunal was brought by Dr Aye Maung, the same politician who

---

[29] Law No 2/2015 on the Referendum Law for the Approval of the Amendment Bill of the 2008 Constitution of the Union of Myanmar.

[30] 2008 Constitution, ss 390–391.

[31] Ibid, ss 48, 4, 38(a) respectively.

[32] Ye Mon and Lu Min Mang, 'NLD to help expelled members get citizenship', 20 March 2015, *The Myanmar Times*, www.mmtimes.com/national-news/13636-nld-to-help-expelled-members-get-citizenship.html.

in 2013 proposed that white card holders be denied the right to vote, and other members of the Amyotha Hluttaw. The applicants challenged the provision of the Referendum Law concerning who could vote in a referendum.[33] The applicants sought clarification of the constitutional provisions on the right to vote and to be elected, and the process and eligibility of a citizen to vote.[34] They argued that the Constitution did not mention temporary registration card holders only citizens and so the Referendum Law was inconsistent with section 198(a) of the Constitution. Their application failed to note that the Constitution is inconsistent, sometimes referring to 'any person' who has rights and other times to 'citizens'. The definition of a citizen in the Constitution[35] limits the concept of 'citizen' to a person whose parents are from one of the official national races and were born in Myanmar, or a person who had already been granted citizenship at the time the Constitution came into force. The applicants noted that sovereign power resides in *citizens*, according to section 4 of the Constitution. On this basis, they argued that only citizens should have the right to vote in a referendum on constitutional amendment. In short, instead of conceiving sovereign power as residing in 'the people' in a broad sense, sovereign power was restricted to full citizens. Further, they emphasised that under the Burma Citizenship Law 1982, both associated and naturalised citizens must swear an oath of loyalty and allegiance to the state.[36] They also noted that associate and naturalised citizens enjoy rights of citizenship unless they are restricted by the state.[37]

The Ministry for Immigration and Population was invited to make a submission to the Tribunal. While the Ministry clarified the role and function of white cards, it agreed that white card holders should be allowed to vote. The Union Attorney General's Office also made a submission that referred to the constitutional categories of people who have no right to vote,[38] including members of a religious order and those in jail (discussed above). The final general category, a person who has been disqualified by law, could be read to suggest that disqualification needs to be explicit in law. The Attorney General pointed out that white card holders are not specifically listed in section 392 of the Constitution as a category of persons who have no right to vote. This could be taken

---

[33] 2008 Constitution, s 11a.
[34] Ibid, ss 38(a), 369, s 391(a).
[35] Ibid, s 345.
[36] Burma Citizenship Act 1982, ss 24, 46(a).
[37] Ibid, ss 30(c) and 53(c).
[38] 2008 Constitution, s 392.

to imply that white card holders can vote, but the Tribunal did not come to this conclusion.

Instead, the Tribunal noted that the 1982 Citizenship Law allows associate citizens and naturalised citizens to have the same rights as citizens, unless this right is limited by the state. It observed that the law does not, however, offer the same rights to white card holders. The Tribunal held that the provision of the Constitutional Amendment Referendum Law allowing white card holders the right to vote was invalid because it was inconsistent with sections 38(a) and 391 of the Constitution. Yet the actual decision of the Tribunal did not refer to the right to vote[39] and so it appears to have avoided making any determination on the constitutional rights issue.

The question before the Tribunal was not whether legislation had failed to protect the constitutional right to vote and to be elected, but rather whether it had gone beyond the legal scope of the constitutional right. In effect, the applicants were seeking to restrict the constitutional right to vote and to be elected to citizens, to deny white card holders (many of whom are Muslim) from enjoying this right. The political outcome of this case was that the Tribunal lent its authority to those in the legislature pursuing an anti-Muslim and anti-NLD agenda in the lead up to the 2015 elections. The decision contributed to the disenfranchisement of over one million people, most of whom are Rohingya.[40] The Tribunal supported the broader ethno-nationalist agenda of exclusion. This was the first election in which white card holders were officially denied the right to vote in an election and denied the right to run for political office. While in many respects it was not just the Tribunal decision that triggered this legislative reversal against electoral rights for citizens with white cards, it was one more justification for the legislature to pass amendments to legislation based on a restrictive reading of the Constitution.

III. THE PROPOSAL FOR PROPORTIONAL REPRESENTATION

Another debate related to electoral laws is whether Myanmar should shift to an electoral system based on proportional representation. It is generally understood in Myanmar that the Constitution requires a

---

[39] Ibid, s 369.
[40] See also Melissa Crouch (2019) 'States of Legal Denial: How the Rohingya Lost the Right to Vote and the Role of Legal Denial in Myanmar' *Journal of Contemporary Asia*.

first-past-the-post arrangement (although this is not explicit), which means any change to the electoral system requires constitutional amendment.[41] There has been ongoing contestation and debate about the constitutional provisions on the elections and the system for counting votes. This debate dates back to the 1990s, when there was discussion of shifting from a first-past-the-post system to proportional representation.[42] In 2012, the National Democratic Front (NDF) initiated a campaign to change the electoral system to proportional representation.[43] Persisting on this issue, in 2014, the NDF again submitted a proposal for proportional representation.[44] This led to debate over possible changes to the electoral system.[45] In the lead up to the 2015 elections, proportional representation became a key issue.

There were different motivations for this proposal to introduce proportional representation. The USDP and Tatmadaw agreed with this proposal because they thought it would reduce the potential support the NLD might secure at the elections. For some ethnic political parties, there is support for proportional representation because the system is seen to support federalism and greater representation for ethnic minority groups. The NLD argues that the proposal would not help ethnic political parties because some ethnic groups are dispersed over a wide geographic area.

In November 2014, the Pyithu Hluttaw sought the advice of the Constitutional Tribunal. It asked the Tribunal which of eight different electoral voting systems, including first-past-the-post, were constitutional. By way of an Advisory Decision issued by letter to the Pyithu Hluttaw, the Constitutional Tribunal held that only first-past-the-post is constitutional, and the other seven options (including proportional representation) were not constitutional.[46]

In late 2014, a separate application was filed with the Constitutional Tribunal concerning the constitutionality of a draft Bill on

---

[41] This is the subject of some debate as it is not explicit in the Constitution, but this is how the election provisions have come to be understood.

[42] Michael Lidaeur, 'Towards a New State in Myanmar?', in Mikael Gravers and Flemming Ytzen (eds) *Burma/Myanmar: Where Now?* (NIAS Press, 2014) p 82.

[43] Lidauer and Saphy, above n 3, p 217.

[44] DVB, 'Burma to consider proportional representation' 5 June 2014.

[45] Kyle Lemargie, et al, 'Electoral System Choice in Myanmar's Democratisation Debate' in Nicholas Farrelly and Nick Cheesman (eds) *Debating Democratisation in Myanmar* (Singapore: ISEAS, 2014) pp 229–226.

[46] See Constitutional Tribunal, Draft Law Case 5/2014. This correspondence presumably should have appeared in PH2014-11:29 (14 November 2014), although this file is missing from the Parliament's website.

proportional representation, this time by the Amyotha Hluttaw.[47] The Amyotha Hluttaw sought an Advisory Decision on several issues, including whether it would be constitutional for elections to the Amyotha Hluttaw and States/Regions to be based on a proportional representation system. This proposal was part of a draft law that was being debated in the Amyotha Hluttaw. The Amyotha Hluttaw argued that the Tribunal had jurisdiction to decide this matter because it had issued Advisory Decisions previously, and because section 9 of the Civil Procedure Code allows the court to decide any matter unless it is prohibited.

The Attorney General argued that the Constitutional Tribunal had no jurisdiction to consider the matter because the application because the Amyotha Hluttaw was still deliberating on this issue, and no law had been passed. The Attorney General's argument was based on section 322 of the Constitution, which sets out the jurisdiction of the Tribunal and only mentions laws and not draft laws. At the heart of the application submitted to the Tribunal, however, was whether the Tribunal's powers extend to consideration of draft laws and the deliberations of the legislature. The 2008 Constitution and the Constitutional Tribunal Law make no mention of whether the Tribunal can review a draft law.

The Tribunal dismissed the application on the basis that the Tribunal did not have jurisdiction to review a draft law. The Tribunal declined to enter political debates on the merits of proposed bills and the politicised nature of the debate over proportional representation. This case is also an example of the way the Amyotha Hluttaw is adopting an approach based on coercive centralism, that is, by trying to get the Constitutional Tribunal to indicate which electoral option would be constitutional *before* the Amyotha Hluttaw goes ahead and passes the law.

There remain discussions about the need to change the electoral system, particularly with regards to the peace process and claims for greater ethnic recognition. Any proposed change to the method of counting votes would likely require constitutional amendment.

IV. THE ADMINISTRATION OF ELECTIONS

The Constitution locates the power to regulate and conduct elections at the Union level. The Union Election Commission ('Election Commission') administers and oversees elections and referendums, amends

---

[47] Constitutional Tribunal, Draft Law Case 5/2014.

constituencies, compiles voter lists, as well as handles electoral disputes.[48] The Election Commission has a constitutional mandate to postpone an election in case of natural disaster, a veiled reference to the criticism the junta received when it went ahead with the constitutional referendum despite Cyclone Nargis (see Chapter 1). As a key part of the apparatus of the military-state, the Election Commission ensures that democracy remains disciplined. The original law governing the Election Commission was minimal in detail, but then in 2012 the legislature introduced a new law that set out further details about its powers and procedures.[49] The Commission consists of at least five members, although there is no maximum number of members, and these members serve a five-year term.[50] The fact that the terms of the Commissioners are tied to that of the government means that there is the potential for the Election Commission to appear biased in favour of the government of the day.

The president has the power to appoint all Commissioners. Eligibility requirements are the same as that for legislators (see Chapter 5), although candidates must be at least 50 years old and have experience as either a judge of the Supreme Court or a High Court, as a judicial officer of a High Court, an advocate, or in the opinion of the president be an eminent person.[51] This requirement for legal and judicial expertise suggests that the role of the Election Commission is understood as exercising quasi-judicial power. The grounds for impeachment of a Commissioner are the same as for legislators, and the process is initiated by the president who requests the speaker to form an investigation body comprising of members of both the Pyithu Hluttaw and Amyotha Hluttaw.[52]

The Election Commission also organises Union and State/Region elections, but it has no jurisdiction over ward/village-tract elections. Decisions of the Election Commission are final and binding. The Constitutional Tribunal has confirmed that decisions of the Election Commission cannot be challenged in the Tribunal.[53] It has powers to draft laws and make submissions to the legislature, and it also has *suo moto* powers.[54]

---

[48] 2008 Constitution, s 399, Law 3/2012 of the Union Election Commission Law, s 10.
[49] Law No 3/2012 on the Union Election Commission (replacing Law No 1/2010), and later amended by Law No 40/2015.
[50] See 2008 Constitution, Ch IX on Elections.
[51] 2008 Constitution, s 398.
[52] Ibid, s 400.
[53] Constitutional Tribunal, Kachin Race Case No 1/2014 (September).
[54] Law 3/2010 of the Pyithu Hluttaw Election Law, s 53.

Outside of the authority of the Union Election Commission, elections are held for ward and village tract, and Yangon and Mandalay City Development Council. These elections are indirect without universal suffrage and follow different rules that often apply inconsistently. Here I focus on ward and village tract elections, which are required to be regulated by law according to the Constitution. The ward and village-tract are the lowest elected unit of administration in Myanmar. While the government appoints district- and township-level administrators, the residents of ward and village tracts elect local administrators.[55] Each head of a household elects a leader to represent ten households by way of secret ballot (heads of households are always men). These ten-household leaders then vote for the administrators of the ward or village tract ('local administrators'). There are no direct elections, although the introduction of a vote is a shift from past practice when administrators were simply appointed by their superiors within the General Administration Department (see Chapter 3).

Since 2016, the term of office of a local administrator coincides with the term of the government and lasts for five years. The elections for local administrators are supervised by a board of village elders and respected persons.[56] In January 2016, the first election of this kind, there were over 16,000 seats for local administrators contested. These positions are among the most important because a local administrator acts as the key government contact for citizens. Local administrators often play a role in local dispute resolution, as well as issue letters of recommendation that are essential for a person to apply for a range of certificates, permits and licences, such as a household certificate or a national identity card.[57] They also chair the local Land Management Committee, and contribute to the Development Support Committees in relation to development projects. The local administrators both fulfil responsibilities delegated to them from township administrators, as well as communicate to township administrators about the needs of their ward or village tract. This is a wide area of responsibility and is an informal means of military influence given that, up until late 2018, the General Administration Department reported to the Minister for Home Affairs who is selected by the Commander-in-Chief.[58]

---

[55] 2008 Constitution, s 189.

[56] Helene Maria Kyed, et al, *Local Democracy in Myanmar: Reflections on Ward and Village Tract Elections 2016* (Danish Institute for International Studies, 2016).

[57] See Ward or Village Tract Administration Law No 1/2012 (amended 7/2012, 13/2016).

[58] Andrew Selth, *All Going According to Plan: The Armed Forces and the Government in Myanmar*. Griffith Asia Institute. Regional Outlook Paper No 54, 2017, p 12.

Local administrators hold powerful positions and their status has increased in the reform era. Prior to 2012, local administrators did not receive an official wage, although this position was open to abuse for the collection of unofficial wages. Since 2012, local administrators are entitled to a monthly wage from the General Administration Department, as well as related office expenses. The law also attempts to prohibit corruption in this role. Observers have identified a range of features of the election process that inhibit local democracy and may be a focus of reform at a later stage. For example, there are no rules on the process of nominating or announcing candidates, nor clarification on how and when elections are scheduled. While the Union Election Commission has a mandate to resolve electoral disputes, this does not include disputes over local administrators.

V. THE RESOLUTION OF ELECTORAL DISPUTES

The Election Commission has constitutional power to hear and determine all electoral disputes.[59] In this respect, the Election Commission exercises adjudicative or quasi-judicial power. Either a voter or a candidate can submit a challenge to the election results claiming the electoral rules have been breached. Such applications must be made within 45 days of the announcement of the election results concerned. The filing fee for a complaint, and for the filing of a counter-claim, is 500,000 kyat (USD$335). This exorbitantly high fee acts as a deterrent to filing cases and is a significant barrier because it is much higher than official court fees. When a complaint is received, an ad hoc Tribunal is formed by the Election Commission to consider the matter.[60] The ad hoc Tribunal consists of either three Electoral Commissioners, or one Electoral Commissioner and two independent experts. Most hearings are conducted in Naypyidaw and the Attorney General may contribute to proceedings by way of an amicus curiae brief. The proceedings are conducted according to the rules of the Code of Civil Procedure and the Evidence Act, and so in this respect mirror court proceedings.[61] Although an administrative body, the Election Commission effectively exercises judicial power. The Election Commission also plays a key role in investigating any right to recall complaint (below).

---

[59] Carter Centre, *Observing Myanmar's 2015 General Elections: Final Report*.
[60] Law 3/2010 on the Pyithu Hluttaw Election Law, s 69.
[61] Ibid, s 77.

The Election Commission is not constitutionally required to respond to complaints within a set period. As a result, there have been delays for the review of applications in some cases. If the case is unsuccessful, a petitioner can decide to pursue their case by appealing to the Election Commission.[62] The decision of the Election Commission is final and conclusive, as indicated by the privative clause both in the Constitution and in the enabling law. The law is clear that the courts cannot hear election disputes. Not even an application regarding a decision of the Election Commission for the constitutional writs can be brought to the Supreme Court. This dispute resolution practice is typical of many areas of administration. There are also major disincentives to bringing a complaint to the Election Commission. For example, an applicant who loses a case faces potential criminal charges.[63] This is symptomatic of the broader judicial system, where applicants who bring a case and lose are often punished as a form of deterring other potential applicants.

As of February 2017, the Election Commission had received 45 complaints, although decisions had only been handed down in two cases.[64] The complaints concerned all levels of the legislature – both the Amyotha Hluttaw and Pyithu Hluttaw, and contestation of 25 State/Region Hluttaw seats. The complaints include pre- and post-election issues. Pre-election issues raised include allegations of intimidation against candidates and breaches of legal processes and procedures on the election day, including irregularities in counting of the votes. Once a complaint has been made, the notice is posted for 15 days at the Election Commission building in Naypyidaw. This does not act as an effective form of public notification given that the Election Commission is not accessible to a broader public.

After the historic 2015 elections, there was a general agreement among some of the major parties, such as the NLD and USDP, to accept the results rather than challenge them. This informal agreement not to dispute the results is another manifestation of coercive centralism. The Election Commission has not necessarily been the primary forum for electoral complaints. Complaints raising criminal issues have been lodged with police during the campaign period in 2015. Some of these cases, such as those involving serious physical attacks on political candidates, have received wide media attention.

---

[62] Ibid, s 74.
[63] 2008 Constitution, s 64.
[64] Carter Centre Report (2015).

The Election Commission has been willing to investigate and determine extremely difficult and sensitive cases, such as the violent and coercive campaign tactics of leaders of the Border Guard Force (see Chapter 3). For example, in 2009, the New Democratic Army-Kachin (NDA-K) became a Border Guard Force. In 2010, the warlord and leader of the NDA-K, U Zakhung Ting Ying, was elected to the Amyotha Hluttaw as a representative of Kachin State.[65] In 1989, Zakhung was responsible for undertaking negotiations with General Khin Nyunt and agreed to a ceasefire for the area that was known as Kachin Special Region 1. To fulfil the ceasefire terms, Zakhung forced the Burma Communist Party troops to leave, but made the strategic move of quarantining all their weapons. This was the beginning of the strengthening of his armed force. Zakhung is rumoured to be involved in the illegal timber, jade and ruby industry, channelling the income into his private wealth. In 2010, he won against a National Unity Party candidate, with the USDP not fielding a candidate for this constituency. In the lead up to the 2015 elections, competition against Zakhung was fierce with four other contending parties. These parties faced pressure from the NDA-K to cease their activities, and NLD members were physically attacked in one township. Zakhung went as far as to send a letter to the NLD warning them not to enter his territory or campaign there. In response the NLD submitted a complaint to the Union Election Commission.[66] Although Zakhung was declared the winner of the 2015 elections, he was subject to a formal complaint to the Election Commission. The Election Commission held that Zakhung was guilty of several breaches of the elections laws and his electoral win was declared void. The runner up in the election was appointed in his place.[67]

The 2015 elections were by no means completely free. There were issues with advance voting procedures, which did not include local or international observation. Issues arise in areas with a Tatmadaw base. Tatmadaw voters could take advantage of the advance voting procedures

[65] *The Myanmar Times*, 'Kachin State Warlord Ordered to let opponents campaign', 30 Sept 2015, www.mmtimes.com/national-news/16747-kachin-state-warlord-ordered-to-let-opponents-campaign.html.

[66] Thuta Linn, 'Interview with Zahkung Tin Ying Independent MP for Kachin Constituency No 5, BNI Online, 29 October 2015, www.bnionline.net/en/2015-election/kachin-state/item/1031-interview-with-zahkung-tin-ying-independent-mp-for-kachin-constituency-no-5.html.

[67] Sithu Aung Myint, 'The Sunset of a Notorious Warlord', *Frontier*, 2 October 2016, https://frontiermyanmar.net/en/the-sunset-of-a-notorious-warlord.

if they were not present in their constituency on election day. This issue was apparent in some areas where the USDP were successful by only a narrow margin of voters, such as in Hpa-pun District in Kayin State. There were also complaints about the misuse of religion for political gain as part of the campaign process. There have been some cases of losing USDP candidates accusing the NLD of various breaches of the electoral rules, such as defaming the government and the USDP candidate. Among the most serious issues was also the mass disenfranchisement of over one million white card holders, the ultimate step effecting exclusion from the political community.

VI. COMPLAINTS AGAINST LEGISLATORS: THE RIGHT TO RECALL

The right of an electorate to recall its elected representative is a contentious mechanism of accountability in Myanmar. The Constitution is one of few around the globe to include a right to recall of legislators.[68] Myanmar has the lowest threshold for a constitutional right to recall in the world. The right of recall is currently provided for as one of the Basic Principles and in the Citizen's Rights and Duties chapter of the Constitution.[69] The agreement of just one per cent of the electorate of the constituency concerned is required to lodge a complaint with the Election Commission.[70] This rule has been the subject of specific calls for constitutional reform. There is historical precedent for the right to recall in Myanmar, which was included in past constitutions.[71]

The grounds for recall are broad, mirroring the grounds for impeachment of other office holders. Initially the law did not clarify whether the Election Commission has a role in investigating applications for the right to recall.[72] In 2011, the law was amended by the legislature so that the investigation of a right to recall request was specifically listed as a power of the Election Commission.[73] In theory, the Election

---

[68] Andrew Ellis, *The Use and Right to Recall*, International IDEA Working Paper (2005); International IDEA, *Direct Democracy Handbook*, pp 109–123.

[69] 2008 Constitution, ss 38(b), 369(B).

[70] Ibid, s 396(b).

[71] 1947 Constitution, s 78; 1974 Constitution, s 15.

[72] Law No 1/2010 on the Union Election Commission (repealed in 2012).

[73] Law No 6/2011 amending the Union Election Commission law, inserting s 8(j). The right to recall is included in the replacement law, Law 3/2012 on the Union Election Commission, s 10(j).

Commission will investigate a complaint and may conclude that a member is no longer fit to serve in the legislature. The legislature has made several efforts to introduce a law to bring the right to recall into force, however so far, the legislature has been unable to obtain agreement on the Bill.[74]

Two high profile political figures have been the targets of this mechanism: the former Speaker, Shwe Mann, and Centre Executive Committee member of the NLD, Win Htein. Shwe Mann is the former chair of the USDP and was ranked third in the former military regime. He was elected to the legislature in the 2010 elections, and then in 2013 was appointed as chair of the USDP. Shwe Mann became increasingly outspoken and bold in his ambitions to become president after the 2015 elections and his alliance with the NLD began to cause concern within the USDP. In 2012, allegations against Shwe Mann were first raised by the Tatmadaw and USDP members of the legislature. One per cent of voters from Shwe Mann's electorate of Zeyathiri in Naypyidaw submitted a petition to the Election Commission based on the right to recall. The Election Commission declined to investigate because there was no law in place enacting the constitutional provision. Unable to use the right to recall against him, in August 2015, Shwe Mann was instead forced to resign from his position as the chairperson of the USDP, and less than a year later in April 2016, he was officially sacked from the USDP in an internal political coup.

The second political figure who was the target of efforts to exercise the constitutional right to recall was Win Htein. Win Htein is a senior member of the NLD and its official spokesperson, member of the Pyithu Hluttaw (2012–2016), as well as a former political prisoner for close to 19 years (1989–1995, 1996–2008), although he was previously also a Tatmadaw officer (1959–1976).[75] In September 2013, Win Htein witnessed severe violence against the Muslim community in Meiktila, south of Mandalay in central Myanmar. Win Htein called for the police to step in to protect the community and restore order, but they did not. This is an area with a large military base and the Tatmadaw did not prevent the violence. After the incident, he was not afraid to condemn the violence and express his deep shame at being from Meitkila, particularly

---

[74] 2008 Constitution, s 397.
[75] Nyan Hlaing Lynn, 'U Win Htein: Godfather of the NLD', 6 February 2017, *Frontier*, https://frontiermyanmar.net/en/u-win-htein-godfather-of-the-nld.

when a United Nations car was physically attacked.[76] Some members of his constituency disagreed with his condemnation of the violence and tried to initiate the right to recall mechanism by submitting a complaint to the Election Commission. There were concerns over his prospects of being re-elected in 2015 because of this incident, but he later chose not to compete although he remains a leader within the NLD.

The right to recall mechanism has been subject to calls for constitutional amendment by those who consider the threshold for recall too low and open to manipulation. In 2014, during the constitutional amendment process, the NLD's submission to the Constitutional Amendment Committee noted that the threshold for the right to recall should be raised to 20 per cent of the member's constituency.[77] The right to recall debate confirms that no constitutional provision is in force unless an enabling law is enacted. This is because constitutional provisions that note a right is to apply 'according to law' are perceived to require legislative action to be realised. This is a restrictive reading of the Constitution, but it explains why some other provisions of the Constitution that do not yet have enabling laws are not followed.

There are other more common forms of accountability of legislators. Some members have resigned rather than face disciplinary proceedings. For example, in 2013, U Thein Tun, the then Minister for Communications, Posts and Telegraphs, resigned after allegations of corruption;[78] in 2014, U San Sint, the Minister for Religious Affairs was dismissed by the President for misusing state funds;[79] in 2016, U Tun Win, the Deputy Minister for Agriculture, Livestock and Irrigation resigned after alleged infighting within the NLD[80] and in 2017, U Min Min Oo, Chief Minister of Mon State resigned again on allegations of corruption.[81]

---

[76] *The Myanmar Times*, 'U Win Htein stands by comments on Meiktila violence', 23 September 2013, www.mmtimes.com/national-news/8251-u-win-htein-stands-by-comments-on-meiktila-violence.html.

[77] NLD Submission to the Constitutional Amendment Committee 2014, on file.

[78] Aung Shin, 'Sacked telecom minister to contest his hometown,' *The Myanmar Times*, 11 September 2015, www.mmtimes.com/national-news/16438-sacked-telecoms-minister-to-contest-his-hometown-seat.html.

[79] Pyae Thet Phyo and Ye Mon, 'MPs draft petition after former minister jailed for 13 years', *The Myanmar Times*, 17 October 2014, www.mmtimes.com/national-news/11987-mps-draft-petition-after-former-minister-jailed.html.

[80] Nyan Hlaing Lynn, 'Deputy Minister for Agriculture fired after Cabinet dispute', Frontier, 21 November 2016, https://frontiermyanmar.net/en/deputy-minister-for-agriculture-fired-after-cabinet-dispute.

[81] Ye Mon, 'Mysteries of Mon Chief Minister's Resignation', *The Myanmar Times*, 27 February 2017, www.mmtimes.com/national-news/25096-mysteries-of-mon-chief-minister-s-resignation.html.

These instances suggest that the practice of forcing someone to retire or pressuring them to resign in order to save face remains powerful in Myanmar.

VII. CONCLUSION

The reintroduction of elections is an important component of the military-state and the perceived benefits of the Constitution. Emphasis is placed on the realisation of a multi-party system, with relatively less concern over on the lack of representation due to unelected military legislators. The Constitution's detailed instructions on the political and electoral system include requirements of political party loyalty to the three meta-principles of the military-state. The case study of the right to vote indicates how the Constitution has been used by the legislature, together with the Constitutional Tribunal and the government administration, to restrict participation in politics. The legislative disenfranchisement of the Rohingya prior to the 2015 elections constitutes a means of legal exclusion from the political community. Similarly, the debate over the constitutionality of proportional representation was primarily a debate in the legislature, although the Constitutional Tribunal was again called up to clarify the issue.

On the administrative side, the Election Commission oversees and regulates elections at both the Union and State/Region level. It also has jurisdiction over electoral disputes as part of its quasi-judicial powers, and its decisions cannot be challenged in a court. The major issue at present is that the Election Commission is not required to resolve disputes within a set time frame. The Election Commission has not yet exercised its power to investigate complaints concerning the right to recall members of the legislature. This constitutional right and form of accountability has the potential to be manipulated and used against political opponents due to the extremely low threshold of the right to recall. This debate and the failure of the legislature to agree on a bill does offer a useful indication of how the Constitution works – unless there is an enabling law, provisions like the right to recall remain a dead letter. Aside from the Election Commission, the General Administration Department remains an important actor in local elections and will be a critical component of any efforts to reform local elections to ensure they are more representative and democratic.

FURTHER READING

Helene Maria Kyed, et al, *Local Democracy in Myanmar: Reflections on Ward and Village Tract Elections 2016* (Danish Institute for International Studies, 2016).

Kyle Lemargie, et al, 'Electoral System Choice in Myanmar's Democratisation Debate' in Nicholas Farrelly and Nick Cheesman (eds) *Debating Democratisation in Myanmar* (Singapore: ISEAS, 2014) pp 229–226.

Michael Lidauer, 'The 2015 Elections and Conflict Dynamics in Myanmar', in Nick Cheesman and Nicholas Farrelly (eds) *Conflict in Myanmar: War, Politics, Religion* (ISEAS: 2016).

Ardeth Maung Thawnghmung (2016) 'The Myanmar Elections 2015: Why the National League for Democracy Won a Landslide Victory'" *Critical Asian Studies* 48:1, 132–142

Michael Lidauer and Gilles Saphy, 'Elections and the Reform Agenda', in Melissa Crouch and Tim Lindsey (eds) *Law, Society and Transition in Myanmar* (Hart Publishing, 2014).

5

The Legislature

Role of the Legislature – Tricameral Structure – Legislative Power and
Privileges – The Speakers – Legislative Committees

THE OPERATION OF the legislature since 2011 has generated surprise from observers because of its robust debates, the vigorous exchanges between the executive and the legislature, and the legislature's law-making endeavours. Some explanations for the achievements of the legislature have focused on dominant personalities, such as the Speaker of the Pyithu Hluttaw, and the behaviour of its members, particularly the Tatmadaw representatives.[1] Other scholars have analysed the role of the legislature in addressing conflict, seeking to reconcile the way in which the legislature has both tried to reduce conflict but also exacerbate it.[2] In this chapter, I offer a legal and constitutional analysis of the legislature's function.[3]

The legislature consists of three houses: the Pyithu Hluttaw, Amyotha Hluttaw and the Pyidaungsu Hluttaw. Myanmar has a tricameral legislative system at the Union level. Some scholars have used the term 'tricameral' to include the role of the president in the legislative

---

[1] Renaud Egreteau, *Caretaking Democratization* (Hurst & Co Publishers, 2016); Thomas Kean, 'Myanmar's Parliament: From Scorn to Significance' in Nick Cheesman et al (eds) *Debating Democratisation in Myanmar* (Singapore: ISEAS, 2014).

[2] Chit Win, 'The Hluttaw and Conflicts in Myanmar' in Nick Cheesman & Nicholas Farrelly (eds) *Conflict in Myanmar: War, Politics, Religion* (Singapore: ISEAS, 2016) pp 199–220; Chit Win and Thomas Kean, 'Communal Conflict in Myanmar' (2017) *Journal of Contemporary Asia* 1; Melissa Crouch, 'Legislating Reform? Law and Conflict in Myanmar' in Nick Cheesman and Nicholas Farrelly (eds) *Conflict in Myanmar: War, Politics, Religion* (Singapore: ISEAS, 2016) pp 219–239.

[3] This Chapter deals with arts 74–198 (Ch IV The Legislature) of the 2008 Constitution. I use the term 'legislature' in this book to refer generally to the three houses at the Union level.

process, such as the United States.[4] Instead, I use the term 'tricameral' in the more common sense to refer to the existence of three legislative institutions that each exercise legislative power.[5] The Pyidaungsu Hluttaw acts as the dominant and pre-eminent legislative institution. The system is distinct from other bicameral systems because the joint sittings of the Pyidaungsu Hluttaw are not extraordinary but very common, and the sittings occur frequently. The Pyidaungsu Hluttaw presents a united legislative front against the executive and president, which was particularly evident under Thein Sein. The other two houses, the Pyithu Hluttaw and Amyotha Hluttaw, play a role in law-making, executive oversight and judicial control.

In Myanmar's military-state, the legislature is not only under surveillance of the Tatmadaw's watchmen (see Chapter 3), but its frequent interactions with the executive means it is often required to deal with former or active military officers. A constitutional crises arose over the scope of legislative power and the role of 'Union Level Organisations'. While the Constitutional Tribunal made a determination on this issue, the legislature's discontent with the decision led all members of the Tribunal to voluntarily resign. The legislature is the locus and hive of constitutional discussion, and it has exerted considerable influence over the Tribunal.

I. THE UNION LEGISLATURE: A TRICAMERAL SYSTEM

The Basic Principles in the Constitution divide legislative power between the Pyidaungsu Hluttaw, the Pyithu Hluttaw and the Amyotha Hluttaw, and the State/Region Hluttaw, as well as Self-Administered Areas where they exist as sub-units within a state.[6] Chapter IV of the Constitution begins by giving priority to the Pyidaungsu Hluttaw, followed by the Pyithu Hluttaw and then the Amyotha Hluttaw.[7] I first explain why the Pyidaungsu Hluttaw should be understood as the dominant house and how it represents the united interests of the legislature in its dealings with the executive. My definition of the system as 'tricameral' is based on four important observations: the structural symmetry of the system;

---

[4] See Saul Levmore, 'Bicameralism: When are two decisions better than one?' (1992) 12 *International Review of Law and Economics* 145, 151–3.

[5] John Uhr, 'Bicameralism' in RAW Rhodes et al (eds) *The Oxford Handbook of Political Institutions* (OUP 2006) pp. 474–94.

[6] 2008 Constitution, s 12.

[7] See the 2008 Constitution, ss 74–108, 109–140, and 41–160 respectively.

the frequency of sittings; the subject matter of sittings; and the sense of corporate personality of the joint sittings. I explain the core functions of the Pyithu Hluttaw and Amyotha Hluttaw as law-making, executive accountability and judicial oversight. The relationship between the three houses favours collaboration and consensus in decision-making and is a feature of co-operative centralism in the military-state.

A. The Pyidaungsu Hluttaw as the Dominant House

One major question of constitutional design is whether the Constitution provides for a bicameral national legislature. While joint sittings in bicameral systems may have a variety of functions, they generally share two core characteristics: the joint sittings are rare, and the subject matter of the sittings is either symbolic, such as appointing the head of state, or of an extraordinary nature, such as a loss of confidence in the government or a declaration of a state of emergency. In addition, a bicameral Parliament in a federal system may often be designed so that the term of office of the houses are asymmetrical. In contrast, I define Myanmar's Union legislature as a 'tricameral system' because of the frequency of sittings (almost as often as the Amyotha Hluttaw and Pyithu Hluttaw); the subject matter of sittings going beyond extraordinary matters and often involve consideration of legislation; its corporate personality and the symmetrical design of the houses which reduces the role of the upper house as a check on the power of the lower house. The Pyidaungsu Hluttaw plays a dominant role in law-making, executive oversight and judicial control. The Pyidaungsu Hluttaw is more than just the two houses sitting jointly but is understood as a separate, independent and dominant legislative entity. I attribute this tricameral constitutional design and function to the combination of the scope of the Pyidaungsu Hluttaw's powers in the Constitution and the expansive mandate the legislature has adopted. The operation of the Pyidaungsu Hluttaw embodies a model of decision-making that emphasises cooperation and consensus.

The Pyidaungsu Hluttaw includes a maximum 664 members, and of these 166 are from the Tatmadaw. The Pyidaungsu Hluttaw is the apex of the legislative branch and sits parallel to the Office of the President as the apex of the executive branch. The Pyidaungsu Hluttaw plays a key role in resolving any disagreement between the Pyithu Hluttaw and Amyotha Hluttaw in the process of law-making,[8] approving a

---

[8] 2008 Constitution, s 95(b).

presidential ordinance,[9] passing the national budget,[10] and approving treaties submitted by the president, or requesting the president to consider entering into a treaty (on the latter, see Chapter 9).[11] The president sends back comments to the legislature on draft bills (which has occurred under Thein Sein), to the Pyidaungsu Hluttaw rather than the house that initiated the bill. The Pyidaungsu Hluttaw then decides on whether to accept the president's recommendations and, if they decide to reject these recommendations, the law will come into effect within a set number of days. The Pyidaungsu Hluttaw also has power to enact laws for the Union Territories (see Chapter 5).[12]

There is a sense of corporate personality of the Pyidaungsu Hluttaw as an institution that represents the interests of the legislature against the executive and president. This developed under Thein Sein, when the USDP Government was split internally. The Constitution anticipates that a significant amount of discussion and debate will take place in the Pyidaungsu Hluttaw.[13] While it decides on the most pressing national issues, the Pyidaungsu Hluttaw also hears many everyday matters and sits frequently. This is evident from the schedule of the legislature over the 13 sessions from 2011–2016. During this time, the Pyidaungsu Hluttaw sat for approximately two-thirds the length of the houses sitting separately. Often the Pyithu Hluttaw and Amyotha Hluttaw would sit concurrent in the morning, and the Pyidaungsu Hluttaw would sit in the afternoon. The corporate sense of identity of the Pyidaungsu Hluttaw is evident in other ways, such as the legislative records. The speeches of members are recorded without reference to which house they sit in. The affiliation of Amyotha Hluttaw and Pyithu Hluttaw civilian members can only be discerned implicitly. Members are identified by their township constituency (which implies they are from the Pyithu Hluttaw) or by the State/Region they represent (which implies they are from the Amyotha Hluttaw). There is no way of telling which house the Tatmadaw members usually sit, and, in this regard, the Tatmadaw act collectively in the Pyidaungsu Hluttaw rather than representing the interests of their house. Further members themselves do not overtly act in the name of the house that they were appointed to.

---

[9] Ibid, s 104 (b) and (c).
[10] Ibid, ss 102–103.
[11] Ibid, s 108.
[12] Ibid, s 99.
[13] Ibid, s 80.

The Union legislature has authority to pass legislation within eleven broad areas under the Constitution.[14] The list of legislative matters is wide and includes defence and security; foreign affairs; finance and planning; economy; agriculture; energy, electricity, forestry and mining; industry; transport, communication and construction; social sector (education, health); government administration; and the judiciary. The headings in this legislative list offer an indication of which ministries are responsible for which laws, for example, the Supreme Court is responsible for matters under section 11 on the judiciary (see Chapter 7). All residual legislative power lies with the Pyidaungsu Hluttaw.[15] This is a source of disagreement as some States/Regions advocate for a US-style distribution of legislative power where the States/Regions hold plenary legislative power.

The scope of legislative power has been the subject of constitutional amendment in the Pyidaungsu Hluttaw. The Constitution contains a list of enumerated powers for the Union legislature and a narrow list of powers for the States/Region Hluttaw.[16] In July 2015, constitutional amendments approved by the Pyidaungsu Hluttaw set out further details of the legislative and taxation powers of the States/Regions. The reforms add a longer list of powers to Schedules 2 and 5 of the Constitution. This allows the 14 States/Regions to collect income tax, customs duties and stamp duty, levies on services (tourism, hotels private schools and private hospitals) and resources (including oil, gas, mining and gems).[17] This amendment was necessary because the Constitutional Tribunal has previously declined to interpret Schedules 2 and 5 of the Constitution, instead deferring to the Pyidaungsu Hluttaw.[18] The amendments suggest that only the Pyidaungsu Hluttaw has the ability to redefine this list. The Constitutional Tribunal sees these lists as part of the power of the Pyidaungsu Hluttaw and plays no interpretive role regarding Schedules 2 and 5.

The process of law-making is broadly understood as a consensus-building exercise, both between the houses of the legislature and with the government administration. Once a Bill is approved by either the two houses or the Pyidaungsu Hluttaw, the legislature sends a Bill to the President's Office, which then sends the Bill to the ministry responsible to

---

[14] Ibid, Sch 1.
[15] Ibid, s 98.
[16] See 2008 Constitution, Schs 1, 2, and 5.
[17] Law amending the Union of Myanmar 2008 Constitution No 45/2015.
[18] Constitutional Tribunal, Kachin Budget Case No 4/2014.

check as a matter of courtesy and deference to the ministry on the final version of the Bill. If the legislature has changed the Bill substantially, then the ministry may have further comments and suggestions. The president may choose to issue recommendations for change and return the Bill to the Pyidaungsu Hluttaw for reconsideration. If the Bill is approved by a simple majority in the Pyidaungsu Hluttaw, then it comes into force within 14 days, regardless of whether the president approves the final version. As I explain later, during his term, president Thein Sein exercised this weak veto power by returning laws to the Pyidaungsu Hluttaw with suggestions for reform (see Chapter 6).

The operation of the legislature is more open and transparent than the past military regime, and legislative records are public.[19] The Constitution does permit these records to be withheld and does not require reasons to be given for the withholding of records. While legislative hearings were initially closed, sessions are now televised and feature in print media and online. Both governments have kept records of proceedings, initially published in hardcopy and most available later online. On occasion, the Tatmadaw has demanded that words be retracted from legislative records, such as when an NLD member referred to the previous military regime as a dictatorship (see Chapter 10).

Aside from its legislative power, the Pyidaungsu Hluttaw does also consider extraordinary requests by the executive for an extension of a state of emergency. On 20–21 May 2013, a special session of the Pyidaungsu Hluttaw was held to debate the extension of the state of emergency in Meiktila. This was the first and only time a special session has been held. The Constitution does not require legislative checks on the initial presidential act of declaring an emergency, although the Hluttaw is required to approve an extension of a constitutional state of emergency within 60 days. The extension of an emergency is not required to meet any specified criteria. The key debate that emerged was the duration of the extension,[20] whether it should remain open-ended as the president had proposed, or whether it should be subject to a 60-day time limit. Most members in the Pyidaungsu Hluttaw voted in favour of a 60-day time limit, which indicates that some members of the Pyidaungsu Hluttaw from the USDP voted against the proposal of the president, who was also from the USDP. The subsequent extension of the state

---

[19] This applies to the Pyidaungsu Hluttaw, Pyithu Hluttaw and the States/Regions: 2008 Constitution, ss 89, 132, 184.
[20] See PDH2013.

of emergency was approved without any apparent evidence from the Tatmadaw, police or local administration as to what measures had been taken, or progress made, to restore order. The Pyidaungsu Hluttaw acts as a check on the power of the president to extend a state of emergency.

In relation to the other branches of government, the Pyidaungsu Hluttaw has sought to portray itself as the supreme branch and check on executive power (although the Tatmadaw remains as the fourth and dominant branch). The Pyidaungsu Hluttaw as a new institution has greater public legitimacy than the government administration, and part of its credibility stems from the emphasis placed on its members as directly elected representatives (see Chapter 5). The other two houses have distinct but subordinate roles in comparison to the Pyidaungsu Hluttaw. One difference is that there is constitutional silence on whether the Pyidaungsu Hluttaw can have its own committees, though such legislative committees can be created by the Amyotha Hluttaw and Pyithu Hluttaw. I consider the respective roles of the Pyithu Hluttaw and Amyotha Hluttaw, and then discuss the issue of legislative committees.

B. The Pyithu Hluttaw and Amyotha Hluttaw

The Pyithu Hluttaw (lower house) represents electoral constituencies while the Amyotha Hluttaw (upper house) grants equal representation to the 14 States/Regions as a form of territorial and ethnic representation. Each State/Region has 12 representatives in the Amyotha Hluttaw. This design favours the sparsely populated states such as Chin State. The houses are symmetrical in design, that is, they serve the same five-year terms. This contrasts with some bicameral parliaments in federal systems where the terms of the houses may be intentionally asymmetrical. The constitutional role shared by the Pyithu Hluttaw and Amyotha Hluttaw consists of three main functions: law-making, executive oversight, and judicial control.

The main role of these two houses is to make laws. Bills initiated by either the government, committees or individual lawmakers are submitted for debate in one of the houses. From 2011–2015, most bills were initiated by the President's Office,[21] and this pattern is likely to be the same under the NLD Government. Bills can originate from either house, except for budget Bills which the president or someone appointed by him

---

[21] Renaud Egreteau 'Emerging Patterns of Parliamentary Politics', in David Steinburg (eds) *Myanmar: The Dynamics of an Evolving Polity* (Lynne Rienner Publishers, 2015) p 71.

submits to the Pyidaungsu Hluttaw.[22] After being approved by majority vote, a bill is sent to the other house for debate. If the other house agrees without amendments, as is sometimes the case, then the bill goes directly to the President's Office. In a situation where the Pyithu Hluttaw and Amyotha Hluttaw cannot agree on a single version of the bill, then a sitting of the Pyidaungsu Hluttaw is held to resolve the dispute.[23] Related to the law-making process, the Pyithu Hluttaw and Amyotha Hluttaw have constitutional power to establish committees and commissions. These committees may contribute to the legislative process as well as deal with executive matters such as address complaints from citizens. I consider the role of legislative committees later in relation to the concept of legislative power.

Another aspect of the role of the two houses is that they actively oversee and monitor the judiciary. The dominant view among legislators is that they must supervise the operation of the courts. Most local actors – from lawyers to scholars, legislators and even judges – agree that the legislature can and should act as a 'check and balance' on the courts. Some scholars have also accepted without question the view that the legislature can legitimately supervise the operation of the judiciary.[24] It is common in Westminster constitutional systems for the legislature to play a role in the appointment and removal processes for the judiciary as a form of check and balance. It is not usually accepted for the legislature to interfere in the day-to-day function of the courts. There are many ways in which the legislature has used the cover of acting as a 'check and balance' on the courts to justify interference and control over the judiciary. This includes requiring the courts to draft legislation according to its demands; calling the Chief Justice to the legislature; questioning the Chief Justice not only on how many cases the courts are hearing but on *why* the court decided certain cases in the way that it has. The legislature has also criticised the Chief Justice for alleged corruption within the judiciary despite the lack of a substantive investigation. From the perspective of the legislature, this level of scrutiny is warranted because of judicial corruption and public dissatisfaction with the courts, although this overlooks the issue of military influence in judicial affairs (see Chapter 8).

In addition to the Union legislature, the State/Region Hluttaw has also undertaken an oversight role of the courts. For example, in

---

June 2016, the Chief Minister of Mandalay Region Hluttaw gave his consent to a proposal to monitor the courts.[25] This was raised again in December 2016, when an NLD member of the regional legislature suggested that it was necessary to set up specific court observation teams to monitor the courts in the area and guard against corruption.[26] Such measures have not been welcomed by the Chief Justice of the Supreme Court, who responded by arguing that this measure would compromise the independence of the courts. I deal with the role of the courts and the issue of reform in more detail in Chapter 8.

Aside from its role in law-making and as a check on the judiciary, the two houses also act as a check on the executive. Ministers are often called to the legislature to report on certain matters, provide clarification on an issue or give an update on the implementation of a government policy. There have been complaints that this mechanism of accountability is ineffective, because ministers may avoid directly answering the question, may send their deputies instead or may fail to turn up to answer questions, thus avoiding scrutiny. In addition, individual legislators and committees receive and seek to address complaints about administrative decisions and actions, such as historic and contemporary land grabs. In this way, the legislature functions to keep the executive in check.

II. THE LOYALTIES, PRIVILEGES AND RESPONSIBILITIES OF LEGISLATORS

There are up to 664 legislators in the Pyidaungsu Hluttaw. The number of legislators in the State/Region Hluttaw may vary and presently ranges from 20 seats in Kayah State to 137 seats in Shan State. The Constitution demands the loyalty of legislators, and this conditions how members relate to their constituency. Constitutional immunities and privileges shield legislators, who are under the oversight of the Speaker. The Speakers are crucial leaders and a key point of communication with the president.

The position of legislators is not entirely free from limitations under the Constitution. All legislators must adhere to the three meta-principles of the military-state (see Chapter 3). This loyalty requirement is not

---

[25] *The Myanmar Times*, 'Chief Minister Rubber Stamps Court Monitors', 3 June 2016, www.mmtimes.com/national-news/mandalay-upper-myanmar/20660-chief-minister-rubber-stamps-court-monitors.html.

[26] *The Myanmar Times*, 'Court Observation Teams Unnecessary', 20 December 2016, www.mmtimes.com/national-news/mandalay-upper-myanmar/24290-court-observation-teams-unnecessary-mdy-chief-justice.html.

only in the Constitution but is contained in every law concerning the legislature.[27] These principles are included in the oath sworn by legislators. In this way, elected representatives remain bound by the military's ideological commitments in the Constitution.

There is no recognised constitutional principle of 'representative government' in Myanmar. Legislators vary in their responsiveness to their constituency, with Facebook as the main form of communication. Receiving and responding to the complaints of their constituency, and often mediating, investigating or solving these disputes, has increasingly become part of the role of legislators. For members from remote constituencies, the difficulty of responsiveness is compounded by the fact it may take several days travel from Naypyidaw to their local constituency. Since 2012, the legislature has placed a greater emphasis on ensuring that legislators are reaching out to their constituency. To facilitate this, laws were amended to clarify that each Hluttaw representative can open an office in the relevant township and can expend funds for this purpose.[28] This includes legislators at the State/Region level.[29]

There are incentives for legislators to spend time and initiate projects on behalf of their constituency, such as the Constituency Development Fund. Launched in November 2013 by Shwe Mann, the Speaker for the Pyithu Hluttaw, the Constituency Development Fund allocates 100 million kyat for the State/Region Hluttaw to distribute to each township.[30] This is a quick means of releasing funds for small community projects. Legislators have direct control over the management and expenditure of these funds. In other countries, such a strategy risks the misuse of the funds for vote buying.[31] Concerns were raised by President Thein Sein that the Pyidaungsu Hluttaw would breach the Constitution by giving executive power to legislators. This issue has not been brought before the Constitutional Tribunal. The Constituency Development Fund has become a means for legislators to exercise executive power by deciding how to allocate these funds in their township. The Constituency Development Fund scheme has not led to meaningful fiscal decentralisation and the scheme remains within the system of coercive

[27] See Pyidaungsu Hluttaw Law No 11/2010; Pyithu Hluttaw Law No 12/2010; Amyotha Hluttaw Law No 13/2010; Region or State Hluttaw Law No 14/2010.
[28] Pyithu Hluttaw Law No 23/2012 s 1(l) and s 64; Amyotha Hluttaw Law No 24/2012 s 1(l) and s 64.
[29] State/Region Hluttaw Law No 22/2013, s 81.
[30] Pyithu Hluttaw Law No 23/2012, s 13; Amyotha Hluttaw Law No 24/2012, s 13. Law No 9/2014 on Pyidaungsu Hluttaw Development Funds, amended by Law 48/2014.
[31] Bart Robertson et al, *Local Development Funds in Myanmar*. Discussion Paper Series No 9 (The Asia Foundation, 2015).

centrism by giving oversight to the Pyidaungsu Hluttaw rather than the States/Regions.

The wide constitutional powers of legislators sit alongside constitutional measures that appear to ensure accountability. The Constitution is designed to preserve and protect the privileges of legislators. This has its origins in Westminster systems in terms of the language of privileges and immunities. But the constitutional provisions go further than this to leave accountability at the discretion of the Speaker. Legislators are granted constitutional legislative privileges in terms of freedom of speech and immunity for anything said in the legislature.[32] This is further elaborated upon in legislation. Legislators are immune from any legal action taken against them, except under the relevant law.[33] They cannot be arrested or summoned as a witness in court without the permission of the Speaker, which is an example of the Speaker's ability to either protect or discipline legislators. The original idea appears to have been borrowed from the Westminster constitutional tradition. In part, it allows legislators to discuss any issues without concern for negative consequences.[34] This privilege is a form of immunity and protection for legislators from any civil or criminal liability. This immunity does not just operate while undertaking their legislative duties but appears to apply *at any time*. Legislators enjoy parliamentary inviolability at the discretion of the Speaker. Legislators have sought to protect this immunity and reputation by prosecuting individuals who have criticised them on Facebook, under section 66(d) of the Telecommunications Law 2013.[35] There remain some limits on the freedom of speech that legislators enjoy, as their speech cannot threaten the three meta-principles of the military-state.[36] All past legislative bodies under the military regime also enjoy complete immunity under the Constitution.[37]

The Speakers are the most powerful members of the legislature and have developed a strong public profile. The Constitution gives power to the Speakers of the Amyotha Hluttaw and Pyithu Hluttaw for the day-to-day running of the legislature.[38] During the five-year term, the Speaker of

---

[32] 2008 Constitution, s 92(b) (Pyidaungsu Hluttaw), s 113 (Pyithu Hluttaw), s 185 (Amyotha Hluttaw).

[33] Eg, Law on the Pyidaungsu Hluttaw 11/2010, s 11(a).

[34] Josh Chafetz, *Democracy's Privileged Few* (Yale University Press, 2006); William R Mackay et al. (eds) *Erskine May's Parliamentary Practice: The Law, Privileges, Proceedings and Usage of Parliament* (London: Butterworths, 2004).

[35] Telecommunications Law No 31/2013.

[36] Pyithu Hluttaw Law 23/2012, s 47 and Amyotha Hluttaw Law 24/2012, s 47.

[37] 2008 Constitution, s 445.

[38] Ibid, s 112.

one house also serves as the Speaker of the Pyidaungsu Hluttaw, and then part way through the term the other Speaker takes over. The Speaker of the Pyithu Hluttaw and Amyotha Hluttaw play a key leadership role in legislative proceedings, from determining the agenda, to setting the daily schedule and keeping sessions on track. The Speakers also play a facilitative role with the executive as the primary point of contact and communication between the legislature and the president.

The role of the Speaker is partly administrative, but also highly political. The Speakers ensure the legislature sits at least once per year,[39] and have a significant level of control over its agenda and conduct. The Speakers determine the focus of the plenary sessions, identify which questions will be asked and answered, and the timing of when and how long bills are debated. Voting methods are at the discretion of the Speaker and may either be oral, by standing up, or by a secret ballot. An optimistic view of this orchestrated process is Chit Win and Kean's description of the legislature as 'stage-managed'.[40] A more sober view is that legislative proceedings are marked by a high degree of control and restraint over its members and at times an absence of free speech. The Speaker is a key element in the constraints imposed on legislators through the notion of disciplined democracy, according to section 6(d) of the Constitution.

In the early years of the transition (2011–2012), the Speaker urged legislators to actively participate. This is in contrast with the period of military rule, when it was often better to do nothing unless you were specifically required to act. Shwe Mann was the Speaker of the Pyithu Hluttaw (2011–2015) and Speaker of the Pyidaungsu Hluttaw (2013–2016). Early in his term, Shwe Mann implored legislators to voice their opinions.[41] In his role as Speaker, Shwe Mann sought to enhance and justify the role of the legislature as the representatives of the people and as a check on the government. Shwe Mann emphasised the power of the legislature to request information from the government, the government's responsibility to respond to legislative requests, with reference to section 228 of the Constitution.[42] In this way, Shwe Mann as Speaker ensured the legislature acted as a check and balance on the power of the executive.[43] Since 2016,

[39] Ibid, ss 77, 79, 80.

[40] Chit Win and Kean, above n 2.

[41] *The Irrawaddy*, 'The People have ultimate power, says Shwe Mann', 13 June 2012, www.irrawaddy.com/news/burma/people-are-the-ultimate-powerful-says-shwe-mann. html.

[42] In June 2011, Shwe Mann made a speech to the Yangon Region Hluttaw that was later censored, and not reported in state run media.

[43] Ian Holliday and Su Mon Thazin Aung, 'The Executive', in Ian Holliday et al (eds) *Routledge Handbook on Contemporary Myanmar* (London, Routledge, 2018) p 245.

U Win Myint, Speaker under the NLD, has acted as mediator with the Tatmadaw, USDP, and ethnic political parties, as well as keeping NLD legislators in line. In 2018, due to the resignation of the president and subsequent appointed of Win Myint as president, U T Khun Myat, a Kachin Christian, was appointed as Speaker of the Pyithu Hluttaw. This was controversial because he is the alleged leader of the People's Militia in Northern Shan State (see Chapter 3), ally of Shwe Mann and participant in the constitution-making process in the 2000s. The Speaker sits on the National Defence and Security Council, so the appointment of T Khun Myat raised concerns that Suu Kyi had given one of the Council seats over to a Tatmadaw sympathiser, potentially tipping the voting majority of the Defence Council in favour of the Tatmadaw.

III. THE SCOPE OF LEGISLATIVE POWER

The legislature's role in law-making and executive oversight has proved contentious, with controversies over the role of legislative committees and Union Level Organisations. These two issues are linked by conceptual confusion about the scope of legislative power and the areas of overlap with administrative power. This has a broader impact on the nature of the distribution of powers in Myanmar. The emphasis is on cooperation and collaboration between the legislature and administration, as a feature of coercive centralism.

A. Legislative Committees and Commissions

Since the establishment of the legislature in 2011, legislative committees, commissions and other Union Level Organisations have been significant actors in the process of legislative reform. The Constitution provides for four permanent legislative committees in the Pyithu Hluttaw: the Bills Committee, the Public Accounts Committee; the Hluttaw Rights Committee and the Government Guarantees, Pledges and Undertakings Vetting Committee.[44] The Constitution also allows for an ad hoc Defence and Security Committee, or any other ad hoc committee that may be required. Joint Committees between the two houses are also permitted.[45]

---

[44] 2008 Constitution, s 115(a)–(c).
[45] Ibid, s 116.

The Constitution is silent on whether the Pyidaungsu Hluttaw can form its own committees, and this has become a source of controversy.

The legislative committees are often the engine room of the legislature. This is where elected legislators, and some outside appointees, sit alongside Tatmadaw officers and discuss key issues of law and policy. Controversy has arisen over the relationship between legislative committees, the President's Office and government ministries in the law-making process. Under Thein Sein, many laws originated from the President's Office but also from legislative committees, rather than soliciting laws from ministries with the relevant mandate. This has been a source of tension between the legislature and the administration. It occasionally results in ministries preparing and submitting their own versions of a draft law to the legislature, and the legislature having to decide between two draft versions of a law. In doing so, the process marginalises the administration and experience of the ministries.

Several legislative committees have been created to address specific issues and have been led by high-profile personalities. For example, the Rule of Law and Tranquillity Committee was created by the Speaker as a gesture of goodwill to Aung San Suu Kyi after her initial election to the legislature (2012–2016). She used this Committee as her platform to promote the rule of law, which included establishing legal training centres for lawyers, government officials and civil society. Another example is Shwe Mann's appointment as chairperson of the 57-member Legislative Affairs Committee (2011–2015), which had responsibility for reviewing all legislation before it was submitted to the legislature. The Committee drew up a centralised list of laws to be repealed, amended or replaced, which shaped the legislative agenda. Shwe Mann was unsuccessful in the 2015 elections, although this was no bar to his participation in the Committee. The Constitution allows legislative committees to include representatives who are not members of the legislature, so Shwe Mann was re-appointed to the same Committee in 2016. In this way, the Constitution grants significant power to committees that may have unelected members. While this allows the legislature to appoint experts to committees, it does mean that legislative committees do not necessarily have a mandate to represent the interests of the people. In 2016, Shwe Mann was appointed by the NLD Government as chair of a 23-member Legislative Committee on Legal Affairs and Special Issues, with a similar mandate to the previous committee. This Committee again is tasked with reviewing all existing legislation and draft legislation. Of the members, 10 out of 23 are former USDP members. Shwe Mann is protected by this appointment because no legal action can be taken against a member of the Committee without permission of the Speakers, according to the constitutional provision on immunity.

There have been suspicions raised that non-elected members of legislative committees have been voting as a means of trying to shift the balance of voting power and undermine the power of the NLD to pass laws. The Constitution stipulates that proceedings of the legislature remain valid *even* if a person who is unable to vote sits in or votes in the legislature.[46] This has been one source of tension between elected and un-elected members of legislative committees.

B. The Unresolved Status of Union Level Organisations

A controversial aspect of the Constitution is the designation of 'Union Level Organisations' (ULO). This issue has raised questions about the relative power of legislative committees in relation to the government administration, as well as the legislative authority of the prior military regime. Although it is not defined in the Constitution, the concept of a 'Union Level Organisation' has been defined in legislation passed in 2010 by the former military regime. The law states that ULO include the following bodies:[47] the National Defence and Security Council; the Financial Commission; the Supreme Court; the Constitutional Tribunal; the Union Election Commission; the Auditor General; the Union Civil Service Board; and 'committees, commissions and bodies formed by either house of parliament or both sitting jointly'. On its face, the law appears to treat all these bodies as having the same status and powers.

The Constitution does specify the powers of a ULO. A ULO has the power to draft bills and submit them to the legislature[48] on matters that fall within its authority according to Schedule 1 of the Constitution (which functions as both a list of legislative and executive power).[49] A ULO may be invited by the legislature to attend a session and provide information and clarification on matters within its authority to either house or to both houses sitting jointly.[50] During a hearing, members of a ULO have the right to discuss and explain a bill that is related

---

[46] Ibid, ss 88 and 131.
[47] Law 13/2010 on Amyotha Hluttaw, s 2(h); Law 12/2010 on Pyithu Hluttaw, s 2(h); Law 11/2010 on Pyidaungsu Hluttaw, s 2(f).
[48] 2008 Constitution, ss 100–102.
[49] Ibid, s 100a.
[50] Ibid, ss 77(c), 112(c), and 160.

to its organisation,[51] and can make other submissions with the permission of the Speaker.[52] This requirement for express permission to do something is a key feature of coercive centralism. Like legislators, persons representing a ULO are granted privileges in terms of freedom of speech and immunity for anything they say in the legislature.[53] ULO also play a crucial role in their power to create rules and regulations under laws relevant to their mandate.[54]

However, on the issue of which bodies have status as a ULO and whether all ULO have the same powers, legal opinion is divided. In 2012, these questions were brought before the Constitutional Tribunal.[55] The case was submitted by the president, represented by the Attorney General. The president argued that legislative committees do not have the power to propose legislation. The Attorney General argued that while the Constitution specifically grants certain powers to ULO, it does not grant these powers to Hluttaw committees. He therefore drew a distinction between the role of ULO and the functions of Hluttaw committees. This was in the context of delays over the passage of the foreign investment law due to concerns raised and amendments proposed by legislative committees as ULO. The respondents included the speakers of the Pyithu Hluttaw and Amyotha Hluttaw, and so this was a dispute between the executive and legislature.

A key issue in this case was whether the Tribunal can interpret laws passed by the former State Peace and Development Council (SPDC, pre-2011). Section 443 of the Constitution states that all work done by the SPDC prior to the enactment of the Constitution is in accordance with the Constitution, and so implies that such laws cannot be questioned by a court. The Tribunal held that it does not have power to interpret such laws. This decision shows extreme deference to the past regime and remains a way for the Tatmadaw to ensure compliance with rules it introduced. The consequence is that the only way to challenge laws passed pre-2011 is via amendment or repeal in the legislature. The implication of this decision is that the Tribunal can only consider the constitutionality of laws after 2011.

Some constitutional provisions acknowledge that ULO may have the right to appear before the legislature or its committees. The president

---

[51] Ibid, ss 90, 140 and 160.
[52] Ibid, s 91.
[53] Ibid, ss 92(b); s133(b).
[54] Ibid, s 97(a)(i).
[55] Constitutional Tribunal, Legislative Committees Case 1/2012.

argued that these provisions amounted to a distinction between ULO and Hluttaw committees. The Tribunal also noted that while the Constitution allows the Pyithu Hluttaw or Amyotha Hluttaw to decide on the members and terms of any ad hoc committee, the president has the power to submit the number of members for a ULO to the Pyidaungsu Hluttaw (according to National Convention records). In interpreting the Constitution, the Tribunal stressed that Pyithu Hluttaw and Amyotha Hluttaw Committees are fundamentally different to ULO. The Constitutional Tribunal held that 'Union-Level Organisations' fulfil an *administrative* function by submitting proposals to the legislature, so ULOs could not also exercise the power to submit *legislative* amendments. The decision of the Constitutional Tribunal raised concerns among legislators for two reasons: the decision was perceived to reduce the power of legislative committees vis-à-vis the executive, and there were concerns that the decision had been unduly influenced by the President's Office.

On 27 August 2012, a motion was initiated in the Amyotha Hluttaw to impeach the entire bench of the Constitutional Tribunal based on the grounds of inefficient discharge of duties.[56] By the afternoon, this motion was debated in the Pyidaungsu Hluttaw.[57] Over 20 legislators made speeches, including three Tatmadaw members. The Tatmadaw members opposed impeachment, while members from the USDP, ethnic political parties and the NLD supported the motion. The Tatmadaw argued that the Constitutional Tribunal is the guardian of the Constitution, and such a motion would suggest that the legislature is above the judiciary. They argued that it would damage harmony and cooperation between the three branches of government. They also implied that legislative committees and their members were trying to gain the privileges of an ULO while in office and that this would negatively impact the budget.

Those in favour of the motion offered a wide range of arguments to support the impeachment.[58] There were three preliminary arguments offered concerning why the Tribunal should not have heard the case. The first was a complaint that the Attorney General should not have submitted the application on behalf of the president. This complaint seems weak and unsubstantiated because the Attorney General represents the executive in every case brought against it in the Constitutional Tribunal. The second was that the president made an application to '*interpret*' based on section 322(a), rather than an application

---

[56] 2008 Constitution, s 334(a)(v).
[57] See PDH2012-4:11.
[58] Ibid.

to '*decide*',[59] but the application did not specify the interpretation of a section of the Constitution. This second debate is complex, and whether an 'interpretation' is different from a 'decision', and whether both or only the latter is final, remains a matter of debate in Myanmar. Generally, however the power to interpret is understood as a separate and distinct power from an application to 'decide'. The third argument was that the Constitution does not give the Constitutional Tribunal power to review and interpret laws made by SPDC. This means that the Tribunal must uphold, rather than ignore, laws passed by the SPDC. This was an argument of convenience to support the interests of the legislature: some representatives who supported this motion did not generally believe that SPDC laws should be above challenge in the Tribunal.

Many legislators referred to the separation of powers and the need to give section 11(a) of the Constitution an expansive definition.[60] Many argued that the legislature was of equal status to the executive and so, if the executive bodies had ULO status, then so should legislative bodies. Some went further and argued that the legislature is the primary branch of government. Some members depicted legislative committees as necessary to check the power of the executive, and the need for ULO status to enable them to fulfil this function. They also complained that the executive was acting like the king and gave examples such as the actions of some branches of the General Administration Department (Chapter 3), which had put up signs prohibiting members of the legislature from entering its buildings.

The Chairperson of the Constitutional Tribunal was also called to the legislature to give his response and defend the Tribunal's decision. Nevertheless, the motion was passed by 447 votes to 168 with 4 abstentions. Several days later, on 6 September 2012, the Pyithu Hluttaw voted to impeach the Constitutional Tribunal, although the vote was split 308 to 101 (the latter being Tatmadaw members). On the same day, the entire Tribunal bench submitted its resignation, avoiding impeachment proceedings.

After this case, in November 2012 the legislature passed several amendments to the law.[61] They inserted a new section clarifying that ULO can discuss proposed bills relating to their organisation at a Hluttaw session or Hluttaw Committee session. ULO also have the

---

[59] This is a crucial distinction in Burmese between အနက်အဓိပ္ပါယ်ဖွင့်ဆိုခြင်း (to interpret) and ဆုံးဖြတ်ခြင်း (to decide).

[60] See PDH2012-4:11.

[61] Pyithu Hluttaw Law No 23/2012, s 50; Amyotha Hluttaw Law No 24/2012, s 50.

responsibility of responding to any request relating to their duties by a Hluttaw Commission and may be required to submit reports to the Hluttaw Commission on its performance. This amendment suggests that the legislature wanted to clarify the powers of ULO and ensure that ULO were more directly accountable to it.

In 2017, the Tribunal heard a second case concerning the powers of legislative committees.[62] This case was the first time that the Tatmadaw was the primary applicant to the Tribunal, without any civilian legislators. This shows a willingness on the part of the Tatmadaw to use legal means to resolve some disputes. This case was a covert attempt to abolish the powerful Legal Affairs Committee headed by Shwe Mann. This follows from the objections of the Tatmadaw to the creation of this Committee. The applicants argued that the Pyidaungsu Hluttaw did not have the power to appoint legislative committees, and that legislative committees could only be appointed to the Pyithu Hluttaw and Amyotha Hluttaw according to the Constitution. The Constitution is silent on whether the Pyidaungsu Hluttaw can form its own committees. The submission from the Attorney General's Office defended the ability of the Pyidaungsu Hluttaw to create a legislative committee. The Tribunal held in favour of the Pyidaungsu Hluttaw (discussed further in Chapter 9). This decision strengthens the power of the Pyidaungsu Hluttaw and means it can continue to form joint committees.

IV. CONCLUSION

Myanmar's legislature has forged an important and central role for itself within the political system under the Constitution. The legislative system at the Union level is tricameral, with the Pyidaungsu Hluttaw as the dominant house at the apex of the legislative system. The symmetrical design of the Pyithu Hluttaw and Amyotha Hluttaw means that when both houses are dominated by the party forming government, the upper house is unlikely to act as a check on the power of the lower house. Contrary to other bicameral systems where joint sittings are reserved for extraordinary matters, the Pyidaungsu Hluttaw sits *regularly* and has the final decision on legislative affairs. In the minds of legislators, the Pyidaungsu Hluttaw has an independent and corporate personality so that it can represent the interests of the legislature against the executive and president. The Pyithu Hluttaw and Amyotha Hluttaw play a supportive role in

---

[62] Constitutional Tribunal, Legislative Committees Case 1/2017.

law-making, executive oversight, and judicial control. While law-making has been the primary activity across both governments, executive oversight was stronger under the Thein Sein Government due to his rivalry with the Speaker Shwe Mann. Under the NLD, the legislature's role in judicial oversight has become stronger, in part because of the Suu Kyi's emphasis on the rule of law and reducing corruption. The operation of the Pyidaungsu Hluttaw reinforces the system of coercive centralism in Myanmar's military-state.

The dominant understanding of the role of the legislature in relation to other branches of government in Myanmar is that it can legitimately act as a check and balance on both the executive and on the judiciary. The role of the legislature to keep the executive accountable may be justified due to the formal separation between the legislature and executive at the Union level, as mandated by the Constitution. The role of the legislature as a check on the judiciary reverses the standard assumptions of the separation of powers. Rather than the legislature simply acting as a check in relation to appointment and removal of the judiciary, the legislature's actions border on interference with the courts.

The first major constitutional crisis, leading to the resignation of all Constitutional Tribunal members exercising their right to resign, is one indication of the pressure the legislature has been able to exert over the Tribunal when dissatisfied with its decisions. This issues also suggests wider ambiguity between the idea of legislative and administrative power in Myanmar. This is demonstrated in the unresolved debate over which institutions are 'Union Level Organisations' and the way the debate over the appropriate function of these organisations blurs conceptions of the separation of powers.

FURTHER READING

Nick Cheesman et al (eds) *Debating Democratisation in Myanmar* (Singapore: ISEAS, 2014).

Melissa Crouch, 'Legislating Reform? Law and Conflict in Myanmar' in Nick Cheesman and Nicholas Farrelly (eds) *Conflict in Myanmar: War, Politics, Religion* (Singapore: ISEAS, 2016) pp 219–239.

Renaud Egreteau, *Caretaking Democratization: The Military and Political Change in Myanmar* (Hurst & Co Publishers, 2016).

Chit Win and Thomas Kean, 'Communal Conflict in Myanmar: The Legislature's Response 2012–2015' (2017) *Journal of Contemporary Asia* 1.

6

The Executive

Executive Power – The President – Union Territories – The Union – State
Counsellor – The Economy

E XECUTIVE INSTITUTIONS AND the exercise of executive power have
undergone significant change. Thein Sein's term was an example
of constitutional accommodation of strong executive power in
the President's Office in tension at times with the legislature. While
executive power is of central importance under the National League
for Democracy (NLD) Government since 2016, the focus of power
has shifted from the President's Office to a new position, the State
Counsellor. The president has become like a head of state and the
State Counsellor is now the de facto head of government. This arrangement is temporary, because the position of State Counsellor is specific
to Aung San Suu Kyi, Nobel Laureate and leader of the NLD. The
Tatmadaw disagrees with the creation of the Office of State Counsellor
on the basis that it is unconstitutional.

In this chapter I focus on the main actors and institutions that
constitute the executive, and the source and scope of executive power
under the Constitution.[1] While some scholars argue that the function
and operation of executive institutions is determined by elite behaviour
in Myanmar,[2] this chapter demonstrates that the Constitution and its
operating principles also matter. Executive power is divided between the
elected government and its ministers, and the Tatmadaw, its ministers,
government administration and security apparatus. The constitutional
allocation of executive power remains highly concentrated in the Union
Government.

---

[1] This chapter deals with ss 199–292 of the 2008 Constitution (Ch V The Executive).
[2] Marco Bünte, 'Perilous Presidentialism or Precarious Power-sharing? Hybrid Regime
Dynamics in Myanmar' (2017) 24 *Contemporary Politics* 1.

The executive branch does not have power or control over the Tatmadaw and, to complicate matters, an estimated 80 per cent of the senior civil service have military backgrounds.[3] Executive power is fragmented between the Tatmadaw and executive actors and institutions (Chapter 3). The president has wide-ranging powers over most high-level positions through appointment and accountability processes. The role of the president has changed over time, particularly since 2016 and the creation of the position of State Counsellor through legislative reform for Suu Kyi and in reliance on the president's authority to confer executive power.[4] The president oversees Union Territories, such as Naypyidaw the capital city.

The Union Government holds significant power and there is a formal separation between the executive and legislature. The Constitution makes a commitment to a market economy and prohibits nationalisation and demonetisation. This is an example of the way the Constitution speaks directly to issues of past executive maladministration, although fails to address the Tatmadaw's monopoly of the economy since the 1990s.

I. THE PRESIDENT AS HEAD OF THE UNION

The Basic Principles in the Constitution designate the president as the head of the executive and the head of the Union.[5] Alongside the president and two vice-presidents, the Constitution identifies ministers and the Attorney General as the core of the executive branch.[6] Constitutional disputes have arisen over the appointment and impeachment process for the president; the role and powers of the president; and the relationship between the president and other branches of government. Even if the president is from the same party as the government, Thein Sein's term demonstrates that factions within a party (particularly the USDP) may lead to tensions between the President's Office and the legislature.

---

[3] Email communication with Maung Aung Myoe 2019. This estimate includes civil servants at the level of Director or above in 2015, but excludes senior civil servants in universities.

[4] The NLD justified the Law on the State Counsellor No 26/2016 with reference to ss 96 and 217 of the Constitution.

[5] 2008 Constitution, ss 1, 16.

[6] Ibid, s 200.

A. Indirect Appointment and Impeachment Processes

From the outset, the constitutional requirements for presidential candidates have been the subject of criticism. Under the Constitution, there are seven criteria that presidential (and vice-presidential) candidates must meet.[7] A candidate must demonstrate loyalty to the Union and to its people, and must meet the citizenship requirements of Myanmar (see Chapter 8). A candidate must be at least 45 years old and meet the qualifications of a candidate for the Hluttaw (see Chapter 5). Three criteria have attracted scrutiny. First, a presidential candidate must have lived in Myanmar *continuously* for 20 years. In 2016, there was debate over whether Henry Van Thio, a ethnic Chin who had lived in New Zealand for a period of time, could become vice-president.[8] Despite breaching the continuous residency requirement, his appointment was approved for the office, perhaps because he is from a minority ethnic and religious group.

The second controversial criterion is that the president must be familiar with a range of political and economic issues, as well as military affairs. It was initially assumed that a candidate must have *worked* in the Tatmadaw, which would effectively limit the position to men and to Tatmadaw officers. There was no specific requirement that the candidate be an active or retired officer, and some speculated a degree in strategic studies would be enough.[9] U Htin Kyaw (once Suu Kyi's driver) is not a former military officer and cannot claim familiarity with military affairs. Nevertheless, in 2016, he was appointed as president. The Tatmadaw remains strategic in selecting its legal battles with the NLD and appears willing to overlook potential constitutional infringements where it is unlikely to affect the Tatmadaw's core interests.

The third issue is that the selection criteria for president only allows candidates who do not hold foreign citizenship, and nor can their parents, spouse or children, commonly referred to as 'section 59f'. This requirement is understood as barring Aung San Suu Kyi from this post because her children and deceased husband are UK citizens. There has been past speculation that if her children renounced their UK citizenship, then Suu Kyi could be eligible. As her deceased husband had foreign nationality, it is generally understood that she is ineligible. Proponents of section 59f argue that this rule has historical precedent

---

[7] Ibid, s 59.

[8] See PDH2016-1:7.

[9] Kyaw Yin Hlaing, 'Setting the Rules for Survival: Why the Burmese Military Regime Survives in an Age of Democratization' (2009) 22:3 *The Pacific Review* 271.

and is not a rule that was designed to target Aung San Suu Kyi because it predated her. There has been no case in the Constitutional Tribunal clarifying the meaning of any provisions related to the selection criteria of the president and vice-presidents. The NLD has failed to bring a case to the Constitutional Tribunal to seek an interpretation of these provisions. In 2012, U Myint Swe, a retired general and former Yangon Region Chief Minister was expected to be appointed as vice-president upon the retirement of another. However, he was not appointed as it was believed he had a son-in-law with Australian citizenship. His son-in-law's Burmese citizenship has since been reinstated,[10] and in 2016 the Tatmadaw appointed U Myint Swe as vice-president.

According to the Constitution, the process for selecting the president is by Presidential Electoral College, rather than direct elections. The Electoral College appoints three candidates, one for president and two for vice-president.[11] The candidates are initially appointed by three groups: elected representatives from the Pyithu Hluttaw and the Amyotha Hluttaw, and the unelected Tatmadaw members respectively. While other systems have some form of electoral college,[12] the twist is that the design of the Electoral College in Myanmar enables Tatmadaw legislatures to propose a least one candidate. All the Pyidaungsu Hluttaw representatives sit as the Presidential Electoral College to vote on which of the three candidates will be president.[13] The president serves five years and is limited to a maximum of two terms in office.

There is a formal separation between the executive and legislature at the Union level. Once appointed, the president and vice-presidents must *vacate* their legislative seats.[14] The president and vice-presidents also cannot be active in a political party.[15] This constitutes two degrees of separation between the executive and legislature. In practice, this formal division is not strictly adhered to. For example, in 2011, Thein Sein was appointed as president but failed to step down as chairperson of his political party, the USDP. He claims he was *inactive* in the USDP, and so was not in breach of the constitutional provision against holding these two positions simultaneously. Finally, in May 2013, Thein Sein did step

---

[10] Sean Gleeson, 'Myint Swe revealed as military VP pick', *Frontier*, 11 March 2016, https://frontiermyanmar.net/en/news/myint-swe-revealed-as-military-vp-pick.

[11] 2008 Constitution, s 60(a)–(b).

[12] Nils-Christian Borman and Matt Golder, 'Democratic Electoral Systems around the World, 1946–2011' (2013) 32 *Electoral Studies* 360.

[13] 2008 Constitution, s 60(e).

[14] Ibid, s 62.

[15] Ibid, ss 63–64.

down to allow Shwe Mann, the Speaker, to take over as chairperson of the USDP. Some within the USDP wanted Thein Sein to remain as chairperson, or at the least were reluctant to allow Shwe Mann to become chair. There were threats made by some legislators to bring a case to the Constitutional Tribunal to decide whether a member of the government can simultaneously be the non-active head of a political party, but a court case never materialised. In 2015, Shwe Mann was deposed of his position as chair of the USDP in an internal coup. The person who replaced Shwe Mann as chairperson was a loyalist of Thein Sein and this was a means for Thein Sein to regain control of the USDP.

Since 2016, a similar issue has arisen under the NLD Government. Suu Kyi holds several executive positions, including as the Minister for Foreign Affairs and Minister for the President's Office. She has failed to give up her position as chairperson of the NLD. Technically, holding an executive position and post in a political party concurrently is unconstitutional. There have not been efforts to challenge Aung San Suu Kyi's position in this respect. This is partly because, aside from the Tatmadaw, it is widely accepted that family lineage, such as the sons and daughters of key independence leaders or prominent ethnic leaders, is a factor favourable to holding high public office.

In this respect, there is dissatisfaction with the constitutional rule prohibiting executive members from holding a position in a political party. In 2015, the legislature debated whether to abolish the prohibition on simultaneously holding positions in the executive, legislature and political party. The debate was primarily between the USDP and the Tatmadaw.[16] USDP members were in favour of deleting provisions from the Constitution that prohibit the president and vice presidents from retaining their legislative seats and prevent them from taking part in party activities. The Tatmadaw indicated that it would vote against this proposal and argued that the provisions need to be retained to uphold the formal separation of powers between the executive and legislature. The Tatmadaw expressed concern that deleting these provisions would violate the Basic Principles of the Constitution. This suggests that the Tatmadaw is committed to a formal separation between the executive and legislature.

---

[16] Ei Ei Toe Lwin and Htoo Thant, 'Struggle for control of USDP enters Parliament', *The Myanmar Times*, 1 July 2015, www.mmtimes.com/national-news/15283-struggle-for-control-of-usdp-enters-parliament.html.

No president has had impeachment proceedings brought against them,[17] though there has been one voluntary resignation. To trigger impeachment requires a motion signed by at least one quarter of the members in the Amyotha Hluttaw or Pyithu Hluttaw, and support by at least two thirds of members in that house. The grounds for impeachment are the same as that for ministers, judges and other high-level officials. In March 2018, U Htin Kyaw voluntary resigned as president, according to section 72 of the Constitution. The vice-president with the highest number of votes served as the acting president for one week, according to section 73, until U Win Myint (then Speaker of the Pyithu Hluttaw) was appointed as president.

B. Executive Decision-maker and Weak Legislator

Under the Constitution, the president is recognised as the constitutionally superior and preeminent person in the country.[18] Yet the president is made subservient to the three meta-principles of the military-state, which are included in the presidential oath.[19] Suu Kyi has rejected the idea that the president takes precedence over all people. There are two contradictory provisions concerning the accountability of the president. On one hand, Thein Sein emphasised the constitutional provision that he as president cannot be held liable or responsible in any way to the legislature.[20] On the other, during the Thein Sein era, the legislature emphasised that the Constitution requires the president to be responsible to the Pyidaungsu Hluttaw (the two houses sitting jointly).[21]

The president's power has two main dimensions: central executive power and weak legislative power. The president's central executive power includes appointment and oversight powers, and high-level administrative decisions. The president has significant power over the structure, appointment and accountability of executive agencies.[22] The president determines the number and shape of ministries.[23] Under Thein Sein, there were 36 ministries, and most of the ministers who were appointed were military generals. The president has the power to form the cabinet.

[17] 2008 Constitution, s 71.
[18] Ibid, s 58.
[19] Ibid, s 65.
[20] Ibid, s 215.
[21] Ibid, s 203.
[22] According to Constitutional Tribunal Legislative Committees Case 1/2012, the Union ministries are civil service personnel organisations formed under s 227 of the Constitution.
[23] 2008 Constitution, s 202(a).

Some observers suggest that under Thein Sein the cabinet became the most powerful executive body, surpassing the National Defence and Security Council.[24] Given the lack of details in the Constitution, the power and composition of the cabinet may change from government to government. Under the NLD Government, the number of ministries was initially streamlined from 36 to 21, although in 2017 the president used his constitutional powers to expand to 23 ministries.[25] The two new ministries are the Ministry for International Cooperation, and the Ministry for the Union Government,[26] both designed to play a greater role in coordination of international agencies and ministries respectively. President Htin Kyaw has also used his powers to abolish all deputy minister positions, but again these were later reinstated for some ministries.

In terms of appointment powers, the president is responsible for major executive and judicial appointments (see Chapter 7). The president appoints representatives to the Union Election Commission, who serve the same term as the government (see Chapter 4). The president selects three of the nine members to the Constitutional Tribunal, with another three chosen by the Pyithu Hluttaw and Amyotha Hluttaw. Many executive and judicial agencies are directly responsible to the president, and this includes the Attorney General, the Financial Commission, the Union Election Commission, the Supreme Court, the Union Civil Service Board,[27] the Auditor General, and the Constitutional Tribunal.[28] All ministers report to the president, rather than the legislature.[29] The president has the power to initiate impeachment proceedings against judges of the Supreme Court and Constitutional Tribunal, as well as the Election Commissioners.[30] The president, appointed by a legislative majority, has significant influence over civilian appointments. Under Thein Sein, many civilian positions were filled with former military officers. However, the Union Government is dependent on the Tatmadaw for security and to implement policy through the government administration.

[24] Ian Holliday and Su Mon Thazin Aung, 'The Executive', in Ian Holliday et al (eds) *Routledge Handbook on Contemporary Myanmar* (London, Routledge, 2018) p 231.

[25] 2008 Constitution, s 202.

[26] *The Myanmar Times*, 'Two New Ministries, Revamp Anti-Graft Body Proposed', 21 November 2017, www.mmtimes.com/news/two-new-ministries-revamp-anti-graft-body-proposed.html.

[27] 2008 Constitution, s 208.

[28] Law 15/2010 on Union Government, s 16(b).

[29] 2008 Constitution, s 232h.

[30] Ibid, ss 261(a), (b); 263.

Aside from the role in appointments, oversight and removal, the president contributes to day-to-day executive decisions. The president may give an official address to the nation,[31] and this is an opportunity to set the tone and direction of government, such as on New Year's Day or Armed Forces Day. The president has the power to pardon prisoners,[32] a power which Thein Sein used to release many political prisoners. The president has power to initiate or revoke international or bilateral treaties and conventions (see Chapter 8) and can redraw territorial boundaries (see Chapter 7). Unlike other presidential systems, the president is not the Commander-in-Chief of the armed forces. There is no civilian control of the Tatmadaw and this is a key feature of the military-state (chapter 3). Although the president chairs the National Defence and Security Council, the Tatmadaw members retain six of eleven seats, and so hold a majority of the votes.

In addition to the president's central executive power, he also has a role in the legislative process. The president has the power to submit the most important bill, the Union Budget Bill, to the Pyidaungsu Hluttaw.[33] The president is required to approve all legislation. While he cannot reject a bill outright, he can return a bill to the Pyidaungsu Hluttaw with recommendations. The Pyidaungsu Hluttaw is under no obligation to incorporate these suggestions and can choose to approve the bill without amendments. The bill will then come into effect within 14 days, even if the president does not give his final approval on the bill. An example of this weak veto power in action arose in 2012, when Thein Sein returned the foreign investment bill to the Pyidaungsu Hluttaw with 11 recommendations to make the bill less protectionist and more investor friendly.

Another aspect of the president's legislative power is the ability to issue ordinances, but these require approval of the Pyidaungsu Hluttaw within 60 days.[34] The president can only issue an ordinance if the legislature is not in session and it requires the president to have a sense of immediacy of action.[35] These presidential ordinances are only temporary in duration. An ordinance will come to an end if it is not approved by the Pyidaungsu Hluttaw, if the Pyidaungsu Hluttaw expressly rejects

---

[31] Ibid, s 210.

[32] Ibid, s 206.

[33] Ibid, s 218.

[34] 2008 Constitution, s 104. This ordinance power is similar to s 123 of the Indian Constitution.

[35] In India, ordinances are considered to be an exercise of legislative power by the executive and are not held to the standard of review of executive power: Shubhankar Dam, *Presidential Legislation in India* (CUP 2014).

the ordinance in a vote, or if the ordinance is withdrawn directly by the president. The president's role in the legislative process also includes being able to call an emergency session of the Pyidaungsu Hluttaw.[36] In May 2013, the president exercised this power to call an emergency session for the first time in relation to the Meiktila state of emergency (see Chapter 3).

In undertaking these duties, the president has wide immunity under the Constitution, which absolves him from any form of criminal accountability.[37] This was a provision in the 1947 Constitution, although some see yet another example of a loophole in the Constitution that can be exploited by the Tatmadaw. In 2014, the Constitutional Tribunal had the opportunity to consider whether the president can be the subject of a case in the Tribunal in relation to section 215, which states that the president is not answerable to any court.[38] The applicants argued that the president cannot be a party because it is a form of suing the president that would breach section 215. The Tribunal held that the president can be named as a party in a constitutional case because the case was brought in his official capacity as a representative of the Union Government and not as an individual. Concerns to protect the president or former presidents again surfaced in 2016, when a law was passed by the outgoing Thein Sein Government that granted lifetime security and other privileges to former presidents (that is, to himself).[39] The law authorises the Ministry of Home Affairs to provide a bodyguard for former presidents. It also stipulates that no court proceedings can be brought against a former president for lawful acts undertaken as part of their presidential duties. This was perceived to be necessary given the outgoing president Thein Sein's disagreements with Shwe Mann, as well as uncertainty over what the incoming NLD-led Government would do in office.

II. THE CENTRALISING MANDATE OF THE UNION GOVERNMENT

The Union Government includes the president and two vice-presidents, the Union ministers (including three appointed by the Commander-in-Chief) and the Attorney General. The Constitution does not specify

---

[36] 2008 Constitution, s 211.
[37] Ibid, s 215.
[38] Constitutional Tribunal, Kachin Race Case 1/2014.
[39] Former Presidents' Security Law No 25/2016.

details concerning cabinet, and so there has been experimentation in the structure, composition and function of the cabinet over time. Union Ministers are appointed by the president and serve the same term length as the president.[40] The requirements for eligibility are the same as that for legislators (see Chapter 5), except that the person must be at least 40 years of age. Once appointed, civilian Union ministers are directly responsible to the president,[41] although the legislature has the power to determine their responsibilities. Impeachment proceedings can commence if one of five grounds are met (see Chapter 5) and the process mirrors that for the impeachment of the president or vice-presidents.[42]

The Constitution requires a formal separation between the executive and the legislature by requiring any minister to vacate their seat in the legislature. A minister must also retire from the civil service and cease contributing to 'party activities' if they are a member of a political party.[43] This suggests these ministerial positions are intended to be above partisan politics, like other high-level executive positions. There has been significant debate over the meaning of party activities and the inconsistencies between the Constitution and many pre-2011 laws. This has been the subject of verbal discussion in the legislature, with the legislature seeking the opinion of the Constitutional Tribunal. In June 2015, a USDP member of the Pyithu Hluttaw raised a question about the constitutional meaning of the term 'party activities' in relation to constitutional provisions[44] that prevent the president, vice-president or ministers from undertaking party activities while they are in office.[45] The chairperson of the Constitutional Tribunal, U Mya Thein, was summoned to the legislature to respond to this question. The USDP member pointed out that discrepancies exist across many laws that permit certain members of the executive to carry out 'party organisational work' that appear to be in contradiction to the constitutional prohibition on undertaking 'party activities'. This includes members of the Naypyidaw Council; the Chief Justice and judges of the Supreme Court; members of the Constitutional Tribunal; the Attorney General; the Auditor-General and Deputy-Auditor General; and the Chairperson of the Union Civil Service Board (USCB).[46]

---

[40] 2008 Constitution, s 235.
[41] Ibid, s 232(h).
[42] Ibid, s 233.
[43] Ibid, ss 232(i), (j) and (k).
[44] Specifically, ss 64 and 232(k) of the 2008 Constitution.
[45] See PH2015-12:66.
[46] See 2008 Constitution, ss 285(g), 300(a), 333(e), s237(h), s242(g), s246(b)(vi); Naypyidaw Council Law, s 6(d); Union Judiciary Law, s 29; Constitutional Tribunal Law,

In the legislative hearing, Mya Thein as chairperson pointed out that the legislature was effectively asking the Constitutional Tribunal to determine the validity of seven laws passed by the prior regime. The chairperson reiterated the restrictive nature of the Tribunal's mandate, but then went on to emphasise that the Tribunal can only determine the validity of laws enacted since 2011. The chairperson also noted that any request should be submitted to the Tribunal and conducted according to the judicial process (rather than in the legislature). In addition, the chairperson suggested that the terms 'party activities' and 'party organisational work' are general terms that can be read widely. He deferred to the administration by noting that the relevant organisations responsible for overseeing these laws are required to provide the definition and limits of these terms so that people know how to comply with the law. This approach by the chairperson of course overlooks the fact that the term 'party activities' is in the Constitution and should be within the remit of the Constitutional Tribunal to interpret.

The three ministerial positions appointed in consultation with the Commander-in-Chief – the Ministers for Defence, Border Affairs and Home Affairs – are accountable to the Commander-in-Chief, not the president (see Chapter 3).[47] They are assigned duties by the Commander-in-Chief. There are further exceptions that apply to these positions – they can remain active in Tatmadaw service and are not required to retire from the Tatmadaw (unlike other ministers who must give up their position in the Tatmadaw or in the civil service).[48]

The absence of detail in the Constitution concerning the Union Government has allowed new administrative leadership positions to be created below ministers and deputy ministers. In 2015, the Thein Sein Government created the role of permanent secretary to sit under ministers but above director generals, who were formerly the highest ranked civil servants. The position of permanent secretaries was created under the government's power to appoint civil servants,[49] although this office has a history in Myanmar.[50] Permanent secretaries facilitate relations between the ministries and the legislature, play a key leadership role in

---

s 11; the Attorney-General of the Union Law, s7(b); the Auditor-General of the Union Law, s 7; the Union Civil Service Board Law, s 7(b).

[47] 2008 Constitution, s 232.

[48] Ibid, s 232(j)(i).

[49] Ibid, s 227.

[50] John S Furnivall, *The Governance of Modern Burma*, (Institute of Pacific Relations 1960), pp 14–5, 62–5.

the evaluation of policy-making, and oversee capacity building within the bureaucracy. While president Thein Sein marketed this as part of his administrative reforms, many former Tatmadaw officers and long-term civil servants were appointed to these positions. This raised concerns that this legal innovation was a way for the outgoing government to retain control and intelligence over the administration regardless of who won at the next elections.

Aside from permanent secretaries, there is direct evidence of former Tatmadaw officers being appointed to the position of director general or deputy director general, as well as in the civil administration more broadly.[51] This is another means of the indirect influence of the Tatmadaw in the administration.[52] In 2015, public criticism focused on the transfer of 13 Tatmadaw officers to the Ministry of Health, four of whom had no medical credentials.[53] A social media campaign decrying this practice was effective in stopping up to 350 officers being transferred into the civilian service. Tatmadaw transfers into the civilian administration has increased in recent years, although sometimes the officers are new graduates from the Defence Services Academy who are not accepted into the higher ranks of the Tatmadaw.

The UCSB is appointed by the president and has responsibility for appointments and training of the civil service.[54] The UCSB consists of five to seven members who are appointed by the president and serve the same term as the president. The criteria for eligibility to serve on the Civil Service Board is the same requirements as for legislators (see Chapter 5), although it requires slightly more senior candidates of at least 50 years old. The Basic Principles of the Constitution state that civil service personnel must not be involved in politics in any way, and there is an (unenforceable) commitment on the part of the state to care for civil service personnel.[55] The USCB plays a role in formulating policy and procedures for the civil service.[56] The Constitution provides that all matters to do with appointments, promotions, discipline and dismissals of civil servants are required to be regulated by law.[57]

[51] David Hook et al, *Conceptualising Public Sector Reform in Myanmar* (Yangon, The Asia Foundation, 2015) p 13.

[52] See also Kyaw Yin Hlaing, above n 9.

[53] Shwe Yee Saw Myint, 'Military backs down on jobs for soldiers', 13 August 2015, *The Myanmar Times*, www.mmtimes.com/national-news/15971-ministry-backs-down-on-jobs-for-soldiers.html.

[54] 2008 Constitution, s 246. Union Civil Service Board Law 24/2010.

[55] Ibid, s 26.

[56] Eg, Notification No 12/2014 on Civil Service Personnel Rules.

[57] 2008 Constitution, s 290.

The Attorney General is part of the Union Government under the Constitution.[58] There is no Ministry of Law nor a Law Reform Commission. The Union Attorney General's Office plays a significant oversight role in legislative affairs and prosecutions. The central Union Attorney General's Office (UAGO) is in Naypyidaw, with regional branches known as Advocate General's Offices in each of the 14 States/Regions, 72 District Law Offices and 330 Township Law Offices. Since 2011, the UAGO has been divided into four departments: the Legislative Vetting and Advice Department; the Legal Advice Department; the Prosecution Department; and the Administration Department.[59] The Attorney General is appointed by the president. The eligibility requirements are the same as for legislators (see Chapter 5), but the person must be at least 45 years old and have experience as a judge of a High Court, as a judicial officer at the State/Region level, as an advocate, or in the opinion of the president be an eminent jurist.[60] Most Attorney Generals, and many officers within this department, have either been former Tatmadaw officers or have worked as part of the administration for the former military regime. Like other former Tatmadaw officers now in the civilian administration, this raises questions about their loyalty and independence. The Attorney General remains responsible to the president, and the same procedures for impeachment apply as for Ministers. The Attorney General is also the chair of the Myanmar Bar Association, an institution that lacks any independence from the government.

Although Myanmar experienced socialist rule from 1962–1988, it did not establish a procuracy like other socialist regimes. Today, the Prosecution Department plays a significant role within the Attorney General's Office, dealing with many cases under the Penal Code. Under the 2008 Constitution, the UAGO must act on behalf of the government in writs cases in the Supreme Court and constitutional review cases in the Constitutional Tribunal (see Chapter 8). The other major department is the Legislative Vetting and Advising Department, which is responsible for reviewing all draft bills before they go to the legislature, although the focus is on form over substance. The Attorney General can also make submissions in cases before the Union Election Commission (see Chapter 4). Like all government offices, the officers within the UAGO do not develop specialised expertise because they are subject to

---

[58] Ibid, s 200(d).
[59] UAGO, 'Moving Forward to the Rule of Law: Strategic Plan 2015–2019' (Naypyidaw, 2015), p 7.
[60] 2008 Constitution, s 237.

the rotation system for civil servants. The UAGO is responsible for the annual publication of laws, rules and regulations, as well as the translation of laws into English. Given the demand for access to the law in the post-2011 era, the UAGO's role is of increasing importance.

III. CONSTITUTIONAL COMMITMENTS TO A MARKET ECONOMY

The role of the Union Government in financial reform is regulated by the broader economic commitments of the Constitution. In terms of fiscal authority, all bills concerning the budget are submitted by the Union Government and discussed in the Pyidaungsu Hluttaw.[61] The Union Government is required to consult with the Union Financial Commission in the drafting of the budget Bill.[62] The Financial Commission consists of 21 members, including all 14 State/Region Chief Ministers, the president and vice-presidents, the Attorney General, Auditor General, Naypyidaw Council Chief, and the Minister of Finance.[63] They serve five-year terms, reinforcing the symmetrical and centralised design of the political system. The Financial Commission reviews the budgets of all Union Ministries and Union Level Organisations. The Financial Commission has some level of budgetary oversight of the Constituency Development Funds (see Chapter 5). The Union Government also has power to collect taxes that do not fall under the list of State/Region taxes in Schedule 5.[64]

The Constitution is important for its economic and financial commitments. The Constitution is a public guarantee that the government cannot resort to the past strategies of the Tatmadaw that crippled the economy. The three key constitutional promises concerning the economy are the guarantee of a market economy (rather than a socialist economy), the promise not to demonetise the currency and the commitment not to nationalise industries.[65]

The Constitution requires the country to be based on a market economy, closing the door on remnants of the policies and practices under socialist rule. A tendency towards socialist economics was evident in the early post-colonial years and was a means of ensuring the economy would be in Burmese control, rather than foreign control, be they British, Indians or Chinese. While efforts to reorient toward a market

---

[61] Ibid, ss 101(b), 103.
[62] Ibid, s 221.
[63] Ibid, ss 229–230.
[64] Ibid, s 231.
[65] Ibid, ss 35, 36(d)–(e).

economy pre-date the Constitution, this provision plays a role in reinforcing the principle of a market economy. It stands as a constitutional guarantee that no future government can demonetise the currency again. The demonetisation decisions of the 1960s and 1980s had a devasting impact on people across the country, many of whom lost their savings without warning. The explicit mention of a market economy in the Constitution distinguishes it from its predecessor, the 1974 socialist Constitution that enshrined a socialist economy. The period of socialist rule from 1962 to 1988 ended in economic ruin.[66] Myanmar joins a growing number of countries from Afghanistan to Cambodia and Romania that explicitly enshrine the market economy in the constitution. The inclusion of a 'market economy' provision in a constitution is an overt effort to distinguish economic reforms from the past and to embed the concept of the market economy in the Constitution, as a form of 'higher' law.

In the 1990s, the Tatmadaw made some legislative commitments to a market economy as a deliberate turn away from socialist era policies, but this did not take off due to Tatmadaw control of the economy, a growing black market and the effect of Western sanctions.[67] The Tatmadaw's monopoly of many sectors and industries restricted who could participate in the economy and how.[68] An example is some ministries were referred to by the area of command because they were led by ministers who were also regional military commanders, such as the ministry of agriculture being known as the 'Ministry of Southwest Command'.[69] This is one indication of how ministries were run like a corporation under the personal control of the minister who was a military regional commander.

Change has been slow in this regard, and the growth of the market economy remains limited by the advantages that the Tatmadaw and its cronies have enjoyed. One example is the opening of the telecommunications market in 2013 to competitors, reducing the monopoly the government-run MPT had over the sector. These reforms may lead to

---

[66] Myanmar's economic downfall is contradicted by the outstanding contribution of a handful of key Burmese economists, such as U Hla Myint: see Sean Turnell, 'Sayagyi and Sage: Hla Myint' (2014) *Sojourn* 29(3) 621.

[67] Catherine Renshaw, 'Top-down Transitions and the Politics of US Sanctions' in Melissa Crouch (ed) *The Business of Transition* (CUP 2017). pp 228–254; Morten Pederson, *Promoting Human Rights in Myanmar* (Rowman & Littlefield Publishers, 2008).

[68] Susanne Prager Nyein, 'The Armed Forces of Burma' in Marcus Mietzner (ed) *The Political Resurgence of the Military in Southeast Asia* (Routledge, 2012) pp 24–44.

[69] Maung Aung Myoe, *Building the Tatmadaw: Myanmar Armed Forces Since 1948* (Singapore: ISEAS, 2009) p 69.

new forms of economic competition by the Tatmadaw, such as in 2018 with the launch of a new telecommunications company majority-owned by the Tatmadaw in an effort to reassert control over the sector.

Since 2011, the constitutional principle of a market economy has been used to support the passage of legislation, showing the importance of the legislature in constitutional debates. Many laws aim to achieve economic and commercial reform. Some existing laws have also been repealed where they contradict the market economy principle. For example, in 2014, a proposal to repeal the socialist-era Law Defining the Fundamental Rights and Responsibilities of the People's Worker was introduced in the Pyithu Hluttaw.[70] Introduced by the Minister for Labour, part of the purpose of repealing the law was to remove any impediments to foreign investment.[71] Under the law, an employer found in breach of orders issued under the law was subject to imprisonment, with no flexibility in the form of punishment. The Attorney General's Office also supported the repeal of this law. During debates in the Pyithu Hluttaw, reference was made to section 35 of the Constitution concerning the market economy to justify the repeal of the law. Affirmation of the market economy runs beyond the legislature to the Tatmadaw itself. On the 70th Anniversary of Armed Forces Day, the Commander-in-Chief referred to the importance of the market economy and the shift from nationalisation to privatisation.

Distinctive to Myanmar is the constitutional promise not to demonetise the currency, as previous regimes had done in the 1960s, and most recently in 1987–88, with devastating consequences. It was the demonetisation policy of the late 1980s that was part of the tipping point that lead to widespread protests for democracy and against the socialist regime. Many of the protestors in the 1988 demonstrations (see Chapter 2) were students who had lost their savings and been unable to pay for the coming year's university tuition fees. The anxiety and trauma of demonetisation has arisen in relation to debates related to monetary policies. For example, in 2017, the Pyithu Hluttaw received a proposal from an NLD member that the image of General Aung San (the father of Aung San Suu Kyi and independence hero) should be printed on currency notes.[72] During the discussion, another NLD member referred to section 36(3) of the Constitution to endorse the proposal because it does not in any way intend to demonetise the currency.

---

[70] See PH2015-12:67.
[71] See AH2011-2:34, p 38.
[72] See PH2017-6:13.

Finally, the constitutional provision prohibiting the nationalisation of economic enterprises has also surfaced in legislative debates. For example, in June 2015, a USDP member proposed that property that had been confiscated during the socialist era should be returned to the owner justified by section 36(d) of the Constitution, which prohibits nationalisation.[73]

The Constitution also permits cooperatives, joint ventures and other economic initiatives.[74] The Constitution does not, however, prohibit the Tatmadaw from being involved in the economy. The economy remains dominated by cronies, military owned corporations and active and retired military officers. Two military owned conglomerates maintain a large commercial presence across a wide range of sectors: the Myanmar Economic Corporation (MEC) and Union of Myanmar Economic Holdings Limited (UMEHL).[75] There has not been any major effort at reform in this regard. The Constitutional Tribunal has not been given the opportunity to hear any cases on the economic provisions of the Constitution.

IV. AUNG SAN SUU KYI AND THE OFFICE OF THE STATE COUNSELLOR

In 2016, at the start of the term of the NLD Government, a new executive position known as the State Counsellor was created. The State Counsellor is defacto leader of the *government*, not defacto leader of the *country* as some outside observers have presumed. The State Counsellor is more powerful than the president, but still subservient to the Commander-in-Chief who is regarded as the defacto leader of the *country*. The Tatmadaw claims that the State Counsellor has no constitutional foundation.[76]

The origins of the Office of the State Counsellor are directly related to the leadership issue the NLD Government faced. In 2015, Aung San Suu Kyi was re-elected as a member of the legislature. But she could not be appointed by the electoral college as president. The NLD had to find a way to justify her leadership of the government constitutionally. At first, a prominent lawyer and legal advisor to the NLD, U Ko Ni, argued that the legislature could appoint Suu Kyi as president if the

---

[73] See PH2015-12:67.

[74] 2008 Constitution, ss 36a and 455.

[75] The UMEHL was formed as tax exempt under the Special Company Act 1950. MEC was formed under Law No 9/1989 as amended in 1997. See Maung Aung Myoe, *Building the Tatmadaw*, pp 176, 181.

[76] Holliday and Su Mon Thazin Aung, above n 24, p 234.

legislature first *suspended* section 59(f) of the Constitution (the provision that is regarded as barring Suu Kyi from becoming president, see above). This option was risky and did not have a clear constitutional basis, though it has historical antecedents. An alternative option was a law to establish a new and unprecedented executive position. The NLD acted on this second proposal and introduced a law to establish the position of the State Counsellor.[77] This law was justified based on the constitutional power of the Pyidaungsu Hluttaw to pass laws and to delegate executive power.[78] Some have suggested that section 217 of the Constitution, which allows the Pyidaungsu Hluttaw to confer executive power on any institution or person, is a constitutional loophole. This provision would have allowed two former military generals – General Than Shwe (sometimes referred to as 'Number 1') and Maung Aye ('Number 2') – to share executive power. The NLD utilised section 217 to create the new executive Office of the State Counsellor, one not anticipated by the constitution-drafters. There are no discernible limits on the power of the Pyidaungsu Hluttaw under section 217.

Both the Tatmadaw, and some observers, have suggested that the State Counsellor is unconstitutional.[79] The Tatmadaw legislators fiercely opposed the creation of the Office of the State Counsellor because they understood this reform as tantamount to unauthorised constitutional change. The Tatmadaw raised objections in legislative hearings and threatened to challenge the constitutionality of the State Counsellor Law in the Constitutional Tribunal, although this has not occurred to date. They also made some more nuanced claims, for example, that the State Counsellor should have been made accountable to the president, rather than to the Pyidaungsu Hluttaw. Their objections were ignored, and the law was passed by the majority NLD Government.

The creation of the State Counsellor role re-adjusts the way people understand the Office of the President in Myanmar. The State Counsellor draws attention and authority away from the Office of the President, reducing its status and influence. The law specifies that only Suu Kyi can hold the position of State Counsellor, so no other person can occupy this office unless the law is amended. The State Counsellor has four explicit functions: to foster a market economy, to enhance democracy, to promote peace and development, and to work towards federalism. The goals of building a market economy and promoting peace and

---

[77] Law on the Office of the State Counsellor No 26/2016.
[78] 2008 Constitution, ss 96 and 217.
[79] Holliday and Su Mon Thazin Aung, above n 24, p 234.

development are consistent with the wording and intentions of the Constitution and National Ceasefire Agreement. However, the goal of fostering democracy may be at odds with the Constitution's more qualified version of disciplined democracy. The goal of working towards a federal system is arguably inconsistent with the Constitution, which does not explicitly claim to uphold federalism as a fundamental principle. In this respect, the State Counsellor Law gives Suu Kyi an expansive mandate that goes beyond the aspirations of the Constitution.

As State Counsellor, Suu Kyi appropriated many leadership functions that were previously undertaken by the president. Technically she reports to the Pyidaungsu Hluttaw. Suu Kyi has established and spearhead the new 'Union Peace Conference – 21st Century Panglong' ('21-Panglong'), named after the 1947 Panglong Agreement orchestrated by her father General Aung San (see Chapter 2). She is the chairperson of the Union Peace Dialogue Joint Committee that facilitates and manages the ongoing peace talks (see Chapter 10). She occasionally issues announcements, such as granting an amnesty for political prisoners, which is a task former president Thein Sein previously undertook. She has also established the Development Assistance Coordination Unit to oversee and coordinate with international donors, a role that was previously undertaken by president Thein Sein and his Myanmar Development Cooperation Forum.

The power of Suu Kyi's role is not only derived from her office as State Counsellor. She was also appointed as minister to the President's Office,[80] and Minister of Foreign Affairs.[81] The latter position grants her a seat at the National Defence and Security Council (see Chapter 3). Suu Kyi plays a significant role in international relations, meeting with foreign ambassadors and other foreign dignitaries. It is not always clear whether she is acting in her capacity as Minister for Foreign Affairs or State Counsellor. Further, the international community clearly sees Suu Kyi, rather than the president, as the leader of Myanmar. A clear example of this is the Rakhine State crisis after August 2017, when the international community called upon Suu Kyi to speak out in support of the Rohingya and to acknowledge and address the grave humanitarian crisis. None in the international community implored the president, U Htin Kyaw, to speak out in support of human rights on this issue.

---

[80] The position of minister to the President's Office is distinction from that of the president. It has been suggested that this position is similar to a position of a Prime Minister in other systems.

[81] Initially she held four positions, although she later gave up the Minister for Education and Minister for Energy.

The State Counsellor has also taken it upon herself to establish special commissions. She is the chairperson of the Central Committee on the Implementation of Peace, Stability and Development of Rakhine State. The most controversial move has been to establish the Advisory Commission on Rakhine State, which was chaired by former Secretary General of the UN, Kofi Annan. The Advisory Commission commenced in September 2016 and had responsibility for investigating the Rohingya crisis in Rakhine State, including challenges for development, human rights and security. Soon after the Commission was formed, in September 2016, a proposal was submitted to the legislature to abolish the Commission. The proposal was supported by the ANP, the USDP and by all Tatmadaw members. The proposal was ultimately unsuccessful as it did not have the support of the NLD Government.[82] However, a similar proposal was then submitted to the Rakhine State legislature, and this proposal was successful. While the Rakhine State Hluttaw did not have the power to formally abolish this Commission, its vote set a clear tone of defiance towards the Commission and its purpose of investigating the Rohingya crisis.[83] The Commission's mandate was limited, as it was established before the first major insurgent attack on 9 October 2016 by the Arakan Rohingya Solidarity Army (ARSA). The Commission's final report also generated further controversy, with speculations that the second major round of attacks by ARSA against police stations on 25 August 2017 was timed to coincide with the release of the Commission's Final Report.

The controversy that the Office of State Counsellor has attracted has come at a great price to the NLD. On 30 January 2017, U Ko Ni, the lawyer mentioned earlier who was one of the architects of the State Counsellor Law, was brutally assassinated. Despite his ordinary background as a traditional civil and criminal law lawyer,[84] he had taken the risk to speak out against the undemocratic elements of the Constitution and to advocate for the constitutionality of Suu Kyi's position as State Counsellor. His role in the creation of the Office of State Counsellor was one of the reasons for his assassination. The trial against the four accused resulted in the death sentence for two of the accused, although the fifth accused and alleged mastermind remains at large.

---

[82] See PH2016-2:27.

[83] This issue is acknowledged directly in the report, see Advisory Commission on Rakhine State, *Towards a Peaceful Fair and Prosperous Future for the People of Rakhine*. Final Report August 2017, p 16.

[84] On the legal profession in Myanmar, see Melissa Crouch 'The Legal Profession in Myanmar', in Richard Abel et al (eds) *Lawyers in Society* (2nd edn, vol II) (Hart Publishing, forthcoming, 2019).

V. THE ADMINISTRATION OF UNION TERRITORIES

The president exercises executive power over Naypyidaw, the capital city, as a constitutionally designated Union Territory.[85] Naypyidaw is governed by a council who are directly responsible to the president.[86] Naypyidaw is the territorial embodiment of the military-state and a visible manifestation of its scale, scope and ambition. It is an expression of the former regime's defiant isolationism. The capital opened in 2006, with the sudden relocation of most of the civil service. Without any schools, health care or basic infrastructure, many civil servants reluctantly left their families and children behind in Yangon. This move literally tore apart the lives of many civil servants and forced them to lead an isolated and exhausting existence, many choosing to travel the seven hours by bus back to Yangon every weekend. In Naypyidaw itself, the centrepiece is the new Union legislature, housed in a sprawling legislative complex that includes 31 separate buildings, complete with an expansive moat. The complex is accessed via an extended bridge next to a 20-lane highway, which is rumoured to double as an emergency launch area for planes.

From 2006–2011, the Tatmadaw regime and its administration had five years in Naypyidaw to prepare for the commencement of the legislature under the Constitution. There are multiple theories as to why the capital was built, ranging from an astrologer who predicted a grand capital would emerge, to General Than Shwe's desire to build a capital as a legacy of his rule like that of past kings, to fears of US invasion. The capital was built with the help of the Chinese at an estimated cost of US$4 billion and has underground bunkers and tunnels built with the assistance of North Korea. This is one example of the blurred line between fact and fiction, conspiracy and reality. The sheer remoteness of the capital adds to the difficulty of governing and the ongoing isolation of the central government administration from its people. No foreign embassy has moved its office to Naypyidaw.

Aside from Naypyidaw, the Constitution anticipates the creation of new Union Territories. The Constitution provides in broad terms that if an issue arises that threatens national security, the government or the economy then the Pyidaungsu Hluttaw can pass a law designating an area as a Union Territory under the oversight of the president.[87]

---

[85] 2008 Constitution, ss 49(o), 51(i), 50(a)
[86] Ibid, ss 284–285.
[87] Ibid, ss 50(b), 99.

The Constitution is clear that Union Territories do not have extra representation in the Amyotha Hluttaw.[88] Union Territories do have their own district courts and township courts, but they do not have a separate High Court. Instead, the relevant court is the High Court of the State/Region in which the Union Territory is located.[89] The Council is the executive body of a Union Territory, although it is not elected directly by the electorate.[90] A state of emergency can be declared in relation to a Union Territory.[91] If there is a dispute between a Union Territory and a State/Region, or a Self-Administered Area, the Union Government has authority to mediate such disputes.[92] In addition, the Supreme Court also has jurisdiction to hear non-constitutional disputes regarding a Union Territory.[93] The Constitutional Tribunal has jurisdiction to consider the constitutionality of decisions made by the president concerning Union Territories.[94]

Aside from the administrative convenience of the president having control over the capital Naypyidaw as a Union Territory, there is little indication of how or why the constitution-drafters included these provisions. Similar constitutional arrangements are found in the Indian Constitution, which designates the capital city Delhi as a Union Territory, as well as a range of other regions. Like some dormant aspects of the Constitution, how these provisions will work or the purpose it might be used for beyond Naypyidaw remains to be seen.

VI. CONCLUSION

The Constitution maintains a symbolic separation between the 'party politics' of the legislature and the neutrality of the permanent administrative institutions of the state and high-level executive positions. This formal constitutional separation between the executive and legislature is designed to uphold the *political* neutrality of the state. However, the executive and the administration are not independent or separate from the Tatmadaw. The Tatmadaw has demonstrated a willingness to overlook instances in the formation of government and selection of the

---

[88] Ibid, s 144.
[89] Ibid, s 307(b).
[90] Ibid, s 394(a).
[91] Ibid, ss 410, 412.
[92] Ibid, s 226(b).
[93] Ibid, s 295(a)(iii).
[94] Ibid, s 322(f).

executive that appear to breach the Constitution, such as the appoint-ment of the vice-president under the NLD. Many of these controversies are open to interpretation, such as the debate over the constitutionality of the Office of the State Counsellor. The Constitution and enabling laws facilitate collective action and this is its main role (rather than constrain-ing behaviour). Since 2016, the president has become like a head of state and the State Counsellor is the de facto head of government, while the Commander-in-Chief remains defacto head of the country.

The executive in Myanmar is marked by a wide scope of discretion, the centralisation of power in the Union Government and the relative absence of limits on executive power. A large portion of executive power lies with the Tatmadaw or with the administration who often have loyal-ties to the Tatmadaw, outside the control of the government. This creates tension within the executive. The constitutional provisions in favour of a market economy, non-nationalisation and non-demonetisation remain in tension with the Tatmadaw's monopoly over many sectors of the economy. Future efforts by the Union Government towards establishing a market economy will depend on cooperation by the Tatmadaw to end its monopoly over the economy.

FURTHER READING

Ian Holliday and Su Mon Thazin Aung, 'The Executive', in Ian Holliday et al (eds) *Routledge Handbook on Contemporary Myanmar* (London, Routledge, 2018).

Marco Bünte, 'Perilous Presidentialism or Precarious Power-sharing? Hybrid Regime Dynamics in Myanmar' (2017) 24 *Contemporary Politics* 1.

Melissa Crouch, 'Authoritarian Straightjacket or Vehicle for Democratic Transition? The Risky Struggle to Change Myanmar's Constitution' in Tom Ginsburg and Aziz Huq (ed) *Implementing New Constitutions* (CUP forthcoming, 2019).

7

Subnational Governance, Federalism and Ethnic Recognition

Territorial Recognition – Sub-national Governance – Distribution of Power – Secession – National Races – Subverting Self-determination

THERE HAS BEEN significant debate over whether and if so, how, the Constitution is federal in nature. The Constitution does not explicitly mention the term 'federal', and this is a deliberate omission in constitutional design. Careful consideration of the Constitution in its historical context suggests that the dependent relationship between the Union and State/Region governments is in contrast to the era of direct military rule, when regional commanders had significant decentralised power.[1] While comparative analysis of the English text may appear to indicate that the 2008 Constitution is 'quasi federal', this is not how people in Myanmar understand the Constitution. Federalism in Myanmar, particularly for ethnic armed organisations, has come to stand for ideas such as the autonomy of states from the Union Government including in appointments, functions and accountability; the right to have state constitutions; state control over natural resources; the right to be part of a federal army, and significant representation of the States in the Union legislature, among other federal proposals. The Tatmadaw prefers a Union rather than a federal system, although views within the military are not monolithic and at the 21st Century Panglong Conference, one Tatmadaw representative argued that the 2008 Constitution is in fact already federal.[2]

---

[1] Maung Aung Myoe, *Building the Tatmadaw: Myanmar Armed Forces Since 1948* (Singapore: ISEAS, 2009).
[2] Maung Aung Myoe (2018) 'Partnership in Politics: The Tatmadaw and the NLD in Politics in Myanmar in 2016', in Gerald McCarthy, Justine Chambers, Nicholas Farrelly and Chit Win (eds) *Myanmar Transformed? People, Places, Politics*. ISEAS.

Local advocates like U Ko Ni argue that the Constitution is not federal, and that the States/Regions are clearly placed in a subordinate position and required to render assistance to the Union Government.[3] There are several features of the Constitution that delegate limited power to the sub-national level, but this is insufficient to constitute federalism in intent or in practice. The delegation of power is extremely limited and subunits must remain loyalty to the Three Main National Causes of the military-state. The co-optation of the term the 'Union' is seen by many as a misnomer, with calls instead for a new 'federal Union'. The lines of accountability for sub-national institutions and actors remain centralised in keeping with the emphasis on coercive centralism. In this chapter, I consider the ways three forms of recognition – the seven States/Region, the creation of Ministers for National Races Affairs, and the Self-Administered Zones or Regions – remain subordinate to the Union Government and the leading role of the Tatmadaw. Calls for expanded recognition for ethnic groups and 'genuine' federalism remain.

I. TERRITORIAL REPRESENTATION: STATES AND REGIONS

Within the Union, the constitutional design at the sub-national level includes State/Region, district, township, ward, village tract and, in some states, self-administered zones.[4] The organisation of seven States and seven Divisions was first established in the 1974 Constitution. This designation of territorial power is retained in the 2008 Constitution. Only minor changes were made, with the renaming of the 'Divisions' to 'Regions', and the addition of the new capital, Naypyidaw, as a Union Territory.[5] The designation of seven ethnic-based States and seven Burman-based Regions is symmetrical in that all have equal recognition or, to put it another way, the ethnic States do not have any form of special recognition compared to the Burman Regions. The States/Regions are the second tier of government, although remain closed connected to and dependent upon the Union Government. The designation, equal status and executive power of the seven States/Regions is recognised in the Basic Principles of the Constitution.[6]

---

[3] He makes this argument with reference to ss 248, 250 of the Constitution, see Ko Ni (2013) *Pwesipone ache-kan ubade-ko, Beh lo pyin-kya hma-le.* [How to Amend the Constitution?]. Yangon.
[4] 2008 Constitution, see ss 288–89, and Ch II, s 51.
[5] Ibid, ss 50, 285–287.
[6] Ibid, ss 9(a), 13, 17(a).

A. The Distinctiveness of the Seven Ethnic-Based States

To appreciate the territorial differences between the seven Burman Regions and the seven ethnic-based States, I offer a brief overview of the people and culture of the seven ethnic-based States and their relationship to the Burman majority. To the west of the country is Rakhine State, known pre-1989 as Arakan State. Rakhine State shares a border with Bangladesh and opens onto the Bay of Bengal. Rakhine State was first created under the 1974 Constitution. The population of Rakhine State is two-thirds ethnic Rakhine, most of whom are Buddhist or animist. Up until 2016, it was estimated that one-third of the population were Rohingya Muslims, a minority group that does not fit in the government's official classification scheme. Many now reside either in internally displaced camps or camps in Bangladesh. The Rakhine Buddhists have historically had grievances both with the ethnic Burman majority, and with the Rohingya.[7] Rakhine State is the poorest State/Region in Myanmar. The Arakan Army (an ethnic Rakhine Buddhist armed organisation) are still fighting against the Tatmadaw and have not signed the National Ceasefire Agreement.

Bordering Rakhine State to the west is Chin State, also known as one of the poorest states. The Chin are a diverse people, speaking many languages that share no commonalities.[8] Most Chin are Christian. Chin State is home to less than half a million people. During colonial rule, the Chin Hills were administered as part of Arakan Division. The Chin signed the Panglong Agreement in 1947. Aspects of customary law are still practiced in these areas.[9] In 2015, the Chin National Front (CNF) signed the National Ceasefire Agreement.

Kachin State reaches to the northernmost tip of Myanmar, sharing external borders with India and China. The Kachin are mostly Christian, although some are animist or Buddhist. The Kachin fought with the British against the Japanese in World War II and have held on to the British promise of autonomy.[10] The Kachin signed the Panglong Agreement in 1947. The Kachin Independence Army is the largest ethnic

---

[7] For a balanced account, see ICG, *The Politics of Rakhine State* (Report No 261, International Crisis Group, 2014).

[8] Frederick K Lehman, *The Structure of Chin Society* (University of Illinois Press, 1963).

[9] P Polianskaja and Mai Len Nei Cer, *Hosts and Guests. Gender Dynamics in Chin Customary Law* (NINU, 2018).

[10] Mandy Sadan, *Being & Becoming Kachin* (OUP, 2013); Edmund R Leach, *Political Systems of Highland Burma* (Berg publisher, 1973); Bertil Lintner, *The Kachin* (Chiang Mai: Teak House, 1997).

armed group. Up until 2018, it has not signed the National Cease-fire Agreement. There has been ongoing fighting and displacement since 2011.

Kayah (Karenni) State has the smallest population of any State/Region, with just over 286,000 people. Part of eastern Myanmar, Kayah State shares a border with Thailand. The Karenni people, also known as Red Karen, are part of the Sino-Tibetan family. In 1875, a treaty was signed between the British and King Mindon acknowledging the independence of the Karenni States. The recognition of one Karenni State in 1947 (a merger of three Karenni States) came with the possibility of secession after ten years. In 2012, the Karenni National Progressive Party (KNPP) did sign a bilateral ceasefire, but it has not yet signed the National Ceasefire Agreement.

Kayin (Karen) State also shares a border with Thailand in the east. Most Karen are Buddhist or animist, although about one third are Christian.[11] The Karen are descendants from Mongolians and constitute the second largest minority ethnic group after the Shan. The Karen National Union (KNU) is the largest insurgent group. The Karen fought with the British against the Japanese in World War II. The Karen did not participate in the Panglong Agreement and boycotted the Constituent Assembly over their demands for a separate state.[12] While the 1947 Constitution granted them recognition as a state, the territory was not as inclusive as was demanded and no right of secession was given. The KNU were among the first to rebel against the government.[13] The KNU is a signatory to the National Ceasefire Agreement, although in 2018 the KNU suspended its participation in the Joint Monitoring Committee. The population of Karen State today is over 1.5 million, although many Karen live outside of the state.

Mon State borders three States/Regions and shares a small border with Thailand, before opening into the Andaman Sea. The capital, Moulemein, was a colonial outpost since the second Anglo-Burmese war and is home to a large Muslim community. The main ethnic armed group that has fought against the government is the New Mon State Party (NMSP). In 1995, the NMSP entered into a ceasefire agreement with the Tatmadaw, and then in 2015 it signed the National Ceasefire Agreement.

---

[11] Harry Marshall, *The Karen Peoples of Burma* (Columbus: Ohio State University Press, 1922).

[12] Ardeth Maung Thawnghmung, *The Other Karen in Myanmar* (New York: Lexington Books, 2012).

[13] Ashley South, *Burma's Longest War: Anatomy of the Karen Conflict* (Transnational Institute, 2011).

Finally, Shan State is of significance because it is the largest state and covers almost a quarter of the total land mass of Myanmar.[14] Most of Shan State is rural, rich in mineral resources and famous for its precious stones and metals. Shan State is also infamous for producing a large portion of the world's opium and heroin.[15] Due to the borders it shares with China, Shan State is strategic for security and economic reasons. The Shan are the largest minority group in Myanmar, most of whom are Buddhist. Only about half of the population of Shan State are ethnic Shan, while other major ethnic groups that live in Shan State include the Pa-O, Palaung, Kachin, Danu, Lahu, Inthar, Wa, Kokang and Akha. The differences within the population of Shan State are more geographical than linguistic or religious. The area was not part of British India until 1922 when the Federated Shan States were formed. By 1937, when the Government of Burma Act 1935 came into effect to separate the administration of Burma from British India, the *saopha* Shan leaders were given representation in the government.[16] The Shan signed the Panglong Agreement, and under the 1947 Constitution were given the right of secession. But in 1952 the government declared a large part of southern Shan State under military administration and brought in Burmese troops. This was on the pretext of suppressing Kuomintang forces, but also worked to undermine the power of the *saophas*.[17] Fighting between the government and various ethnic armed organisations in Shan State broke out in the 1960s, and continued in the following decades, until a number of ceasefire agreements in the late 1980s and early 1990s.[18] Five of the six Self-Administered Areas are located in Shan State. Shan State is home to many ethnic armed organisations, though the most powerful of these have not signed the National Ceasefire Agreement.

The seven ethnic-based States are primarily highland, border areas that occupy a different place in the political imagination compared with the seven Regions in the lowlands. The Regions are majority Burman-Buddhist. The difference between the ethnically plural and sparsely populated highlands, and the more ethnically and religiously

---

[14] Chao Tzang Yawnghwe, *The Shan of Burma: Memoirs of a Shan Exile* (Singapore: ISEAS, 1987).

[15] Bertil Linter, 'The Shans and the Shan State' (1984) 5(4) *Contemporary Southeast Asia* 403–45.

[16] Sai Aung Tun, *History of the Shan State: From its Origins to 1962* (Silkworm Books, 2009) p 224.

[17] Linter, above n 15, p 411.

[18] Martin Smith, *Burma: Insurgency and the Politics of Ethnicity*, 2nd edn (White Lotus, 1991).

homogenous Burman lowlands is relevant to the debate on federalism and has been central to demands for self-determination.

B. The Constitutional Role of the Chief Minister and the Executive

The State/Region executive remain subordinate to the Union Government. The executive is led by the Chief Minister[19] who is selected by the president from among elected Hluttaw members.[20] Many argue that the Chief Minister should be chosen by the State/Region Hluttaw to reduce centralised control over the States/Regions and enhance local representation. In 2015, an unsuccessful attempt was made to amend the Constitution so that Chief Ministers could be appointed from among members of the legislature. The demands for federalism, or at least greater devolution of power and independence of the State/Region Hluttaw from the Union Government, may lead to reform in the future.

The Chief Minister plays a direct role in the legislative process by sitting in the legislature. However, the Chief Minister is subject to the control of the Speaker of the Hluttaw. This matters because, since 2016, the Rakhine State and Shan State legislature have an NLD-nominated Chief Minister but a Speaker who is not chosen by the NLD. The Chief Minister, unlike the president, has no right to veto legislation. Instead, the Chief Minister has seven days to sign the draft, otherwise it becomes law.[21]

There is overlap between the executive and legislature, with the Chief Minister and other ministers retaining their seats in the legislature. The cabinet consists of the Chief Minister and several civilian members, the Advocate General and the head of the General Administration Department (GAD).[22] The GAD forms the core of the administration and the head of the GAD at the State/Region level is the Secretary of the Cabinet at the State/Region level. This effectively means that the Union-level Government controls the administration and implementation of State/Region laws. This is lack of legislative autonomy is another reason the system is not considered to be federal.

Under the Thein Sein Government (2011–2016), 10 out of the 14 Chief Ministers were former Tatmadaw officers, and all affiliated

---

[19] 2008 Constitution, s 247.
[20] Ibid, ss 261–264.
[21] Ibid, s 195.
[22] Ibid, ss 248, 260.

with the Union Solidarity and Development Party (USDP). In contrast, under the NLD Government (2016–2021) most Chief Ministers were NLD members. There have been concerns that the Chief Ministers under the NLD take orders from the party at the Union level and have neglected to allow for full participation or deliberation of Parliament at the State/Region level. There are reports that the executive makes decisions and proposes laws with little consultation with the legislature. Executive power is concurrent with legislative power in Schedule 2 and includes any matters the sub-national government is allowed to undertake according to Union law.[23] The State/Region government has the authority to submit a budget Bill to the legislature, although because it must be in accordance with the Union Budget[24] it is largely determined by the Union Government. State/Region governments also have limited taxation powers under Schedule 5 of the Constitution.[25]

The Chief Minister plays an important coordination and communication role between the Union Government and the State/Region government. In terms of hierarchy, the Chief Ministers are on the same level as Union Ministers. The Chief Minister is ultimately responsible to the president[26] and this has led to concerns that the Chief Minister is too close to the president. The Chief Minister does not have the power to determine the number of Ministers, instead the president, with the approval of the State/Region Hluttaw, wields this power.[27] The Hluttaw is led by the Speaker, who is chosen by the Chief Minister.

The Constitution provides that the Chief Minister selects the ministers of the States/Regions with the formal approval of the president. Since the Chief Minister is appointed by the president, the president can influence the choice of ministers. The qualifications for minister, and the rules of impeachment, are like that for the Pyithu Hluttaw (see Chapter 5), including the requirement of loyalty to the Union, and by implication loyalty to the Tatmadaw and the Three Main National Causes of the military-state.[28] There have been impeachment proceedings initiated against ministers. For example, in December 2017, the Speaker of Rakhine State Hluttaw created an investigation team to consider allegations that the Municipal Affairs Minister had failed to perform his duties. The complaint was lodged by 17 legislators from a cross-section

---

[23] Ibid, s 249.
[24] Ibid, s 252.
[25] Ibid, ss 254–259.
[26] Ibid, s 262 (l)(i).
[27] Ibid, s 248.
[28] Ibid, s 262.

of political parties, including the Arakan National Party (ANP), NLD and USDP members.[29] The complaint concerned the alleged failure of the minister to consult the legislature on the state budget and the failure to seek legislative approval on development projects. In early 2018, a vote was taken and the proposal to impeach the minister was approved.

The main points of tension at the State/Region level have been between the executive and legislature, or more specifically between the Chief Minister and the Speaker of the legislature. For example, in August 2012, the Ayeyarwaddy Hluttaw Speaker threatened to dismiss the entire Ayeyarwaddy Government (the Chief Minister and his ministers in cabinet).[30] This came after concerns that the government was pressuring other members not to ask questions, or not responding adequately to their questions, and that some members were being followed by the Special Branch (see Chapter 3).

C. The State/Region Hluttaw and its Limited Legislative Powers

The 2008 Constitution is the first time that the States/Regions have a unicameral Hluttaw, although its representativeness and independence is qualified by the condition that Tatmadaw personnel hold 25 per cent of seats in the sub-national Hluttaw.[31] The prominent lawyer U Ko Ni was strategic in arguing that even if Tatmadaw representation in the Pyidaungsu Hluttaw was necessary, there was no good reason for the States/Regions to be required to allocate seats for the Tatmadaw. Tatmadaw seats in the State/Region Hluttaw reduces both the democratic and federal nature of these subunits. Leaving aside these reserved Tatmadaw seats, the unicameral State/Region Hluttaw consist of elected representatives from townships. As townships are based on population size, the number of seats of the State/Region Hluttaw vary widely, from Chin State of 24 members to Shan State of 137 members. There is no upper house, so the State/Region Hluttaw are not designed to represent its internally diverse population.

The State/Region Hluttaw have limited legislative powers. The State/Region Hluttaw can pass laws related to any matters that fall under

---

[29] Moe Myint, 'Rakhine Lawmakers push for regional ministers Impeachment' 6 December 2017, *The Irrawaddy*, www.irrawaddy.com/news/rakhine-lawmakers-push-regional-ministers-impeachment.html.

[30] *The Myanmar Times*, 'Ayeyarwaddy Hluttaw moves to sack Government', 1 October 2012, www.mmtimes.com/in-depth/2014-ayeyarwady-hluttaw-moves-to-sack-govt.html.

[31] 2008 Constitution, s 14.

Schedule 2 of the Constitution.[32] These matters primarily include issues such as finance and planning (including the State/Region budget), the local economy, development, agriculture, industry, energy, electricity, mining, forestry, transport, communication, construction and the social sector. The main law passed by State/Region Hluttaw concerns municipal councils.[33] Although the first two years of the transition saw little activity from the State/Region Hluttaw, by late 2013 the President's Office indicated its support and encouragement for the States/Regions to actively fulfil their duties in administration and governance.

The State/Region governments function in a distinctly different way from the Union Government for three main reasons. The State/Region Hluttaw are unicameral, not bicameral, which means there is no second house to act as a check on the legislature. The Chief Minister, as leader of the State/Region executive, and cabinet members retain their positions as active members of political parties and as legislators. This contrasts with members at the Union level who are required to vacate their seat or cease political party activity. Unlike the formal separation between the legislature and executive at the Union level, the States/Regions are modelled on a unitary form of government closer to a Westminster system. This means the executive has stronger influence over the legislature and the legislature does not act as a check on the executive.

Further, because the Chief Minister is appointed by the president, and is usually from the political party of the president, the Chief Minister is often accused of acting upon instructions either from their political party at the Union level or the Union Government, rather than initiating their own policies. The subservience of subnational governments to the Union is a feature of coercive centralism and means there is a degree of conformity, rather than diversity, among policies at the State/Region level. This has been a complaint against the NLD since 2016, that is, the president chose to appoint Chief Ministers who were members of, or perceived to be sympathetic to, the NLD and these Chief Ministers take orders from the central NLD.

The Constitution requires the State/Region governments to help the Union Government maintain stability and peace in the country.[34] This implicit reference to the Three National Causes reinforces the subordination of the State/Regions to the Union and to the Tatmadaw. The division of powers between the Union and State/Region governments,

---

[32] Ibid, s 188.
[33] The Municipal Council Law 5/1993 was finally repealed in 2018, after all State/Region Hluttaw had passed their own Municipal Council laws.
[34] 2008 Constitution, s 250.

or between the legislature and executive at the State/Region level, has not gone undisputed. The Constitutional Tribunal has been called upon to resolve disputes concerning the State/Region Hluttaw. The deference shown by the State/Region Hluttaw towards the Union Government is evidence of coercive centralism.

In 2014, the Constitutional Tribunal was asked to determine a dispute about the State budget and the scope of legislative power within the Kachin State Hluttaw. The Speaker of the Kachin State Hluttaw asked the Tribunal to decide whether a decision of the Kachin State Government to refuse to approve the State budget was constitutional. The Speaker also asked the Tribunal to consider whether the decision of the government to fund the construction of a garden is beyond the legislative power of the State Government under Schedule 2 of the Constitution.[35] This case involved the Constitutional Tribunal exercising its powers to determine the rights and duties of various levels of government, or disputes between different levels of government.[36] At the State/Region level there is a State Hluttaw, that is, all members including Tatmadaw members, and a State Government, led by the Chief Minister, appointed by the president. In this case the Tribunal had to decide whether the Kachin State Hluttaw has the power to amend or reject a budget Bill proposed by the Kachin State Government under section 193 of the Constitution.[37] The Kachin State Government argued that the Kachin State Hluttaw must pass the budget on the grounds that the state budget has been approved by the Financial Commission and the Pyidaungsu Hluttaw and that the Kachin State Hluttaw had no power to reject or curtail the state budget. The Tribunal held that the Hluttaw had the power to approve or reject a budget bill in relation to matters that fall under s 193(b) of the Constitution (and so partly agreed with the applicants). This is one example of how the Tribunal has intervened to resolve disputes at the sub-national level.

The Tribunal declined to decide on any other issues raised in the case, effectively leaving it to the Pyidaungsu Hluttaw to decide how to interpret the legislative lists in the Constitution. In the constitutional amendment Bill proposed in 2015,[38] a long list of additions to Schedule 2 (and Schedule 5) were proposed to clarify the law-making powers of the State/Region Hluttaw. These were approved by vote in

---

[35] Constitutional Tribunal, Kachin Budget Case 1/2014.
[36] 2008 Constitution, ss 322(d)–(e).
[37] Ibid, s 193.
[38] Draft Law to Amend to Constitution of the Union of Myanmar 2015, published in *Myanma Alin*, 12 June 2015.

the legislature. This has led to an unusual situation where the Pyidaungsu Hluttaw must define the scope of legislative power via constitutional amendment. The Constitutional Tribunal has effectively deferred to the Pyidaungsu Hluttaw on the meaning of the legislative list, which means that the Pyidaungsu Hluttaw has significant opportunity to read down the powers of State/Region Hluttaw.

The Constitutional Tribunal has also considered whether States/ Regions can pass laws on municipal councils. In 2012, the Speaker of the Mon State Hluttaw submitted a case to the Constitutional Tribunal.[39] The question was whether the Municipal Law,[40] as a law passed by the former SLORC regime, was unconstitutional or should be repealed. Mon State Hluttaw sought to enact a new Municipal Law in order to revise the regulation of local councils, known as municipal councils or development councils.[41] They argued that the State Hluttaw had the power to do this because 'municipal affairs' was listed as part of the State/Region Hluttaw's legislative power in section 8(a) of Schedule 2.[42] The Constitution provides that any existing laws remain in operation until they are repealed or subject to amendment by the legislature.[43] Mon State Hluttaw sought clarification on whether the Pyidaungsu Hluttaw must repeal the Municipal Law before the States/Regions can pass their own municipal laws. The president argued that the Municipal Law should be repealed after the States/Regions and Self-Administered Areas had all introduced new Municipal Laws. That is, the State/Region Hluttaw were permitted to legislate in areas allocated to them under Schedule 2, even if there was a prior Union law that would later need to be repealed by the Union Government. The Tribunal agreed with the president on the recommendation that the Municipal Law should be repealed after all new Municipal Laws had been created. Implicitly, this meant that Mon State was permitted to go ahead and pass a new Municipal Law. In its decision, the Tribunal upheld the importance of the State/Region Hluttaw and their respective legislative power. This has been an important decision and has provided certainty for other State/Region Hluttaw to pass Municipal Laws.

---

[39] Constitutional Tribunal, Municipal Law Case 3/2012.

[40] Municipal Law No 5/1993.

[41] The word used to refer to 'local councils' is **စည်ပင်သာယာရေး**. However, this is sometimes translated as 'development', such as in Yangon City Development Committee. See the 2008 Constitution Sch 2 (8a), Sch 3(4) and Sch 5(17) which use the term 'development affairs', but Sch 2(1e) uses the term 'municipal' taxes (rather than 'development taxes').

[42] 2008 Constitution, s 188 and Sch 2.

[43] Ibid, s 446.

The symbolic recognition of seven ethnic-based States and seven Burman-majority Regions permits a basic form of unicameral government while allowing the Union Government to maintain control over the State/Region executive. In this chapter I have only considered the legislature and executive, and I turn later to the State/Region courts (Chapter 8) and identify various calls for reform of the States/Regions (Chapter 10).

II. SUB-NATIONAL LEGISLATIVE REPRESENTATION OF NATIONAL RACES

For the first time, the 2008 Constitution creates special additional seats in the State/Region Hluttaw for representatives of official ethnic groups over a certain size population in a designated area. The Basic Principles mandate that there will be national race representatives in the State/Region Hluttaw and the Self-Administered Areas.[44] These Ministers for National Races Affairs advocate for ethnic claims such as language recognition, and freedom to express their culture and traditions. This form of special representation diversifies the sub-national Hluttaw and, because of the Burman populations in ethnic areas, allows Burmans to have representation in some ethnic States.

Past constitutions have featured some form of special representation. For example, under the 1947 Constitution, the Chamber of Nationalities reserved 125 seats based on ethnicity in proportion to the population, which included seats for Shan, Chin, Kayah, Kachin and Karen representatives. The other 62 representatives were Burmans. The subsequent 1974 Constitution and its unicameral legislature did not offer any form of legislative representation for ethnic groups. It was only in the 1990s, at the National Convention to draft a new constitution, that the Ministers for National Races Affairs positions was created to acknowledge that many ethnic groups are scattered throughout the country and do not reside in the State after which their ethnic group is named. This includes Burmans in ethnic areas, more than two thirds of Karen living outside of Karen State[45] and Kachin in Shan State, among others. The position was a concession to some ethnic groups that could not satisfy the criteria for an 'Area' (see below). The Constitution provides for a national race

---

[44] 2008 Constitution, s 15.
[45] Ardeth Maung Thawngmung, *The Other Karen: Ethnic Minorities and the Struggle without Arms* (Lexington Books, 2012).

recognised by the government to have representation at the State/Region or Area level, if it forms at least 0.1 per cent or more of the population.[46] The Constitution allows the president the power to assign responsibilities to the Ministers for National Races Affairs.[47]

One role that the Ministers for National Races Affairs have adopted is to advocate for the realisation of certain provisions in the Constitution concerning traditions, customs and language rights.[48] In 2015, a Committee of the Pyithu Hluttaw submitted a Bill that was approved to realise the constitutional rights of national races and create a new Union Ministry for Ethnic Affairs.[49] These Ministers are allowed to contribute in the Hluttaw and are presumed to exercise executive power to the extent necessary to undertake their responsibilities on behalf of national races.[50] However the Constitution anticipates that these Ministers will only be invited to contribute to cabinet from time to time, that is, constitutionally they are not permanent members of cabinet.

In 2016, there were 29 Ministers for National Races Affairs. This allocation of ministers is based on unreliable statistics prior to the 2014 census. The number of ministers is one indication of the ethnic diversity within each State/Region. Shan State has the most ministers with seven non-Shan ministers, which is not surprising given that the Shan barely constitute a majority in that area; Kachin State has four ministers; Karen and Mon State each have three. The Ayeyarwaddy, Yangon and Sagaing Regions have two ministers each. Lastly, there are two States – Rakhine and Karenni State – and four Regions – Magwe, Mandalay, Bago and Tenasserim Regions – that have just one minister. Chin State is the only one that does not have any ministers, which is because there are many Chin sub-groups but none that are large enough to be given a Minister for National Races Affairs.

Two ethnic groups, the Burman and the Karen, each have five Ministers to represent them across the States and Regions. This allows the Burmans to have representation in the Hluttaw of five out of seven ethnic-based States. The Chin and Shan both have three representatives; the Pa-O, Rakhine and Lisu have two each; and then a handful of

---

[46] 2008 Constitution, ss 161(b) and (c). This only applies to the 135 national races recognised by the government.

[47] Ibid, s 262(g).

[48] Eg, the Union Government must facilitate the development of local dialects, the preservation of culture and promote socio-economic development of disadvantaged races (ss 22, 27).

[49] Rights of National Races Protection Law No 8/2015.

[50] 2008 Constitution, s 17(c).

ethnic groups have one representative.[51] The main difference between the Thein Sein and NLD Governments is the political party affiliation of the ministers. Under the Thein Sein Government, the ministers were closely affiliated with the Tatmadaw, with most of the representatives (17) being members of the USDP. Another two ministers are from the National Unity Party, a political party also known to support the Tatmadaw. Of the remaining ministers, nine are from ethnic-based political parties. The remaining minister is independent.

In some States/Regions, these ministers were given subordinate portfolios, or were in an inferior position to other ministers. This issue was raised in a case heard by the Constitutional Tribunal.[52] The legal issue was whether the larger benefits conferred on other ministers by law, in comparison to the reduced benefits given to Ministers for National Races Affairs, was constitutional. Members from the Amyotha Hluttaw challenged a law that would have effectively prevented Ministers of National Races Affairs from receiving the same privileges as other State/Region ministers. Under the law, Ministers of National Races were entitled to K1,000,000 per month (the same as High Court judges), while general ministers were entitled to double that amount, K2,000,000 per month.[53] General ministers receive free accommodation and security guards, while ministers for national races do not.[54] The State/Region Government Law was clear that Ministers of National Races Affairs do not form part of the cabinet, and only have the right to attend a cabinet meeting if invited.[55] The Attorney General argued that Ministers of National Races Affairs are not equal to other ministers, as set out in legislation. The Attorney General based this on the fact that the Constitution requires the Chief Minister to confer on ministers' responsibilities over ministries,[56] while the president assigns duties to Ministers of National Races Affairs. The Attorney General argued that the entitlements of Ministers of National Races Affairs were commensurate with their relative responsibilities. The applicants argued that Ministers of National Races Affairs should be considered as equal to other ministers. They argued that just because Ministers of National Races Affairs are assigned duties by the president, and do not have a ministry, does not necessarily mean that they are not equal with other ministers.

---

[51] These are the Kayan (Padaung), Kachin, Mon, Rawang, Lahu, Akha and Inn.
[52] Constitutional Tribunal, Ministers for National Races Affairs Case 2/2011.
[53] Law No 3/2011 relating to the Emoluments, Allowances and Insignia of the State/Region Level Person, ss 4–5.
[54] Ibid, ss 16–17.
[55] State/Region Government Law No 16/2010, ss 4(c), 48.
[56] 2008 Constitution, s 262.

The Constitutional Tribunal agreed that Ministers of National Races Affairs were of the same status as other ministers and rejected the submission of the Attorney General's Office. It held several provisions in the Emoluments Law[57] to be inconsistent with section 262 of the Constitution. The Tribunal referred to the Basic Principles of the Constitution that entitle national races to participate in the State/Region Hluttaw and in the affairs of national races.[58] The Tribunal referenced records of the National Convention, which state that ministers of the States/Regions are of the same status and entitled to the same privileges as Union ministers. These records however, do not mention Ministers of National Races Affairs. The Tribunal stretched the meaning of the National Convention records to approve an expanded understanding of the status of Ministers of National Races Affairs that was not the explicit intention of the previous regime, as evidenced by legislation passed in 2010 by the SPDC.

This was the first case in which the Tribunal used its power to invalidate sections of a law. Its decision also had the effect of reinforcing the equal status of national races, which was perceived as a win for recognised ethnic groups that make up less than 20 per cent of the population. In fact, the Tribunal appears to have gone beyond the intention of the constitution-drafters, expanding the meaning of the Constitution in a show of nationalist sentiment. The legislature followed this decision by amending the law accordingly.[59]

In a subsequent case, the Tribunal decision regarding ministers of national races affairs was challenged by the president who attempted to bring an appeal or revision case to the Tribunal regarding a previous decision.[60] The Constitution does not mention whether the Tribunal also has power to hear cases on appeal. The president sought a right to appeal from a decision of the Tribunal on the basis that the Tribunal, like the Supreme Court, should be bound by the Civil Procedure Code and the common law and permit a right to appeal. If this preliminary argument was accepted, the president further argued that the decision of the Tribunal was incorrect, and that ministers of national races affairs were in fact lower in status than other ministers. The Tribunal determined that it cannot entertain applications for appeal of its own decision and rejected

---

[57] Namely, ss 5 and 17 of Law No 3/2011 relating to the Emoluments, Allowances and Insignia of the State/Region Level Person.

[58] 2008 Constitution, ss 15, 17(c).

[59] Law 6/2013 amending the Law relating to the Emoluments, Allowances and Insignia of the State/Region Level Person.

[60] Constitutional Tribunal, Right to Appeal Case 2/2012.

the case, so the presidents' arguments were not considered further. Although the Tribunal did not consider the merits of the presidents' second claim, the decision was taken as further affirmation of the original decision on the equal status of ministers of national races affairs.

The government must be able to identify voters based on national race in order to fill the ministers of national races affairs positions.[61] There was significant controversy over the 2014 census, and a delay in the release of certain results. The census also marks a change in population that would affect which ethnic groups receive special representation, while some groups may lose their existing representative. However, in the 2015 elections the prior calculation was still used and as a result the current designation of ministers does not reflect the 2014 census data. In 2016, the Thein Sein Government also recognised a new category, although designated this a sub-set of 'Burman' group (to retain the 135). This is contradicted by the Ministry for Immigration, which has claimed that there are in fact only 108 races left (the others it claims are extinct).[62] Many groups feel that they have not been classified appropriately, while other groups are not recognised on the list at all.

In a later 2014 Tribunal case, there was debate about which ethnic groups are eligible for status and representation by a minister of national races affairs.[63] An ethnic Kachin member of the Pyithu Hluttaw, Daw Dwe Bu, and 50 other legislators brought a case to the Tribunal. While there were multiple constitutional issues in the case, here I focus on the issue related to the ministers of national races affairs. The question of the applicants was whether these ministers are appointed from the eight races (Burman, Shan, Kachin, Karen, Kayah, Mon, Arakan, Chin), or whether the ministers are appointed from among the 135 sub-groups, according to section 161 and 262 of the Constitution. The background to this case was that a person was appointed as a Minister of Rawan Affairs and Minister of Lisu Affairs (in Kachin State) and a separate person was appointed as Minister of Lisu Affairs (in Shan State).

The applicant argued that in Shan State the position should have been for the category of Kachin generally, not the sub-category of 'Lisu' specifically (which is listed as one of 12 sub-groups of Kachin according to the government). The Constitutional Tribunal held that it was

---

[61] Jane M Ferguson, 'Who's Counting? Ethnicity, Belonging and the National Census in Burma/Myanmar' (2015) 171 *Bijdragen tot de Taal-, Land- en Volkenkunde* 1.

[62] This is according to the ministry's submission in the Constitutional Tribunal, Citizenship Case 1/2015.

[63] Constitutional Tribunal, Kachin Race Case 1/2014 (Sept).

the responsibility of the Union Election Commission and the complaint should have been sent to it. This is because the Election Commission has responsibility for deciding which ethnic groups are eligible for representation as a minister of national races affairs.[64] In doing so, the Tribunal was taken to have affirmed the idea that it is sub-groups (that is, one of the 135 groups) that may possibly be granted a minister of national races affairs if they meet the 0.1 per cent threshold. That is, the position is not to be held in the name of the eight mega-categories of national races.

One proposal that has been raised in relation to constitutional amendment is for the position of minister of national races affairs to only be occupied by people who can prove they are from the ethnic group of the population they are elected to represent. Another slight variation on this proposal is for these ministers to only be drawn from the political party(ies) of the ethnic group they represent. This concern reflects the recognition that most positions have either been held by USDP members or NLD members. Both proposals, however, would create further difficulties in terms of how to decide who is from a certain ethnic group, given that many have mixed heritage. There is a future need for empirical research around what these ministers do and the constitutional principles and aspirations concerning language, culture and tradition that they embody and promote.

III. SPECIAL GOVERNANCE ARRANGEMENTS FOR SIX AREAS

The 2008 Constitution designates Self-administered Zones and Divisions (hereafter 'Areas'), thereby granting a form of limited self-governance. This has similarities to the proposals put forward in the AFPFL Draft Constitution and also resonates with the concept of autonomous zones in the former USSR and China. The Basic Principles of the Constitution specifically name the six Areas and the townships that each include.[65] The introduction of any new Areas or the expansion of existing areas into new townships would require constitutional amendment.

These Areas are a limited form of self-governance that exist within the Union. The oath sworn by leaders of the Area requires them to uphold the non-disintegration of the country.[66] The process of determining which national races received Area status was partly mathematical

---

[64] 2008 Constitution, s 399 (this role seems to be implicit only).
[65] Ibid, s 56.
[66] See Law 17/2010 establishing the Self-Administered Areas.

and based on unreliable population data. At the National Convention in the 1990s, there were 16 groups that applied for self-administered status. The conditions that a group was required to meet to obtain this status were largely numerical: first, an ethnic group must make up most of the population in at least two townships; and, second, the townships must be located adjacent to each other. If the application included more than two townships, the ethnic group had to form a majority of the population in all these townships. The final two conditions that needed to be satisfied were that the application could only be made by one ethnic group, that is, it could not be a coalition of groups. A further limitation is that ethnic groups that already had a State were not allowed to apply for this status (even if they satisfied the above criteria in areas outside their States).

The application process began in the early 1990s and by 1995 the Self-administered Areas were announced.[67] This lends weight to my earlier claim that the age of the Constitution and its ideas date back to the 1990s. Fifteen years later, on 20 August 2010, the Areas were officially proclaimed. Six Areas were established: the Naga, Kokang, Danu, Palaung, Pa-O and Wa Areas.[68] Each of these Areas includes between two and six townships. The Areas, in theory, have legislative, executive and judicial power.[69] The name of a Self-Administered Area can be changed, and the constitutional procedure is the same as that for changing the name of a State or Region.[70]

A. Constitutional Powers of the Self-Administered Areas

The Areas are allocated certain powers and functions of limited self-governance under the Constitution. Legislative and executive power is administered by the Leading Body of the Area.[71] The terminology here is important, as the 'leading body' is a common term used in socialist states. The Leading Body has at least ten members, including Ministers for National Races Affairs and Tatmadaw personnel (who are assigned duties by the Commander-in-Chief himself). These members are appointed for a period of five years. Within the Leading Body, a smaller unit known

---

[67] The Detailed Basic Principles for Prescribing Self-administered Divisions or Self-administered Zones as laid down by the National Convention Plenary Session held on 7 April 1995.

[68] 2008 Constitution, s 56.

[69] Ibid, ss 12, 17, 18.

[70] Ibid, s 55.

[71] The powers of the Leading Body of the Zone are set out in the Constitution (ss 274–283).

as the Executive Committee must be formed, which consists of between three and five members. All the existing Areas have three members, except for Naga Area and Pa-O Area, which have five each. The Leading Body is organised within this system of coercive centralism and must remain loyal to the Union and the unity of the state. The Leading Body has a constitutional mandate to maintain social order and uphold the Union. Areas also have no constitutional right to secede from the Union.[72]

The Leading Body is coordinated by a chairperson who is chosen on the consensus of the Body itself, or by a secret vote if there is a dispute. The role of the chairperson is to oversee the function and activities of the Leading Body, and the president can also assign responsibilities to the chairperson, in the same way that the president determines the duties of the Ministers for National Races Affairs. The position of the chairperson is subject to removal by the president on the same set of grounds as other members of the executive or judiciary.[73] One of the privileges of this position is that the chairperson has the power to submit a question to the Constitutional Tribunal, although this has never occurred. More broadly, the Executive Committee has administrative responsibility to oversee the civil service and is also supposed to be responsible for initiating the annual budget.[74]

In terms of legislative power, the ability to pass laws is granted to the Leading Body of the Area.[75] The legislative power covers a narrow list that includes matters such as the provision of electricity and the prevention of fires. The list is composed of three types of matters: local development and public services; the environment; and the local economy. Even if an Area does legislate in these areas, an Area law is subordinate to both State/Region law, as well as Union Government laws.[76] In terms of the judiciary, the Areas should include an Area-level court, the District Court (in Wa Division) and the township courts.[77]

B. Conflict and Ceasefires in the Wa, Kokang, Pa-O and Palaung Areas

Four Areas – the Wa, Kokang, Pa-O and Palaung – emerged from ceasefire deals of the 1990s. Of these Areas, it is the Wa that pose the most

---

[72] 2008 Constitution, s 9.
[73] Ibid, s 61(a).
[74] Law No 17/2010, ss 38, 45, 41.
[75] 2008 Constitution, s 275, Sch 3.
[76] Ibid, s 198(c) and (d).
[77] Union Judiciary Law No 20/2010, s 42(b) and (c).

significant threat to a contemporary nationwide ceasefire given their relative strength, wealth and self-sufficiency from the Union Government. The Wa and Kokang Zones share a similar history in terms of their relations with the Union Government and both are in Shan State. Up until the late 1980s, both were part of the Communist Party of Burma (CPB), until they entered ceasefire deals with SLORC and received certain concessions in return. The constitutional status as a Zone was granted to these two groups as part of the broader process of the ceasefire deals with these ethnic armed organisations.

From the 1960s until late 1980s, the Wa were one of the biggest forces in the CPB, which posed the most significant military threat to the regime at the time.[78] By January 1968, the CPB had also entered the Kokang area. Support for the CPB waned in the late 1980s, however, after it took steps to oppose the drug trade, which many national races relied on as a source of income. In March 1989, the Kokang opposed the leadership of the CPB. In April 1989, Wa troops took the strategic base of Panghsang and drove the CPB leadership across the border into China. Because of the break with the CPB, new lines of communication were opened with the military junta. In 1989, the Kokang entered into a ceasefire agreement with the Tatmadaw. The Kokang could keep their arms and control of all their territory, known as the Shan State Special Region 1 (North). The Tatmadaw also provided the Kokang army with money, cars and food, and permitted the growing of opium.[79]

In 1989, the Wa with the assistance of Lo Hsing-han, a former drug lord from Shan State, entered a ceasefire deal with the regime as represented by General Khin Nyunt. The United Wa State Army (UWSA) was similarly given food, fuel and funding by SLORC, and could continue its drugs trade and the extraction of natural resources in Shan State Special Region 2 (North).[80] As the Wa were part of the first round of ceasefires, they benefited from higher rewards and a lack of restrictions in comparison to later ceasefire deals. The UWSA is the largest armed organisation and is infamous for recruiting child soldiers and engaging in the illegal export of weapons. The gap between the elite leaders and the rest of the Wa community is stark. One reason for this is the challenges caused by a lack of citizenship. The 2014 census found close to 95 per cent of the

---

[78] See Bertil Linter, *The Rise and Fall of the Communist Party of Burma* (Ithaca, NY, Cornell University Press, 1990).
[79] Zaw Oo and Win Min, *Assessing Burma's Ceasefire Accords* (Washington, DC, East-West Center, 2007) 15; Linter, above n 78, p 53.
[80] Ibid.

population does not have a national registration card and most derive a livelihood from subsistence agriculture. The high levels of food insecurity, illiteracy and an absence of land rights perpetuates a cycle of poverty.[81]

The ceasefire deals were generous and extended beyond the territorial boundaries of the recognised regions of each group. The Wa and Kokang were given profitable jade mines in Kachin State, because areas like the Wa Hills have no minerals of its own.[82] The ceasefires also came with significant concessions for a handful of elite ethnic leaders. The past two decades have seen these leaders amass terrible wealth. For example, in 2009, Wei Xuegang, a leader of the Wa, is alleged to have built a house worth $60 million near Panghsang, close to the border of Yunnan province. While ethnic armed leaders have in recent decades accumulated significant wealth, and with that power, they remain closely dependent on China. The Wa region is often likened to the 'Crimea' of China or even a colony of China.[83] Some leaders of the Wa and Kokang do not speak Burmese, and many also live in China itself. Both the Wa and Kokang maintain close ties with China, including with officials and intelligence agents from Yunnan. Some Chinese have been granted Myanmar identity cards with their ethnicity noted as Wa or Kokang.[84]

There continue to be disputes between the Union Government and the Wa. For example, in 2008, the Wa Region was the only part of the country that returned a majority 'no' vote in the constitutional referendum, even refusing access to election authorities prior to the poll, resulting in the ballot being cancelled in areas not under Union Government control.[85] In the Wa Area, there is no Self-Administered Area structure as elections were not able to be held.[86] In these regions, institutions of the Union Government are minimal or non-existent.

The Wa aspire to greater powers of autonomy, with reference to the autonomous zones of China. In 2010, the UWSA submitted a proposal

---

[81] Naomi Hellman, 'Separation and Integration on the Sino-Burmese Frontier: Wa Autonomous Spaces', paper presented at ANU Update 2017.

[82] Magnus Fiskesjö, 'Mining, History, and the Anti-state Wa' (2010) 5(2) *Journal of Global History* 241–264.

[83] Hellman, above n 81.

[84] Mary Callahan, *Political Authority in Burma's Ethnic Minority States* (Washington, DC, East-West Center, 2007), p 21.

[85] Transnational Institute, 'A Changing Ethnic Landscape: Analysis of Burma's 2010 Polls' (Burma Policy Briefing No 4, 2010), available at www.tni.org/files/download/bpb4final.pdf.

[86] Kim Joliffe, *Ethnic Armed Conflict and Territorial Administration in Myanmar* (Yangon, The Asia Foundation, 2015).

to the Burmese Army for the inclusion of three more townships as part of the Wa Area, on the ground that in 1948 these regions were marked as inhabited by Wa people. In 2011, a new bilateral ceasefire was signed but despite this, there remain calls for greater independence and recognition. Although the Wa attended the 2017 Union Peace Conference, the Wa walked out of the second 21-Panglong Conference due to disagreements. The UWSA had not yet signed the National Ceasefire Agreement.

In 2015, in an unusual move, the Kokang Self-Administered Zone Leading Body relinquished its powers to the Union Government because of the heavy fighting in that area and the declaration of the constitutional state of emergency. On 12 February 2015, a section 144 order was imposed (see Chapter 3). By 16 February 2015, the chairperson of the Kokang body transferred his power over the region to the General Administration Department. The president declared a state of emergency and a military administrative order. Then on 20 February 2015, the president submitted these orders to the Pyidaungsu Hluttaw to seek its approval in accordance with section 212(b) of the Constitution.[87]

Like the Wa and Kokang, the Pa-O and Palaung also share a history of opposition to the Union Government. Since the 1990s, armed conflict has largely ended in favour of a ceasefire, and which again resulted in constitutional recognition. The Pa-O are related ethnically to the Karen; most adhere to Buddhism and primarily live in south-west Shan State. The Pa-O National Liberation Organisation was formed in 1949 and has at times fought against both the Shan and the government.[88] In the late 1950s, the Pa-O National Liberation Organisation was one of the ethnic armies that took up U Nu's offer of 'arms for democracy' and formed a political party known as the Pa-O National Party.[89] But in the mid-1960s, some Pa-O National Party leaders were arrested after the breakdown of the ceasefires. The CPB formed links with the Pa-O and entered into an understanding that the CPB would supply arms in return for being allowed to operate in the Pa-O area.[90] Following the retreat of the CPB to China, in February 1991, the Pa-O National Party agreed to a ceasefire with the Tatmadaw. As part of the ceasefire deal, the Pa-O were granted logging permits and concessions in the gem-mining industry, and a new generation of ultra-wealthy warlords soon emerged.[91]

---

[87] See PDH2015-12:16.
[88] Callahan, above n 84, p 45.
[89] M Smith, *State of Strife* (Washington, DC, East-West Center, 2007) pp 168–69.
[90] Linter, above n 78, p 29.
[91] Ricky Yue, 'Pacifying the Margins: The Pa-O Self-Administered Zones', in Nick Cheesman and Nicholas Farrelly (eds) *Conflict in Myanmar* (Singapore: ISEAS, 2016) pp 91–120.

Unlike the Pa-O, it was not until 1962 that the Palaung formed a resistance army against the regime. The Palaung people are related to the Mon-Khmer, and most identify themselves as Buddhist, with a small percentage being animist or Christian. The population is estimated to number over one million, spread across Shan State with a concentration in the north-west, although they also live in northern Thailand and south-west China. In the late 1980s the Palaung State Liberation Party (PSLP), like many other armed groups, was affected by the junta's 'four cuts' program, a strategy that aimed to target ethnic armies' supplies of food, finances, information and recruits. In 1991, the Palaung State Liberation Army (PSLA) entered a ceasefire, and the area it controlled came to be known as Shan State Special Region 7. The agreement allowed the PSLP to maintain the area it already held and were promised financial and development assistance. Since 2011, there has been ongoing conflict with the armed wing of the PSLP, known as the Ta'ang National Liberation Army (TNLA), and this conflict has displaced over 2,000 people. In addition to conflict, the TNLA are dissatisfied with the borders of their Area. In 2013, the TNLA called for the expansion of the Palaung Area from two to 12 townships, and they contested the official population figures.[92] Similar to the Wa, the Palaung continue to call on the Union Government for greater recognition than has currently been granted, such as by adding more townships as part of existing Area.

In 2010, in all four of these Areas except the Wa, former ethnic armed leaders were appointed into positions in the Area.[93] If the 1990s cessation of conflict and granting of concessions was the first stage of the ceasefire deals, and the second stage was constitutional recognition granted as part of the National Convention process, then the third and final stage was the appointment of ethnic armed leaders to the Leading Body of the Areas.

C. The Danu and Naga Administered Areas

The final two Areas – the Danu and Naga – are the only two Areas that did not arise from 1990s ceasefire agreements. While the Danu Area is in Shan State, it is the only national race of the six that was not in armed conflict with the Tatmadaw. The Danu Zone appears to be largely the

---

[92] Nan Tin Htwe, 'No ceasefire but govt and Palaung agree to further talks', *The Myanmar Times*, 4 August 2013.
[93] Joliffe, above n 86.

result of the numerical formulae for Area status and the population count in the 1990s. The Danu Self-administered Area includes two townships, Pindaya township and Ywangan township. The Danu have never had an armed group.

The Naga Area is located outside of Shan State, and its status reduces the perception that the Areas aimed to undermine unity in Shan State. Outside of Shan State, the Naga Self-administered Area is in Sagaing Region and includes three townships. The Naga were one of the ethnic groups who served in World War II alongside the British. The area populated by the Naga has had a history of conflict and includes the Naga on both sides of the border with India. While there have been past attempts to unite the Naga across the borders, in 1988 the Burmese Naga drove the Indian Naga out of their base. The National Socialist Council of Nagaland fought against the Tatmadaw although never to the same extent as other armed groups in Shan State. In April 2012, a bilateral ceasefire agreement was signed, which included an agreement to stop all fighting and provided for further discussions on steps towards settlement. The Naga have yet to sign the National Ceasefire Agreement.[94]

Most Areas are closer in terms of culture, language and trade to either India or China than to Myanmar. For example, the Indian Government and India-based companies have provided development assistance for education, health and infrastructure projects to the Naga Area. Similarly, China's support for the Wa Zones and Kokang Zones is also evident, although it is not proclaimed in terms of development aid. The designation of the Naga Zone has also seen a renewal of overt government sponsorship of annual ethnic celebrations. For example, on 15 January 2013, as part of the Naga New Year celebration,[95] the Deputy Minister for Border Affairs gave official financial assistance for the development of the Naga Zone. But this practice of publicly reported displays of gifts to national races is not new, and it portrays an image of the Areas as dependent on the goodwill of the Union Government.

There remain issues of contention between the Union Government and the Naga concerning the categorisation of the Naga ethnic group. For example, the Naga contest their classification as one of the 53 Chin tribes. In March 2013, a public statement issued by several

---

[94] *The Irrawaddy*, 'Naga Armed Group Holds Rare Meeting with Govt' 28 Dec 2017, www.irrawaddy.com/news/naga-armed-group-holds-rare-meeting-govt.html.

[95] *Myanmar Update*, 'Naga Self-Administered Zone Organises New Year Celebration on 15 January', 23 January 2013, www.myanmarupdate.com/naga-self-administered-zone-organizes-new-year-celebration-on-15-january/.

Naga organisations based in 'Yangon' called on the government to list the Naga as a separate ethnic tribe on the official government list.[96] The contested nature of the list of 135 national races, as the pretext around which these constitutional forms of recognition are built, highlights the arbitrary nature of this classification system. Further, the status as an Area has not necessarily reduced the demands of national races for greater recognition.

IV. CONCLUSION

When considered in historical context, and with the intention of the constitution-drafters in mind, the purpose of 2008 Constitution was to create a unitary system, not a federal system. The idea of a Union was co-opted to placate ethnic demands, but falls short of ideas first articulated by General Aung San or what is referred to as a genuine federal Union.

For ethnic minorities, the 2008 Constitution does not offer a substantive federal arrangement. Both ideas of federalism and democracy are compromised and weakened at the subnational level. State/Region governments are on a tight leash, being appointed by the president, responsible to the Union Government and must assist the Union Government when required. The lack of substantive legislative powers and the absence of an administrative department that is separate and independent from the Union leaves the State/Region Hluttaw and government weak and dependent. Lines of appointment, allocation of responsibilities and accountability are centralised in the Union Government and president, from the position of Chief Minister to Ministers for National Races Affairs. The Self-Administered Areas also suffer from narrow legislative and executive powers, and the presence of Tatmadaw officers in the leading body.

Calls for a 'genuine' federal Union continue. The existing constitutional structures could be a part of a future federal system if sub-national powers are enhanced, the lines of accountability decentralised and subunits allowed to be fully democratic. This is one reason why it is important to consider how the designation of States/Regions, the creation of

---

[96] Thawng Zel Thang, 'We are an indigenous people in Burma, Naga', *Chinland Guardian*, 16 March 2013, www.chinlandguardian.com/index.php/cartoons/item/1832-we-are-an-indigenous-people-in-burma-naga.

Ministers of National Races Affairs and the Self-Administered Areas have begun to work in practice.

Central to calls for federalism in Myanmar are claims to autonomy and self-determination. Yet the Constitution makes no reference to autonomy or self-determination. In fact, the Constitution explicitly prohibits any possibility of secession. The prohibition on secession is mentioned in the Basic Principles, and applies to the States/Regions, the Union Territories, and the Self-Administered Areas.[97] The issue of a 'non-secession' clause, as a key aspect of any federal bargain, remains a key sticking point for ethnic armed organisations in the 21-Panglong Conference (see Chapter 9). To date, neither the Tatmadaw nor the NLD Government appear willing to accede to this constitutional demand.

FURTHER READING

Mary Callahan, *Political Authority in Burma's Ethnic Minority States* (Washington, DC, East-West Center, 2007).

Nick Cheesman, 'How in Myanmar "National Races" Came to Surpass Citizenship and Exclude Rohingya' (2017) 47:3, *Journal of Contemporary Asia*, 461–483.

Melissa Crouch, 'Ethnic Rights and Constitutional Change' in Andrew Harding and Mark Sidel (eds) *Central-local Relations in Asian Constitutional Systems* (Hart Publishing, 2015) pp 105–124.

Jane M Ferguson, 'Who's Counting? Ethnicity, Belonging and the National Census in Burma/Myanmar' (2015) 171 *Bijdragen tot de Taal-, Land- en Volkenkunde* 1.

Matthew J Walton, 'The "Wages of Burman-ness:" Ethnicity and Burman Privilege in Contemporary Myanmar' (2013) 43 *Journal of Contemporary Asia* 1.

---

[97] 2008 Constitution, s 10.

8

The Judiciary as an
Administrative Institution

Judicial Power – Judicial Independence – Separation of Powers – General
Courts – Constitutional Review

T HE COURTS ARE on the periphery of the constitutional system in
Myanmar. The judiciary features in the Basic Principles of the
Constitution, which identifies the Supreme Court, High Courts
and Self-Administered Area courts.[1] The Basic Principles include three
judicial ideals: independence in adjudication of disputes, to ensure an
open court, and to ensure the right of defence and the right to appeal.
The actual protection of these principles is determined and conditioned
by law passed by the legislature, and so is heavily qualified. There is a
gap between the written portrait of the courts in the Constitution as
a separate and independent branch, and the reality of interference by
other branches of government and by the Tatmadaw. More than any
other part of the administration, the courts are prone to pressure from
the Tatmadaw through the police force and township administration.
A closer look at judges themselves reveals the connections between the
judiciary and the Tatmadaw.

Myanmar's judiciary, like the General Administration Department
(see Chapter 3), is an institution that pre-dates the 2008 Constitution.[2]
The challenge for the courts is whether and how its pre-existing practices
fit with new constitutional statements and institutions. The position of
the courts contrasts with that of the legislature, which is an entirely new
institution. The courts have a conflicted history that at times does not fit
with the constitutional text. In this chapter I consider the constitutional
text and reality of both judicial institutions and judicial power, including

---

[1] 2008 Constitution, s 18.
[2] This chapter deals with ss 293–336 of the 2008 Constitution (Ch VI The Judiciary).

the Supreme Court, High Courts, District and Township Courts, and Township Administrators, as well as the Constitutional Tribunal. The courts form a unitary system and operate as an administrative institution to serve the interests of the political elite in the military-state.

The primary constitutional issue is the numerous challenges to the constitutional statement of judicial independence. The executive determines the make-up of the courts, the legislature oversees the courts in terms of accountability, while the Tatmadaw has an indirect oversight role through the General Administration Department and the police.[3]

I. THE UNION SUPREME COURT

The Supreme Court is the epitome of institutional stasis and illustrates the tendency towards administrative legality that pervades the judiciary. The Supreme Court was re-established in 1988, after the abolition of the socialist-era Chief Court. The period from 1988 to 2010 was marked by military-executive discretion in court affairs in the absence of a constitution.[4] Post-2010, there are constitutional and legal provisions that establish a clearer process for the selection, tenure and removal of judges of the Supreme Court. The executive and legislature have direct influence over the courts, while the Tatmadaw has an indirect influence over the composition and functioning of the Supreme Court.

A. Judicial Appointments and Removal

The constitutional framework grants the executive, as represented by the president, significant powers over the Supreme Court through appointments and removals. The president nominates the Chief Justice of the Supreme Court and the legislature cannot object to the nomination unless the candidate does not meet the selection criteria.[5]

---

[3] This is well-known in Myanmar: see Pyae Thet Phyo and Swan Ye Htut, 'Yellow ribbons seek an end to militarised judiciary', 10 September 2015, *The Myanmar Times*, www.mmtimes.com/index.php/national-news/nay-pyi-taw/16400-yellow-ribbons-seek-an-end-to-militarised-judiciary.html.

[4] Myint Zan, 'The New Supreme Court and the Constitutional Tribunal' in N Cheesman et al (eds) *Myanmar's Transitions: Openings, Obstacles and Opportunities* (Singapore, ISEAS, 2012).

[5] 2008 Constitution, s 299.

In February 2011, U Htun Htun Oo was nominated as Chief Justice, having previously served as Deputy Chief Justice. He is an example of a transfer from the Tatmadaw legal apparatus to the civilian courts. In the 1980s, Htun Htun Oo was a captain in the Southwest military command. From 1990, he served in the Military Advocate's General Office. In 2007, he was appointed as Deputy Chief Justice of the Supreme Court. The personal connection between the Chief Justice of the Supreme Court and the Tatmadaw is one indication of the broader relationship of loyalty shown by the courts to the Tatmadaw.[6]

Aside from the Chief Justice, several judges of the Supreme Court also have military backgrounds. Most members of the bench were appointed in 2011 and worked for decades within the judicial and administrative system of the military regime. This includes former prosecutors; and career judges. In June 2017, for the first time since the 2011 political transition, four new judges were appointed to the Supreme Court bench:[7] one was a former law officer, one a former judge and director-general of the Supreme Court; and two career lawyers. Of these, it is the last two appointments that are unusual, as it has been rare in the past few decades for advocates to be appointed as judges. All current judges on the Supreme Court are men and there has never been a female judge on the Supreme Court, past or present.

There is a centralised appointment process. The president has authority to determine the composition of the bench of the Supreme Court and all 14 State/Region High Courts, providing candidates meet the selection criteria. This creates a structural advantage of executive control over entry to the Supreme Court. The criteria for appointment to the Supreme Court or High Court is relatively broad, allowing the president significant discretion.[8] Candidates must be between 50 and 70 years old, and meet the requirements for legislative candidates (see Chapter 5). A candidate must be loyal to the Union, and this demand of allegiance is implicitly connected to the three principles of the military-state (see Chapter 3). A judge cannot be a member of the Hluttaw, a civil servant nor a member of a political party.[9] This rule effects a formal separation between the judiciary and the other branches in terms of

---

[6] *Mizzima*, 'President changes his Chief Justice Nominee', 17 February 2011, http://archive-1.mizzima.com/news/myanmar/4895-president-changes-his-chief-justice-nominee.

[7] See President's Office Notification on the Appointment of Supreme Court Judges 2018.

[8] 2008 Constitution, s 301.

[9] Ibid, s 300.

political affiliations, which is the same as the formal separation rule between the legislature and executive. A candidate must be a lawyer, judge, law officer (prosecutor) or judicial officer with years of experience depending on their position, or an 'eminent jurist' in the opinion of the President. Only two of the current judges of the Supreme Court are career lawyers, the rest have connections to the former military administration either as military Judges' Advocate General or serving in the civil service under military rule as public prosecutors, judges, law officers or judicial officers.

Once appointed, the tenure of judges of the Supreme Court is until the set retirement age of 70 years.[10] This age limit is important because, as Myint Zan has observed, under the military regime, U Aung Toe served as Chief Justice for 22 years until he was in his 80s.[11] The retirement age has been subject to proposals for constitutional amendment. In 2015, two bills on constitutional amendment were discussed and voted on in the legislature. Part of the proposal was to limit the terms of the judges of the Supreme Court to five years so that the term is tied to the duration of the government (see Chapter 10). Although this proposal was unsuccessful, it indicates a desire on the part of some legislators to further control the courts. This is because the legislature sees itself as a 'check' on the power of the courts, rather than the courts as a legitimate check on the power of the executive and legislature.

There have not yet been efforts to remove judges of the Supreme Court through the constitutional process.[12] The process for removal can be initiated by the president or the legislature. The grounds for removal are the same as for the president. The process requires an investigation body to be established with legislators at either the Union or State/Region level. As head of the executive, the president, or the chief minister of the State/Region, essentially has the power to act as the prosecutor against the accused judge by bringing evidence and witnesses before the investigation body. If the motion relates to a judge of the High Court, the process requires one quarter of the support of the members of the State/Region Hluttaw, which means that Tatmadaw officers, who occupy 25 per cent of seats in the legislature, can bring an impeachment motion without the support of civilian legislators. This is another example of a structural rule in favour of the Tatmadaw.

---

[10] Ibid, s 303.
[11] Myint Zan, above n 4, p 254.
[12] 2008 Constitution, s 302.

B. Role and Function of the Supreme Court

The Supreme Court has five core roles: original jurisdiction; appellate and revision authority; a supervisory role over the lower courts; law reporting; and a law-making function. In its exclusive or original jurisdiction, the Supreme Court can hear matters arising from bilateral treaties, disputes between the Union Government and State/Region governments, or disputes among State/Region governments that are not of a constitutional nature. It also has authority to issue the writs of habeas corpus, mandamus, prohibition, quo warranto and certiorari as remedies against unlawful government decisions (see Chapter 9). Excluded from its authority is the power to retrospectively hear penal cases, a rule which functions to protect the Tatmadaw and former government from prosecutions for past crimes. The Supreme Court also cannot hear matters of constitutional law, although it can refer these matters to the Constitutional Tribunal. The distribution of constitutional review power to the Tribunal is perceived as a diminution of the authority of the Supreme Court and talks of abolishing the Constitutional Tribunal have often been linked to the idea of transferring constitutional review power to the Supreme Court. This reform on its own would not necessarily facilitate greater independence in the hearing of constitutional review cases.

The Supreme Court can hear appeals from the State/Region High Courts. It is the final court of appeal, yet the Constitution allows for several additional ways to seek review of decisions of the Supreme Court. There is a right to appeal in all cases concerning the death penalty and the Supreme Court must approve all decisions for the death penalty (see Chapter 9). There is also an avenue of special appeal for cases heard in the Supreme Court. The Supreme Court has discretion to review a court decision under its revisional jurisdiction although unlike in an appeal, it cannot consider new evidence. In short, there are multiple possibilities for appeal in most cases. These avenues for appeal channel the discontent of the losing party to bolster the legitimacy of the system. This means that appellate institutions support the political purpose of control as intended by the regime. Cheesman has suggested that appeals are in part a result of corruption and the practice of double cropping, where judges at both the original and appellate level can take a cut of bribes.[13]

---

[13] Nick Cheesman, *Opposing the Rule of Law: How Myanmar's Courts Make Law and Order* (CUP, 2015) p 189; Nick Cheesman, 'Myanmar's Courts and the Sounds Money Makes', in Monique Skidmore and Trevor Wilson (eds) *Myanmar's Transition* (ISEAS, 2012).

While this is true in many cases, the provision of multiple opportunities to appeal also operates to justify and reinforce the administrative role of the courts. At the same time as the Supreme Court operates as the final court of appeal, its status as a Union Level Organisation means that its decisions are also 'final and conclusive'. This means that decisions of the Supreme Court cannot be subject to review.[14]

Aside from original and appellate jurisdiction, the Supreme Court has administrative and oversight powers of all fourteen High Courts (one in each State/Region). The supervisory role of the Supreme Court also extends to prisons, which the judges can inspect in order to check that the rights of individuals are being upheld while in detention. The Supreme Court's role in supervising prisons has existed since 1988, yet the scale of political prisoners and the concerns of multiple human rights organisations on the conditions in prison suggest it has not actively exercised this authority (see Chapter 9). The Supreme Court also has the power to submit its own budget to the Pyidaungsu Hluttaw,[15] though in reality this is determined by the Union Government.

In addition to these functions, the Supreme Court exercises legislative power by having authority to draft Bills on certain matters. The Constitution does not specifically grant the Supreme Court legislative power, though many believe it has a role in the drafting process by implication.[16] In the Union Legislative list contained in Schedule 1 of the Constitution, section 11 deals with Judicial Affairs.[17] Any matter that falls under section 11, such as family law matters,[18] insolvency, civil procedure, criminal law and contempt of court,[19] will in the first instance be drafted by a working committee within the Supreme Court. In this respect, the legislature treats the Supreme Court like any other ministry. At times, the legislature has exerted significant pressure on the Supreme Court to draft laws that it has no interest in drafting, or on matters that it disagrees with. This law-making role is left over from the military era, when the Supreme Court had the power to draft laws in a wide range of areas. In addition to its role in drafting legislation, the Supreme Court has the power to issue regulations on court practice and procedure.

---

[14] 2008 Constitution, ss 295(c), 402, 324.

[15] Ibid, s 297.

[16] Ibid, s 298.

[17] See Law 20/2010 on the Judiciary, ss 24 and 65-66.

[18] Melissa Crouch, 'Promiscuity, Polygamy and the Power of Revenge: The Past and Future of Burmese Buddhist Law in Myanmar' (2016) 3(1) *Asian Journal of Law and Society* 85.

[19] Contempt of Court Law No 17/2013.

These regulations are internal documents and are not generally accessible to the wider public.

While the Supreme Court is a judicial institution under the Constitution, it is often treated like an administrative body by the legislature. The constitutional designation of the Supreme Court as a Union Level Organisation (ULO) blurs the separation between judicial and administrative institutions. The legislature has the power to summon judges because the Supreme Court is a ULO.[20] For example, judges of the Supreme Court have been called to the legislature to answer allegations of corruption in the courts. In March 2017, the Pyithu Hluttaw passed a motion directed to the Supreme Court, urging it to rid the judiciary of corruption.[21] When called to the legislature, the Justice, U Soe Nyunt, expressed his concern that the Pyithu Hluttaw was interfering with the judiciary, showing disrespect and insulting the judicial branch without credible evidence. Two months later, in speaking to a session of the Pyithu Hluttaw, the Chief Justice capitulated and conveyed his regret, apologising to the Pyithu Hluttaw.[22] In doing so, the extreme deference of the courts towards the legislature was on display. Judicial submission to the legislature is an example of coercive centralism.

Finally, the Supreme Court has an established practice of annual court reporting. In 2016 there were 12 board members, including four judges of the Supreme Court, the Deputy Attorney General, the Director General of the Attorney General's Office, six judicial officers from the Supreme Court, and one lawyer. The Board determines the selection and reporting of cases for publication in the annual Myanmar Law Reports. The Myanmar Law Reports only include cases of the Supreme Court (not any lower courts), and only include a very small number of cases per year. Unreported cases are generally not made available to the public, although such cases are often summarised and published in books edited by former Director Generals of the court. The accessibility and availability of court decisions may change in the future, depending on the responsiveness of the court to calls for greater transparency. The Supreme Court has begun to build an online public presence, with a website, although its Public

---

[20] 2008 Constitution, s 77(c).

[21] Htoo Thant, 'Hluttaw approves motion to revamp judiciary system after majority votes', *The Myanmar Times*, 9 March 2017, www.mmtimes.com/national-news/nay-pyi-taw/25241-hluttaw-approves-motion-to-revamp-judiciary-system-after-majority-votes.html.

[22] Htoo Thant, 'Supreme Court Judge expresses regret in parliament', *The Myanmar Times*, 24 May 2017, www.mmtimes.com/national-news/nay-pyi-taw/26123-supreme-court-judge-expresses-regret-in-parliament.html.

Relations Facebook page is more active.[23] The Facebook page includes posts on case lists and hearings, advertisements for judicial positions and notifications of judicial promotions or appointments. In the future, this may allow for greater access to court decisions.

II. SUB-NATIONAL COURTS IN A UNITARY JUDICIAL SYSTEM

A. High Courts of the States and Regions

Within this unitary judicial system, there are 14 State and Region High Courts.[24] Each High Court has between three to seven judges.[25] The largest court, Yangon Region High Court, has seven judges, while the smallest, Chin High Court, has three judges. The jurisdiction of the High Courts' extends to original civil and criminal matters, and appeal and revision cases. The High Court can hear civil cases of unlimited monetary value. The Constitution has introduced several major changes for the High Courts, clarified the process of appointment, the criteria for appointment and the process of dismissal.

In 2011, the Thein Sein Government appointed 75 per cent of the High Court judges. In terms of selection criteria, a candidate must be between 45 and 65 years old and meet the requirements of Pyithu Hluttaw candidates (see Chapter 5). They must have work experience as a judicial officer or law officer, or have practised as an Advocate, or be an eminent jurist in the opinion of the president. Like other judges, as well as members of the executive and legislature, High Court candidates must be loyal to the Union and to the three-meta military of the military-state. The Constitution aims to ensure a separation between the courts and other branches by prohibiting judges from being a member of a political party or a member of the legislature. It also requires High Court judges to be free from 'party politics' which, as mentioned in Chapter 5, relates to the portrayal of the Tatmadaw as playing a 'neutral' or apolitical and positive role in governance.[26] The majority of High Court judges are career judges. At least four of the 53 judges previously worked in the Tatmadaw as Judges' Advocates General, three worked in the Attorney General's

---

[23] Facebook is the primary way that people in Myanmar use the internet.
[24] 2008 Constitution, s 305.
[25] Ibid, s 306(a)(ii).
[26] Ibid, s 309(a).

office and seven in the Supreme Court. The majority of High Court judges (72 per cent) are men.

The President has power to appoint the Chief Justices of the 14 State/Region High Courts, in collaboration with the Chief Minister of the State/Region (who is also appointed by the president).[27] The nominee is then approved by the relevant State/Region Hluttaw, although the role of the Hluttaw is token and nominal because it cannot reject candidates who clearly meet the selection criteria. Nominations for judges of the High Court are made by the Chief Minister and the Chief Justice, and the State/Region Hluttaw again approves the nomination.

The retirement age for State/Region High Court judges is 65.[28] This means that the NLD Government will be able to appoint at least 31 High Court judges during its term in office due to retirements alone. The president can initiate the impeachment process of a High Court Chief Justice. The Chief Minister, or one quarter of members of the State/Region Hluttaw, can initiate proceedings against another judge of the High Court.[29] One difference between High Court judges, compared with their lower court counterparts, is that they are not civil servants. This is significant and means they are not bound by the rules of the civil service. High Court judges usually have expertise in the Code of Civil Procedure,[30] the Penal Code, the Code of Criminal Procedure, the Evidence Act,[31] and the Courts Manual 1960. Each High Court oversees the District Courts;[32] Township Courts; and other specialised courts below it, such as the Children's Court.[33]

B. Courts in the Districts and Townships

There are several constitutional and legal differences between the position of judges of the Supreme Court and High Courts, and judges of the lower courts in the military-state. The oversight of the court system is highly centralised and the Union exercises control over sub-national courts. The Constitution leaves all matters to do with the appointment,

---

[27] 2008 Constitution, s 308.
[28] Ibid, s 312.
[29] Ibid, s 311(b), (c), (h).
[30] Code of Criminal Procedure.
[31] Evidence Act 1872, amended Law No 73/2015.
[32] At the same level as District Courts are the six Self-Administered Zone or Division Courts, see Ch 6.
[33] 2008 Constitution, s 314.

discipline and removal of these judges to regulation by the Pyidaungsu Hluttaw.[34] The two main lower courts are the District Courts and Township Courts. The Constitution confirms that District Courts have original criminal and civil jurisdiction, and appellate and revision authority, while Township Courts only have original jurisdiction,[35] dealing with minor criminal offences and civil suits of low monetary value.[36] The primary caseload of the general courts is criminal law matters, and it is the police and prosecutors who exert significant influence over court proceedings of a criminal nature.

Another main difference between these lower courts and the High Court concerns the status of lower court judges as civil servants. Their classification as civil servants mean they are subject to different entrance requirements, promotion, supervision and disciplinary action, according to the Civil Servant Law[37] and regulations. The type of case that can be heard not only depends on the court but also on the status of the judge. There are five levels of judicial service from the District Courts down: District Court judge, Deputy District Court judge, Township Court Judge, Additional Township Judge and Deputy Township Judge. One consequence of being a civil servant is that judges are subject to a rotation system. They may often only serve in one location for three or four years. The location of a judge may depend on whether the purpose of the rotation is for promotion, demotion or disciplinary action, with more rural areas being a means of punishing wayward judges. A more recent change is that judges are now permitted to undertake higher education, which in the past was prohibited. The change in rules means that more judges are obtaining post-graduate education such as masters and diplomas.

There are other consequences of the classification of lower court judges as civil servants. The judges are paid on the same pay scale as civil servants and subject to the same entitlements. It is not possible to increase their pay without also increasing the pay of other civil servants on the same pay scale. This means that efforts to reduce the incentives for corruption by increasing pay are structurally difficult. All matters of selection, promotion and discipline or dismissal are under the responsibility of the Union Civil Service Board (UCSB), not the Supreme Court.

[34] Ibid, ss 317–8.
[35] Ibid, ss 315–6.
[36] Supreme Court Order No 100/2011 and No 101/2011.
[37] Civil Service Law No 5/2013.

The UCSB is appointed and responsible to the president and serves the same five-year term as the government.[38] It has a constitutional mandate to select and train all civil servants. The UCSB is part of the system of coercive centralism, as it ensures Union Government control over civil servants at the sub-national level. The UCSB oversees training at the Judicial Training Institute, although the Supreme Court has also made the training of judges a future priority. There is no debate over whether a judge's status as a civil servant compromises their ability to act independently from the administration.

C. The Judicial Power of Township Administrators

Most people in Myanmar do not have any interaction with the courts. In some disputes, local matters may be adjudicated by township administrators. Like parts of the former British empire, it was common in colonial Burma for executive administrators to also exercise judicial power. This practice continued at the lower levels of government into the parliamentary democracy era. From 1972, the socialist government established a system of People's Courts, although many existing judges were replaced with administrators. This system represented a merger of judicial and administrative functions. After 1988, the power of township administrators (many of whom were military officers) increased and they exercised some adjudicative powers at the local level. In 2011, an historic Constitutional Tribunal case that confirmed that the Supreme Court could no longer delegate first class magistrates' power to the General Administration Department (GAD) because it would breach the constitutional separation of powers. In this case, the Supreme Court questioned the constitutionality of a request of the Ministry of Home Affairs to appoint sub-township administrative officers to adjudicate minor criminal cases. The Supreme Court challenged this request for overstepping the judiciary's role by giving a judicial function to administrative officers. The Supreme Court was successful in arguing that the request of the Ministry of Home Affairs was beyond its power.[39] In its decision, the Tribunal recognised that the previous military regime had appointed administrative officers to positions where they were required to adjudicate minor criminal offences. The Tribunal drew a clear distinction between the previous regime's practices and the requirement of the

---

[38] 2008 Constitution, s 246.
[39] Constitutional Tribunal, Judicial Power Case No 1/2011.

separation of the three branches of government according to the Constitution. Although section 11(a) of the Constitution appears to keep open the potential compromise of the separation of powers, the Tribunal upheld the separation between the judiciary and executive. This was a very significant case. The Supreme Court can no longer delegate first class magistrates' power to the GAD (although as noted below, it is still given some judicial powers under the Penal Code and Code of Criminal Procedure). The Supreme Court issued a directive following this decision to revoke the authority of township administrators to exercise judicial power, although this was understood to only revoke the judicial powers of a first-class magistrate.[40]

The General Administration Department functions as the administration for the States/Regions, according to the Constitution (see Chapter 3). It is a centralised department that until 2019 came under the supervision of the Ministry of Home Affairs. In 2017, a draft Bill on the Township Administration was debated.[41] This draft Bill seeks to upgrade the existing functions of administrators in regulations and rules to the status of legislative mandate. Township administrators would have the power to issue directives for public order, safety and security, and have powers of arrest. Township administrators are delegated powers under the Criminal Procedure Code, and specifically in relation to gambling[42] and habitual offenders,[43] all of which are supposed to be the power of a judge or the police. These powers include: to compel the production of a document or issue a search warrant; to require security for good behaviour or if they are at risk of sedition, intimidation or defamation or other offences under the Penal Code; to issue a warrant for arrest; to issue an order for an unlawful assembly to disperse; to arrest those who refuse to disperse or use military force to disperse the assembly; to regulate or prohibit a wide range of public nuisance issues from trade, commerce to buildings and wildlife; section 144 orders (see also Chapter 3); to make orders concerning interference with property; to order that property be surrendered, or redistribute that property to any person who may have a claim to it or, if not, to sell property.[44] This draft law confers on administrators authority over a wide range of minor criminal offences and local dispute resolution issues.

---

[40] Supreme Court Directive No 232/2011, 18 July 2011.
[41] Township Administration draft law, 2017.
[42] Gambling Act 1990, revised 2014.
[43] The Habitual Offenders Restriction Act 1961.
[44] See Criminal Procedure Code: ss 95–96; 107; 108–9; 127–9; 133; 144; 145–6; 523–5.

Township administrators also have powers under the Gambling Law[45] and the Habitual Offenders Restriction Act.[46] The later law dates from the colonial era and has been used against political opponents. Under the act, a person is put under permanent bail, forcing them to sign in with local authorities daily. For example, in July 1998, the Tatmadaw used this law against NLD legislators (who had not yet been convicted of a crime) to restrict their activities. They were prevented from leaving their house or their area without prior permission from authorities. 79 MPs were detained and charged for refusing to follow this reporting procedure.[47] This is just one example of the significant powers that township administrators have exercised as the institution most proximate to the people in Myanmar.

Finally, it is important to note the superior status and power that township administrators enjoy over the township courts in the military-state. One example in 2018 illustrates this adeptly. A township court had issued a letter to the township administrator summoning them to appear as a witness in a case.[48] The township administrator responded with hostility, reprimanding the court for the lack of respect it showed the administrator. In the letter, the township administrator reminded the court that the administrator was *above* every other institution including the courts. It instructed the court to use more respectful language in future summons letters, to indicate the superiority of the administration. While the NLD has indicated it will transfer the GAD to the Ministry of the Union Government, this is unlikely to change the relationship between township administrators and the courts in the short term.

III. THE CONSTITUTIONAL TRIBUNAL

Sitting distinct in the judicial hierarchy, and removed from the people, is the Constitutional Tribunal. The Tribunal is not a court for the people and it handles very few cases compared to the court system described above. The Basic Principles of the Constitution recognise the Constitutional Tribunal as the forum for all constitutional disputes, other

---

[45] Gambling Law 14/1990, s 4(b).

[46] Habitual Offenders Act 1961, amended by Law No 6/2015.

[47] Human Rights Documentation Unit (HRDU) *Human Rights Yearbook 1998*. National Coalition Government of the Union of Burma.

[48] Letter of the Ingapu Township Administration, 26 March 2018, (on file, in Burmese).

than the constitutional writs.[49] The Constitutional Tribunal is the first *separate* judicial institution in Myanmar to have power to review statutes for unconstitutionality.[50] From 2011 to 2018, the Tribunal heard and published decisions in 13 cases, and issued several advisory decisions. Many have suggested that the low number of cases that the Tribunal has heard is a reason in favour of abolishing the Tribunal. Although Myanmar identifies as a common law legal system, it has a Constitutional Tribunal based on a civil law model. Concerns about the Tribunal's small caseload and civil law attributes are a nominal justification for the strong negative sentiment towards the Tribunal. The real issues relate to the perceived capture of the Constitutional Tribunal by the President's Office, and to a lesser extent its structural features that mean it is an elite institution[51] and is not open to individuals or civil society.[52] In short, the Constitutional Tribunal lacks authority and legitimacy.

The operation and powers of the Tribunal are heavily conditioned by the political environment in which it operates. The Tribunal has imposed its own severe restrictions on its jurisdiction and at times has succumbed to a conservative nationalist agenda.

A. Tribunal Member Appointments and Removals

Both the issue of appointments and removals from the Tribunal are a heated point of contention. The Tribunal consists of nine members and the selection process is in the hands of the legislature and the president. Three of the Tribunal members are chosen respectively by the president, the speaker of the Pyithu Hluttaw and the speaker of the Amyotha Hluttaw.[53] A person cannot be appointed to the Tribunal while they are a member of the Hluttaw, the civil service or a political party.[54] Like the rest of the administration, Tribunal members must be seen to be independent of political parties and the legislature. While this suggests a formal division between the branches of government, there is no time

---

[49] 2008 Constitution, s 46.

[50] Under the 1947 Constitution, the Supreme Court could consider constitutional questions from the President.

[51] Dominic Nardi, 'Discipline-Flourishing Constitutional Review' (2010) 12(1) *Australian Journal of Asian Law* 1–34.

[52] Specific policy suggestions for reform by a local scholar are contained in Khin Khin Oo, 'Judicial Power and the Constitutional Tribunal' in Andrew Harding and Khin Khin Oo (eds) *Constitutionalism and Legal Change in Myanmar* (Hart Publishing, 2017).

[53] 2008 Constitution, s 321.

[54] Ibid, s 330.

limit to prevent a person who is part of the Tatmadaw, executive or legislative branch from being appointed directly to the bench. For example, in 2016, an elected legislator and NLD member was appointed directly to the bench of the Constitutional Tribunal. If they have given up their prior position on commencing their role as Tribunal member, the person meets the relevant requirements. The first Tribunal bench (2011–2012) was elected by a legislature that primarily consisted of the military-backed USDP political party, the 25 per cent of Tatmadaw representatives in the legislature, and ethnic national political parties. Once elected, the length of tenure of the Tribunal members is five years.[55] On expiry of its term, the bench continues until the new president initiates the process for the selection of a new bench. The bench is therefore tied to the current government of the day, reducing both real and perceived institutional independence.

In terms of leadership, the chairperson is nominated by the president, which means that the head of the Tribunal is selected by the executive. The president's nomination can only be refused by the Pyidaungsu Hluttaw if the proposed candidate does not fulfil the requirements under the law.[56] Again, like other judicial appointments, this gives a weak role to the Pyidaungsu Hluttaw in the selection process. These qualifications require a candidate to be over 50 years old; meet the qualifications for Pyithu Hluttaw representations; and must have either served for the required minimum number of years as a judge of a State/Region High Court or as a judicial officer or law officer (public prosecutor) at the State/Region level; as an Advocate (lawyer); or be, in the opinion of the president, an 'eminent jurist'.[57] While attention has been drawn to the potential abuse in allowing the president to appoint an 'eminent jurist' as a vague category, this appeared in the 1947 and 1974 Constitution and may be similar to the tradition of appointing academics as judges. In 2016, the issue over who can appoint an 'eminent jurist' was raised with the Tribunal.[58] Members of the Amyotha Hluttaw (including some Tatmadaw members), challenged the decision of the president to appoint two Tribunal members. There were differences between the constitutional provisions and the Constitutional Tribunal Law over who can elect a member based on the criterion of 'eminent jurist'.

---

[55] Ibid, s 335.
[56] Ibid, s 328.
[57] Ibid, s 333.
[58] Constitutional Tribunal, Eminent Persons Requirement Case 1/2016.

The Constitution suggests that only the president can nominate a member on the basis of being an eminent jurist, while the law suggests that either the president, the Speaker of the Pyithu Hluttaw or the Speaker of the Amyotha Hluttaw can nominate a member as long as the president considers the person to be an eminent jurist. On the other hand, the law suggests that only the president can make such a recommendation of a person who is an eminent jurist.[59] The Tribunal was asked to consider whether it is constitutional for the Speakers of the Amyotha Hluttaw and Pyithu Hluttaw to recommend a person as a member as long as the president considers the person to be an eminent jurist. The applicants argued that it was unconstitutional. The Tribunal held that it was constitutional, but rejected the case on a separate issue.

Controversy has also surrounded the impeachment proceedings and voluntary (or forced) resignation of members. In its decision in 2012, the Constitutional Tribunal was perceived to have sided with the president against the legislature (see Chapter 5).[60] The legislature-initiated impeachment proceedings against the entire bench. By August 2012, a petition for impeachment circulated among the Pyithu Hluttaw. The Amyotha Hluttaw then initiated the formal impeachment process with all non-Tatmadaw members agreeing to the proposal.[61] The Tribunal members were accused of inefficiently undertaking their duties under section 333 of the Constitution. The Pyithu Hluttaw established an investigation committee, but in September the members submitted their resignation in writing to the president.[62] While the Tribunal members exercised their 'right to resign' under the Constitution, the circumstances suggest they resigned rather than be forced out. This necessitated the appointment of an entirely new bench that was established in February 2013.

B. Limited Jurisdiction

The Tribunal's primary mandate is the adjudication of cases for constitutional review of laws and determining the constitutionality of executive decisions. The Tribunal hears cases for constitutional review of laws

---

[59] 2008 Constitution, s 333(d); Constitutional Tribunal Law, s 4(b).
[60] Constitutional Tribunal, Legislative Committees Case 1/2012.
[61] See PDH2012-4:11.
[62] 2008 Constitution, s 331.

issued at either the Union, State/Region or Self-Administered Area level.[63] The Tribunal has clarified that it cannot review draft laws but only laws that have been approved by the legislature and the president. In 2014, this was the key issue in a case concerning the draft Bill regarding proportional representation.[64] As the draft Bill had not been passed, the Tribunal dismissed the case on the basis that it could not review a draft law.

The Tribunal also has power to hear matters concerning executive decisions of the President or other executive actors at the Union, State/Region or Self-Administered Area level.[65] This potentially allows the Tribunal to review any order, decree, regulation or directive of an executive body to determine whether it is in breach of the Constitution. In 2014, a case initiated by the Speaker of the Kachin State Hluttaw asked the Tribunal to decide whether the Kachin State Government's decision to refuse to approve the state budget was constitutional, and whether the decision of the government to fund the construction of a garden is beyond the legislative power of the state government under Schedule 2 of the Constitution (see Chapter 7).[66]

The Tribunal has responsibility for any other duties that the Pyidaungsu Hluttaw chooses to confer on it by law.[67] For example, the Tribunal has been asked to provide advice to the president's office and to provide training to the Tatmadaw on constitutional law.

The Tribunal's authority to issue final decisions has come under repeated and deliberate attack by the legislature. A related issue is whether an application for an 'interpretation' has different consequences to an application for a 'decision', and whether an advisory decision has the same effect as a final decision. The Tribunal has power to make decisions that are final and conclusive under the Constitution.[68] In late 2012, after the impeachment of the Tribunal members the year prior, a USDP member of Parliament in the Amyotha Hluttaw submitted a proposal to amend the Constitutional Tribunal Law.[69] Tatmadaw legislators objected to the amendments proposed on the grounds it would impair judicial independence and contradict the Constitution. This view was also endorsed by the Attorney General. There were five proposed

---

[63] Ibid, s 322(a)–(b).
[64] Constitutional Tribunal, Draft Law Case 5/2014.
[65] 2008 Constitution, s 322(c), (f).
[66] Constitutional Tribunal, Kachin Budget Case 4/2014.
[67] 2008 Constitution, s 322(g).
[68] Ibid, s 324.
[69] See AH2012-5:13.

changes and a majority voted in favour of all five proposals, with the Tatmadaw members voting no. In the Pyithu Hluttaw,[70] Justice Soe Nyunt of the Supreme Court was invited to give his opinion. He argued that the changes would be inconsistent and unconstitutional. The Pyithu Hluttaw nevertheless approved the Bill. After the president approved the law,[71] it was enacted by the Pyidaungsu Hluttaw.[72] This was an effort by the legislature to reduce the effect of Tribunal decisions initiated by legislators, and to control decisions that have binding force through the Supreme Court's referral powers. The effect of the amendment was to reduce the Tribunal's powers to weak form judicial review (except in matters referred by the Supreme Court), although this change did not reduce tensions between the legislature and the Tribunal. From the perspective of the Tribunal, this was *unconstitutional* weak form review because the legislature's amendments ran counter to the Constitution. This change attempted to downgrade the Tribunal's authority from binding to declaratory, damaging the public image of the Tribunal.

In 2014, the Tribunal had the opportunity to reject the legislature's amendments to the Constitutional Tribunal Law. In a case that, among other issues, raised the question of the finality of the Tribunal's decisions after the legislative amendments, the Tribunal held that all its decisions are final according to the Constitution.[73] The Tribunal rejected the legislature's attempt to limit the force of its decisions. The Tribunal's decision ran counter to the opinion submitted by the government, which failed in its bid to argue that the amendments to the law were constitutional. In a turn of events, in 2014 the legislature capitulated and allowed the Tribunal to submit a revised law to the legislature as a Union Level Organisation.[74] In his submission to the Amyotha Hluttaw, the chair of the Constitutional Tribunal, U Mya Thein, emphasised that the Constitutional Tribunal has three different functions: interpretation power; power to scrutinise; and power to determine.[75] After discussion in the Pyithu Hluttaw the Bill went back with amendments to the Amyotha Hluttaw. After the Bill was approved by the legislature, the president sent back several comments to the Pyidaungsu Hluttaw that were further discussed and debated.[76] This shows that the

---

[70] See PH2012-5:13.
[71] See PDH2012-5:7.
[72] Law 4/2013 amending the Constitutional Tribunal Law.
[73] Constitutional Tribunal, Finality Case 1/2014.
[74] See AH2014-10:6, p 17.
[75] See respectively ss 12(a); (b)–(c); (d)–(f).
[76] See PDH2014-11:14, pp 403–17; PDH2014-11:15, pp 431–444.

power of a ULO to draft and submit laws is more than just mere administrative power (Chapter 5). The second amendment as passed reaffirmed the finality of the Tribunal's decisions.[77] The Legislature's deference to the Tribunal seems short-lived. In 2015, the proposed amendments to the Constitution included removing the finality of the Tribunal's decisions (although this proposal failed). Many legal questions remain, such as what is the legal status of decisions made by the first Tribunal bench? Does the decision on ULO have binding force? What is the difference between an advisory opinion and decision? The decision in relation to Union-level Organisations in 2012 is one that has not been followed by the legislature. The issues over finality and a lack of regard for Tribunal decisions by the legislature have undermined the integrity of the Tribunal and the potential authoritative value of its decisions.

C. Access to the Tribunal: Centralised and Elite-Led

The Tribunal has failed to generate support from civil society, public interest lawyers or the people, in large measure because these groups have no right to access the Tribunal. Indirect access rules mean that a person directly affected by a constitutional issue cannot bring a case to the Tribunal. There are three types of indirect access to the Tribunal: executive, judicial and legislative.

Certain executive positions have indirect access to the Tribunal, specifically the president and the Chairperson of the Union Election Commission.[78] At the State/Region level, the Chief Minister of the State/Region and the Chairperson of a Self-Administered Area (who are members of both the executive and legislative branch) can also bring a submission to the Tribunal. The second type of access is from members of the legislature (who are not part of the executive). The respective speakers of the Pyidaungsu Hluttaw (the two houses of the legislative sitting together), the Pyithu Hluttaw and the Amyotha Hluttaw at the Union level, and the Speaker of the State/Region Hluttaw, can initiate cases in the Constitutional Tribunal. Collective submissions can also be made by legislators.[79] An application requires at least ten per cent of all the representatives of the Pyithu Hluttaw or the Amyotha Hluttaw (roughly 44 or 22 members respectively). The Tatmadaw, who make

---

[77] Second amendment to the Constitutional Tribunal Law No 46/2014.
[78] 2008 Constitution, s 325.
[79] Ibid, s 326.

up 25 per cent of the legislature at the Union and State/Region level, can apply. The third type is indirect access by the judiciary, specifically the Chief Justice of the Supreme Court. All these positions are directly appointed by the president (bar the president him or herself).

The Constitution makes access to the Tribunal subject to procedure as determined by law. The legislature has created a centralised system of access to the Tribunal. The Constitutional Tribunal Law requires that a Chief Minister must obtain consent of the president to make an application to the Tribunal; the Speaker of the Region/State Hluttaw must make his/her request through the Speaker of the Pyidaungsu Hluttaw; the Chairperson of the Self-Administered Area must make his/her submission through both the Chief Minister of the State/Region and the president; and if the submission is made by 10 per cent of representatives of one of the houses of the Hluttaw, it requires the consent of the Speaker of that House.[80] In particular, this access rule limits the autonomy of the State/Region Hluttaw by tying its application to the consent of the Pyidaungsu Hluttaw, while the Self-Administered Areas require consent both of the State/Region in which it is based and of the president. In short, access to the Tribunal is centralised and largely determined by the president and the Speakers of the two houses of the Pyidaungsu Hluttaw. This fits with the consensus model of coercive centralism, and largely acts as a communication tool to alert the Union Government about cases.

Members of the legislature have not brought cases on behalf of citizens nor of the concerned electorate. In this respect, there is no formal or informal link between the Tribunal and society, because the Tribunal in effect only interacts with the branches of government when the government initiates such interaction. Members of the Amyotha Hluttaw have effectively brought a case on behalf of Ministers for National Races Affairs, given their shared interests in the national project of promoting the position of national races.[81]

D. The Approach of the Tribunal

The Constitutional Tribunal has exclusive authority to interpret the Constitution. Some lawyers have understood this to mean that the Supreme Court must refer any question on the interpretation of the Constitution to the Constitutional Tribunal. Given that the Supreme Court has

---

[80] Law on the Constitutional Tribunal No 21/2010, s 15.
[81] Constitutional Tribunal, Ethnic Ministers Case 2/2011.

original jurisdiction in writ cases that concern constitutional rights, this should mean that the Supreme Court works very closely with the Constitutional Tribunal. However, the Supreme Court generally does not refer a matter of interpretation in a writ case to the Constitutional Tribunal. Many argue this is because Chapter VIII of the Constitution confers jurisdiction on the Supreme Court in these matters, not the Constitutional Tribunal.

No dominant approach to deciding and interpreting constitutional cases has emerged in the Tribunal. Formally, the Basic Principles in the Constitution are a guide to interpretation of the Constitution and other laws (see Chapter 2).[82] The Constitution also acknowledges the existing law on statutory interpretation, which is the Interpretation of Expressions Law 1973.[83] This law was introduced in the socialist era. Unlike India, Myanmar did not retain the General Clauses Act from the colonial era. The Interpretation of Expressions Law requires any section of a law to be interpreted according to the intention of the legislative authority that passed the law. During the socialist era, this was a reference to the unicameral legislature filled with members of the Burma Socialist Program Party. The provision in the 2008 Constitution to the law on interpretation has been taken by some to mean that the Interpretation of Expressions Law also applies to *constitutional* interpretation. That is, the role of the Tribunal is to interpret the Constitution according to the intention of the National Convention and Drafting Committee at the time the Constitution was drafted. However, the National Convention records do not offer extensive justification for, or explanation of, provisions of the Constitution. There were over 1,000 representatives to the National Convention over a period of 20 years, making it difficult to discern a 'common' intention. Participation and debate in the Convention was not open or free (see Chapter 2). The Tribunal has been inconsistent in the use of Convention records, with only the first bench making explicit use of these records.

There is a larger question of whether a past military regime can bind a court appointed by a new partly elected democratic regime, whether by requiring adherence to the intention as expressed in constitution-making records or by deeming that laws passed prior to 2011 (by the military regime) cannot be reviewed by the Tribunal. In 2012, the Tribunal had

---

[82] 2008 Constitution, s 48.
[83] Ibid, s 453.

to deal with the question of whether it can interpret laws passed by the former State Peace and Development Council (SPDC) (pre-2011). Section 443 of the Constitution states that all work done by the SPDC prior to the enactment of the Constitution must be held to be in accordance with the Constitution.[84] Based on this section, the Tribunal held that it did not have power to interpret laws passed before 2011. This is an example of extreme deference by the Tribunal to the past regime and is a restriction on the scope of the Tribunal's jurisdiction.

The decisions of the Tribunal suggest that at least three approaches to interpretation are evident: a literal approach, a nationalist approach and a restorative approach. The literal approach to constitutional interpretation treats law as black and white text, clear and unambiguous. This is not originalism, as some foreign scholars have suggested, but rather a continuation and mirroring of the approach to law adopted during the periods of socialist-military rule. In this conception, judges presume the law is clear and undertake a role like that of administrators.

The second approach is a nationalist approach, where the Tribunal reads the Constitution in a way that emphasises the rights of official national races to the exclusion of outside groups. The nationalist approach to interpretation is both about the choice of an interpretation that will enhance the outcome for national races but also about the insistence of adopting an ethno-nationalist lens to the interpretation of the Constitution. For example, in the Ministers of National Races Affairs case, the Tribunal found that these ministers are equal in status to other ministers, even though this does not appear to have been anticipated in the Constitution (see Chapter 7).[85] Another example of the nationalist approach is the Citizenship case, in which the Tribunal read the word 'person' restrictively to mean associate or naturalised citizen, and not a temporary identity card holder (see Chapter 4).[86] This was an anti-rights case, in the sense that the applicants were arguing (contrary to past political practice) that the right to vote in a constitutional referendum (and by implication, elections) should only be given to citizens, and not to groups with temporary identity cards such as the Rohingya. In both these cases, the Tribunal's decision reflects populist ethno-nationalist sentiment and arguably goes beyond the literal wording of the Constitution or the intention of the constitution-drafters.

---

[84] Constitutional Tribunal, Legislative Committees Case 1/2012.
[85] Constitutional Tribunal, Ministers for National Races Affairs Case 2/2011.
[86] Citizenship Case 1/2015, dated 11 May 2015.

The third approach to constitutional interpretation has been to return to the 1947 Constitution and the principles of interpretation that were expounded by the Supreme Court at that time. This mode of interpretation is a form of 'restorative jurisprudence', that is, the Tribunal adopts a past approach to interpretation (restoring past jurisprudence) under a previous court and constitutional era. This is a revivalist approach to constitutional law, involving the adaptation of past constitutional principles under a former constitution to an entirely new constitutional context. This approach was evident in a case in 2017[87] where the Tribunal deliberately turned back to principles of statutory and constitutional interpretation of the 1950s, citing jurisprudence of the former Supreme Court of Burma. The Tribunal used past jurisprudence to emphasise that the Constitution should be given an expansive and not a restrictive meaning.[88] It did so in order to find that legislative committees could be formed by the Pyidaungsu Hluttaw, even though this is not mentioned in the Constitution. This demonstrates a willingness on the part of the Tribunal to draw on the history of constitutional law to attempt to forge a new jurisprudence in Myanmar beyond the literal or nationalist approach. This was significant because the applicants were 50 military representatives, and so the Tribunal indicated that it is willing to rule against military legislators.

IV. CONCLUSION

There are several paradoxical principles at the heart of the Constitution in relation to the judiciary, and these principles contradict everyday judicial practice. On one hand, the Constitutional Tribunal has given the separation of powers doctrine in section 11(a) of the Constitution a clear and bold meaning. It has determined that the separation of powers means that judicial power cannot be delegated to the executive. On the other hand, the term of the Tribunal is tied to that of the government of the day. The appointment process means the Constitutional Tribunal is perceived to be influenced by the president. Although Supreme Court judges enjoy long tenure, there has been no fundamental change of

---

[87] Constitutional Tribunal, Legislative Committees Case No 2, 1/2017, dated 21 September 2017.
[88] Ibid.

guards and many have Tatmadaw backgrounds. Also running contrary to judicial independence is that the Supreme Court itself is classified as a 'Union Level Organisation', in effect a defacto government department, and can be called to account by the legislature.

The courts have an indirect relationship with the Tatmadaw, in comparison to the direct relationship between the Tatmadaw and the executive and legislature. But this indirect relationship is perhaps more dangerous because it is unregulated. This indirect connection includes many former Tatmadaw officers as judges and court personnel, including in the two highest courts, the Supreme Court and the Constitutional Tribunal. Tatmadaw transfers into the judiciary continue to take place. This connection is also evident in the influence that the police and General Administration Department have over the everyday operations of the lower courts. The Attorney General's Office prosecutors and law officers also include many former Tatmadaw officers.

The legislature treats the courts, including the Constitutional Tribunal, as a subordinate institution. This means that the courts are consigned to the margins of political and legal influence. To strengthen the separation of powers and judicial independence requires not only a re-consolidation of judicial power within the courts, but also a process of 'demilitarisation' to ensure a decisive break with military influence, and a reassertion of judicial power in relation to the legislature and the courts. Part of this process will require a commitment from the courts to greater transparency and reasoning in decision-making in order to rebuild its public image as an institution that can contribute to building democracy in Myanmar.

I have focused in this chapter on the formal judicial system, although there exists both customary law and non-state judicial systems. The Constitution does not formally acknowledge traditional or customary sources of law. The courts have long acknowledged and developed a system of family law according to religious groups such as Islamic law, Hindu law and Burmese Buddhist law. Some territories are outside of the control of the state and have their own court and justice systems.[89] If discussions of federalism continue, consideration of how to recognise or incorporate these non-state justice systems will require greater attention.

---

[89] Brian McCartan and Kim Joliffe (2016) *Ethnic Armed Associations and Justice in Myanmar*. Asia Foundation.

FURTHER READING

Nick Cheesman, *Opposing the Rule of Law: How Myanmar's Courts Make Law and Order* (CUP, 2015).

Melissa Crouch and Nick Cheesman, 'A Short Research Guide to Myanmar's Legal System' in Melissa Crouch and Tim Lindsey (eds) *Law, Society & Transition in Myanmar* (Hart Publishing, 2014).

Melissa Crouch, 'Democrats, Dictators and Constitutional Dialogue: Myanmar's Constitutional Tribunal' (2018) 16(2) *International Journal of Constitutional Law* 421.

Andrew Harding and Khin Khin Oo (eds) *Constitutionalism and Legal Change in Myanmar* (Hart Publishing, 2017).

Dominic Nardi, 'Discipline-Flourishing Constitutional Review' (2010) 12(1) *Australian Journal of Asian Law*.

Myint Zan, 'Law and Legal Culture, Constitutions and Constitutionalism in Burma' in Alice Tay (ed) *East Asia: Human Rights, Nation-building, Trade* (Nomos Verlagsgesellschaft, 1999).

Myint Zan, 'The New Supreme Court and Constitutional Tribunal: Marginal Improvement or More of the Same?' in Nick Cheesman et al (eds) *Myanmar's Transition: Openings, Obstacles and Opportunities* (ISEAS, 2014). pp 249–268.

9

Constitutional Duties and the Contingency of Rights

International Law – Citizens and Persons – Citizens' Duties – Legislative and Constitutional Qualification of Rights – National Human Rights Commission – Constitutional Writs

THE STATE IN Myanmar has been the subject of sustained criticism for human rights violations over several decades.[1] The Constitution regulates and mediates the extent to which the state recognises international law and human rights. Myanmar remains a dualist country in the application of international law. Under the Constitution, Chapter VIII contains citizens' duties and rights. The constitution-makers did not have international human rights law as their point of reference in terms of constitutional design. Chapter VIII mixes ideas from past constitutions along with military imperatives. The concept of a 'citizen' (as distinct from 'person') is important, and citizens' duties are conceptually prior to rights.

Any consideration of legal rights in Myanmar needs to be prefaced by acknowledgement of the mix of socialist and leftist Marxist ideology and Burmese Buddhist thought with its emphasis on duties rather than individual rights, as considered in the work of Matthew Walton.[2] Further, there is a long history of formal legal defences to individual rights being rendered ineffective against the authoritarian state in Myanmar, as Cheesman and Kyaw Min San's analysis of cause lawyering suggests.[3] Nevertheless, it is critical to understand how rights are

---

[1] See Morten Pedersen, *Promoting Human Rights in Burma* (Rowman & Littlefield, 2008).

[2] Matthew Walton, *Buddhism, Politics and Political Thought in Myanmar* (CUP, 2017).

[3] Nick Cheesman and Kyaw Min San, (2013–2014) 'Not Just Defending: Advocating for Law in Myanmar' 31 Wis. Int'l L.J. 702.

formulated in the 2008 Constitution. Duties are conceptually prior to rights, which are qualified, difficult to defend legally and inherently limited. There are two formal avenues for the protection of rights: the writs in the Supreme Court and the National Human Rights Commission. Both institutions operate under self-imposed restrictions – such as dismissing cases against the police or Tatmadaw – and show little willingness to act as an independent check on the executive. Rights are subordinate to disciplined democracy and the imperative of maintaining the military-state, which affects the overall credibility of the Constitution. While the political opening since 2011 has created space for civil society and advocacy groups to mobilise for the protection of rights, the Constitution does not necessarily feature as a prominent source of inspiration.

I. THE STATUS OF INTERNATIONAL LAW AND CONVENTIONS

For decades, international law had little purchase in Myanmar domestically. This situation was ironic because Myanmar was once a leader of the international community, with U Thant serving from 1961–1971 as Secretary General of the United Nations. As the first non-European to occupy this office, this was a significant and historic appointment. Despite his achievements on the global stage, his contribution was not recognised by the socialist regime and a standoff occurred after his death in 1974 over the issue of whether he should receive a state burial. Myanmar's historical legacy and connection to building the international order contrasts with the government's contemporary relationship with international law.

At the level of international relations, Myanmar has historically been part of the non-aligned movement, and the Constitution specifies that the Union is to remain non-aligned in international affairs.[4] The Constitution does anticipate the ratification of treaties. The process of ratifying a treaty can be initiated either by the Pyidaungsu Hluttaw, which can instruct the president to approve or ratify a treaty, or can be initiated by the president who can submit a request to the Pyidaungsu Hluttaw to ratify a treaty.[5] The role of the legislature in the process of entering or ratifying

---

[4] 2008 Constitution, s 41.
[5] Ibid, s 108.

a bilateral or international treaty is also confirmed in Chapter V on the executive and the president's power to enter into a treaty with the agreement of the Pyidaungsu Hluttaw.[6]

There has been growing international pressure on the government to enter into international treaties, particularly in relation to fundamental rights. In June 2013, the Myanmar National Human Rights Commission sent a recommendation to the president to suggest that the government ratify both the International Covenant on Civil and Political Rights and the International Covenant on Economic, Social and Cultural Rights ('ICESCR'). In 2015, the Thein Sein Government signed the ICESCR and it was ratified on 6 October 2017. Signing the ICESCR was part of the Thein Sein Government's concession to ethnic groups and recognition of cultural claims. The government did make a reservation concerning article 1 on self-determination, noting that this provision does not apply to any people in Myanmar and that it does not affect the operation of section 10 of the Constitution, which prohibits secession.

Myanmar remains a dualist country and an international treaty must be included in national law first before it is enforceable domestically. According to the Constitution, the Legislative List of the Union includes the power and responsibility to finalise and implement international and regional treaties, agreements and conventions.[7] In the past, the courts have held that international law does not automatically form part of Myanmar law, though it may apply if it does not contradict Myanmar law.[8] The courts have emphasised that the government has the authority to incorporate such principles into national law.[9] There is an absence of contemporary jurisprudence on this issue.

The Constitution specifically acknowledges that Myanmar will fulfil its obligations under such agreements signed prior to its enactment.[10] Under the previous regime, some human rights conventions were signed, including the Convention on the Rights of the Child (1991) and the Convention on the Elimination of All Forms of Discrimination Against Women (1997), although the government made a reservation concerning article 29 so it does not accept the jurisdiction of the ICJ. This opened a safe space for advocates and human rights defenders to work on issues

---

[6] Ibid, s 209.
[7] Ibid, Sch 1, s 2(d).
[8] *Evgoni T Kovtunenko v U Law Yone* 1960 BLR (SC) 51.
[9] Min Thein, 'Application of International Law in Myanmar Courts' (2013) 3(3) *Judicial Journal* [တရားရေး ဂျာနယ်] pp 22–31.
[10] 2008 Constitution, s 456.

concerning women and children.[11] In 2011, the Convention on the Rights of Persons with Disabilities was ratified.

A further dimension of the constitutional power to enter into treaties includes permission to sign bilateral trade agreements, which Myanmar has done since 2011 with Japan, Israel and South Korea. However most existing bilateral trade agreements signed by Myanmar date back to the military era, including with Philippines, Vietnam, China, Laos, India and Kuwait.[12] The Supreme Court has jurisdiction over any disputes arising from bilateral treaties,[13] although disputes are far more likely to go to arbitration in places such as Singapore.

II. THE PRE-EMINENCE OF DUTIES

The domestic context heavily conditions the meaning of Chapter VIII of the Constitution. The provisions have not been articulated or clarified in court judgments. Chapter VIII on Citizens Fundamental Rights and Duties is misleadingly named, as some of the provisions in the chapter apply to 'persons' more broadly or contain state duties. It represents a mix of ideas from the 1947 Constitution, the 1974 Constitution and Tatmadaw ideology of the 1990s–2000s. Much confusion and misunderstanding has arisen about the meaning of rights in the Constitution. The provisions in Chapter VIII are subject to the lower threshold for amendment that does not require a referendum of the people. This contrasts with other provisions of the Constitution, such as provisions on the president and Tatmadaw (see Chapter 10), which do require a constitutional referendum. This means the legislature can amend constitutional rights without the assent of the people.

The claims of the Constitution concerning rights are relative and conditional. There are no rights without duties. The pre-eminent duty is to uphold the three meta principles of the military-state, which are conceptually prior to any right. I identify four types of provisions in the Chapter VIII: citizens' duties, citizens' rights, other persons' rights and state obligations (both positive and negative). One reason for the emphasis on citizen's duties over rights is that even citizens are treated with suspicion and perceived as enemies.[14] While non-citizens are the

[11] Cheesman and Kyaw Min San, above n 3, p 715.
[12] These were signed in 1998, 2000, 2001, 2003, 2008 and 2008 respectively.
[13] 2008 Constitution, s 296(a)(i).
[14] Mary P Callahan, *Making Enemies: War and State Building in Burma* (NUS Press, 2004), pp 3, 223.

most vulnerable, even citizens are rarely perceived to hold individual rights to seek protection from the state.

A. The Distinction between 'Citizens' and 'Persons'

The Constitution distinguishes between 'citizens' and 'persons'. This is a trait of other constitutions, such as India and Sri Lanka, although one that has been criticised.[15] The rights in the Constitution that are open to persons include equal pay for women; equal rights for women and children; the right to life and freedom; and criminal safeguards such as a right of defence, no detention for longer than 24 hours, punishment only according to the law and no retrial for the same offence.[16] This is in contrast to the rights of citizens which also include the freedom to publish, the freedom of association and assembly, freedom to practice their language and culture, freedom of movement, freedom to practice literature and traditions, the right to education, the right to vote and run for office and a right to seek protection.[17] This raises the question of the meaning of the terms 'citizen' and 'person' in the Constitution, and how the meaning of citizenship has narrowed over time.

Independence in 1947 led to a whole host of new questions and administrative issues that had to be dealt with by the state. One of these was the issue of citizenship. Like many post-colonial states, Burma struggled with the issue of who was eligible for citizenship. This distinction between 'persons' and 'citizens' was a feature of the 1947 Constitution, which provided for one type of citizenship. There were four possible grounds on which a person could apply for citizenship.[18] First, on the 'parent's race ground', a person could apply for citizenship if both their parents' identified as an indigenous race of Burma. Second, on the 'birth plus one grandparent' ground, a person could apply for citizenship if they were born in Burma and at least one of their grandparents identified as an indigenous race of Burma. Third, on the 'birth plus parents' ground, a person could apply for citizenship if they were born in Burma and their parents were also citizens of Burma. The fourth avenue is the 'birth plus residence' ground, which a person met if they were born in the

---

[15] While courts in countries such as Sri Lanka have determined that the category 'person' includes any incorporated association but not unincorporated associations and so denied trade unions the opportunity to bring claims, this jurisprudence is not common knowledge in Myanmar.

[16] 2008 Constitution, ss 350–51, 353, 373–76.

[17] Ibid, ss 354–55, 365–67, 369–70, 380.

[18] 1947 Constitution, ss 10–11.

dominion, had lived in Burma for at least eight of ten years in the lead up to the war or to independence, had the intention to remain in Burma permanently; and, applied for citizenship following the procedure and within the timeframe set out in law. The legislature retained the constitutional authority to pass any laws necessary on citizenship or create new categories.

In the late 1970s and early 1980s, a new citizenship law was drafted. Beginning in 1976, a Law Commission was formed by the Council of State.[19] One aspect of the draft version circulated was that stateless persons were given the right to make an application to the central authority for permission to hold a foreigners' registration certificate.[20] This provision on statelessness was later removed from the final draft. The law that emerged and remains in force today is the Burma Citizenship Law 1982, which created three categories of citizenship: full citizens, associate citizens and naturalised citizens. Full citizens are national races who can trace their ancestry in Burma before 1823 (being the year before the First Anglo-Burmese War took place). The government maintains a list of 135 races. Associate citizens are person who obtained citizenship under the 1948 Citizenship Act. A naturalised citizen is a person who can demonstrate that they entered and resided in Burma before 4 January 1948 (independence). From 1995, a new 'white card', was issued by the Immigration and Population Department as a temporary registration card. It was given to some, but not all, Rohingya in northern Rakhine State.

Up until 2015, there were four main types of identity: full citizenship, associate citizenship, naturalised citizenship and white cards. Considering these forms of identity, the question in relation to the 2008 Constitution is who qualifies as a 'citizen' or 'person'. The provisions on citizenship come first in Chapter VIII. The Constitution offers two categories of citizens: those whose parents are from national races; and those who had citizenship prior to the adoption of the Constitution. All other matters concerning citizenship are to be regulated by law and there have been no changes to the Citizenship Law.[21] In this way, Cheesman has argued, the concept of national races precedes the idea of citizenship in the Constitution.[22] In a similar way, the concept

[19] *The Guardian Supplement*, 'Suggestions sought in connection with the Burma Citizenship Draft Law' 21 April 1982.

[20] Ibid, s 35.

[21] 2008 Constitution, ss 345–6.

[22] Nick Cheesman, 'How in Myanmar "National Races" Came to Surpass Citizenship' (2017) *Journal of Contemporary Asia* 461–483.

of a section 144 emergency order precedes any constitutional state of emergency (see Chapter 3). These examples show how the persistence of administrative practices of the past military regime often precedes the constitutional text.

The Constitutional Tribunal appears to have set an unusual and negative precedent by deciding that the phrase in section 391, 'persons who have the right to vote', can only include associate citizens or natural-ised citizens (see Chapter 4). The Tribunal has not yet clarified whether this only relates to section 391, or whether all mention of 'persons' in the Constitution are to be read in this way. An ongoing issue remains the processing of those who formerly held white cards. Now holding green cards, these people remain in a precarious position. In the past, excep-tional measures have been taken, such as granting citizenship in 1953 to ethnic Chinese people who were found to live in the Myanmar after the border between Myanmar and China was redrawn, or the promise of citizenship as part of ceasefire deals of the 1990s. This is a precedent for a one off, exceptional measure to address difficult citizenship dilemmas for people groups.

The power to regulate citizenship remains with the Union Govern-ment, although some State/Region Hluttaw have attempted to intervene. For example, in March 2017, the Rakhine State Hluttaw received complaints alleging that the citizenship verification process in some townships in northern Rakhine State had wrongly issued full citizenship to Muslims. These complaints were part of the broader ANP anti-Rohingya agenda in Rakhine State. The State/Region Hluttaw have no constitutional power to review a citizenship verification procedure initi-ated by the Union Government, even if that procedure is being carried out by township officials.[23]

B. Citizen's Duties and Limitations on Rights

Most constitutions today do not mention citizens' duties, with the exception of socialist-inspired constitutions such as Vietnam and African states such as Zambia, Ghana, Gambia and Uganda. In 2011, in a submission to the Constitutional Tribunal in Myanmar, the Attor-ney General's Office commented on the interrelated nature of rights and duties and emphasised that there are no rights without duties.[24]

---

[23] *Asia News Monitor* (2017) 'Parliamentary Committee Contests Full Citizenship for Maungdaw Muslims', 27 March.
[24] Constitutional Tribunal, Ministers for National Races Affairs Case 2/2011.

Rights are conditional and dependent on the observance of duties as defined in the 2008 Constitution.

Given the power of government over citizens, this inverts the common assumption that a constitution is intended to restrain the state. There is an explicit constitutional requirement that all citizens must uphold and comply with the Constitution.[25] Most constitutions simply presume that all people will follow the Constitution, however socialist constitutions mandate this. The Constitution of Myanmar demonstrates a noticeable preoccupation with ensuring that its citizens comply with its terms.

All citizens are responsible for upholding the territorial unity, sovereignty and independence of the country.[26] This obligation binds all citizens to the three meta-principles of the military-state, particularly the exhortation to territorial sovereignty. This is accompanied by a specific prohibition: all citizens must not act in a manner that negatively affects or diminishes national solidarity and the unity of national races.[27] For example, ethnic groups that support a right to secession in the Constitution are accused of threatening national solidarity. The Constitution contains further exhortations to national unity and the duty of citizens to maintain peace and harmony among national races.[28]

There is a constitutional duty for citizens to undergo military training and serve in the armed forces.[29] Like some provisions of the Constitution, this is a hollow provision, because there is no active program of compulsory military service in Myanmar. At best it is an example of a dormant constitutional provision that could be activated in the future, although it is likely that conscription would be very unpopular. Another duty of citizens' is the explicit requirement to pay taxes,[30] although this is something that other constitutions would simply leave to regulation. There is also a vague duty for citizens to support the development of a modern nation-state.[31] The appeal to progress and modernity binds citizens to the agenda of the state. While this is wide open to interpretation, the regime practice of requiring villagers to work for free to construct roads may fall within this duty. There are also several matters in which the citizen is depicted by the Constitution as partnering with the state,

---

[25] 2008 Constitution, s 384.
[26] Ibid, ss 383, 385.
[27] Ibid, s 365.
[28] Ibid, s 387.
[29] Ibid, s 386. See People's Military Service Law No 27/2010.
[30] Ibid, s 389.
[31] Ibid, s 388.

including in environmental conservation, cultural heritage protection and the protection of public property.[32]

The courts have not published court decisions that articulate how these provisions on citizens' duties are to be read and under what conditions citizens' duties would trump any rights considerations. Some of these citizens' duties are taken straight from the 1974 socialist Constitution, while other duties reflect the mantras of the SPDC or mirror the Basic Principles in Chapter I earlier in the Constitution.

The rights provisions are subject to significant limitations according to law; limitations in the Tatmadaw's interests of public order and security; limitations during a state of emergency, and limitations according to other provisions of the Constitution. The phrase that a right shall be enjoyed according to the law or as prescribed by the law arises frequently in the Constitution.[33] This means that the legislature can further define and impose conditions on the content of the right. There has been no consideration by the Constitutional Tribunal on the meaning of individual rights, the relationship between different constitutional rights, nor of the scope of the constitutional limitations on rights. The legislature is given full power and discretion to set the limits of those rights. This means that rights do not exist unless and until the legislature passes a law regarding these rights. In Myanmar, given that the legislature contains 25 per cent Tatmadaw members, these limits on rights are not necessarily determined by a representative of the people. Further, the Tatmadaw is given power through a broad limitation that applies to all rights in Chapter VIII. The Tatmadaw can limit any rights to ensure public order and maintain security.[34] Limitations can also be placed on the opportunity to seek protection of a right or a remedy during a time of emergency or internal or external conflict.[35] Finally, rights are limited by other provisions of the Constitution. Although these limitations are significant, the courts have yet to apply or interpret these limitations.

C. The Contingent Nature of Rights

Citizens' rights in the Constitution include civil and political rights, and economic, social and cultural rights. This division makes two

---

[32] Ibid, s 390.
[33] See, eg, 2008 Constitution, ss 346, 351, 353–57, 359, 365, 370, 372–5.
[34] Ibid, s 382.
[35] Ibid, ss 381 and 378.

things apparent: the overemphasis on cultural rights as opposed to civil and political rights, and the greater limitations on civil and political rights as opposed to social and cultural rights. The core civil and political rights included in the Constitution are freedom of expression and association, freedom of press, freedom of religion, citizenship, right to vote, and the right to equality and non-discrimination. These rights have been the source of political contestation.

The Constitution grants citizens freedom of assembly and the right to form associations.[36] The right to assemble freely is qualified by the phrase that the gathering must be *unarmed*, an indication of the intolerance for ethnic armed organisations. There are clear examples of the limits on the right to freedom of association in legislation, such as in relation to trade unions. On one hand, the Thein Sein administration did introduce new laws to permit the formation of trade unions and to allow the right to protest.[37] However, it can be difficult to obtain permission under these acts, and there remain prohibitions on the formation of student unions. This is because student activism has long been a source of discomfort for the Tatmadaw, particularly due to student protests, most notably in 1962, 1974 and 1988. Another example of limits on the right to association is the Unlawful Associations Act that has been used against a wide range of dissidents, including ethnic armed organisations. One small development has been that signatories to the National Ceasefire Agreement are now removed from the list and recognised as a lawful association (see Chapter 10). Otherwise the act continues to be used against political opponents of the state.

Citizens are free to publish and express their opinions.[38] Under Thein Sein, the former censorship restrictions were lifted, and the censorship board abolished. Newspapers were once again permitted to publish daily (rather than weekly) and this led to the emergence of many new media outlets. However, since 2013, many defamation cases have been filed against people who criticise high-ranking government officials under section 66(d) of the Telecommunications Act.[39] Other laws, such as the Official Secrets Act are also used to curb these freedoms, particularly for journalists. The Official Secrets Act was used to imprison two journalists who allegedly possessed classified information regarding massacres that occurred in 2017 in northern Rakhine State. The rights in the

---

[36] 2008 Constitution, s 354(b)–(c).
[37] Right to Peaceful Assembly and Peaceful Procession Law No 15/2011.
[38] 2008 Constitution, s 354(a).
[39] Telecommunications Law No 31/2013.

Constitution did not protect the accused against a broadly worded law that allows significant discretion in the determination of what is considered a state secret.

The scope of freedom of religion is ambivalent and the rights of members from one religion may weigh up against those of another religion.[40] The Basic Principles acknowledge that citizens have the right to freedom to practise religion.[41] This is then cross-referenced in Chapter VIII, which sets out other limitations on the right in addition to health, morality or public order. The legislature retains the ability to pass any law that has as its purpose the protection of the public, even if it infringes on religious freedom.[42] This allows the state to claim to act in the interests of the broader good (or of the Buddhist majority), even if certain minorities have their right to religious freedom compromised. The state can also choose to aid or protect religions as it sees fit.[43] The Constitution goes on to recognise Buddhism as having a special position, although it also acknowledges other religions such as Hinduism, Christianity and Islam.[44] There is an explicit prohibition and warning against the misuse of religion for political gain, as well as a prohibition on what sounds like hate speech. There have been a range of instances where concerns have been raised about the role and use of religion in political and public life, such as the rise of Buddhist extremism and instances of hate speech and inciting violence against Muslims.[45] In addition to provisions on religion and Buddhism, the preamble to the Constitution refers to the Buddhist calendar. It does so by prioritising the Burmese Buddhist calendar, referring to the date the Constitution was approved with the Western Gregorian calendar in brackets: 10th waxing day of Kasone 1370 M.E. (29 May 2008 AD).[46] The Burmese Buddhist calendar is used in a range of other settings, including in all legislation.

The Constitution contains the right to equality and non-discrimination.[47] There are specific provisions on the rights of women

---

[40] For more on the history of religious provisions in the Constitution, see Melissa Crouch, 'Personal Law and Colonial Legacy', in Melissa Crouch (ed) *Islam and the State in Myanmar* (OUP, 2016). pp 69–97.

[41] 2008 Constitution, s 34.

[42] Ibid, s 360.

[43] Ibid, s 363.

[44] Ibid, ss 361–362.

[45] See Nyi Nyi Kyaw, 'Islamophobia in Buddhist Myanmar' in Melissa Crouch (ed) *Islam and the State in Myanmar* (OUP, 2016) pp 183–210. See also a special issue of the *Journal of Contemporary Asia* (2017).

[46] The abbreviation 'M.E.' stands for Myanmar Era, and refers to the calendar system according to lunar months, based on an adaptation of the old Hindu calendar.

[47] 2008 Constitution, ss 347, 349 and 348.

and children that are framed in the language of equality.[48] Women have the right to equality at work, such as salaries. There is provision for mothers and children to have equal rights as set out by law, though this does not recognise that women and children may need *greater* protections than men. This provision appears to be overpowered by a later provision that declares nothing prevents the government from creating positions only for men. The Constitution does not include any quotas or special consideration for women in the political or judicial system. While the system of family law provides novel approaches to social issues, such as court recognition of inheritance rights for second wives in polygamous marriages under Burmese Buddhist law, this system was placed in doubt in 2015 with the passage of four laws that affect the rights of women.[49]

There is a constitutional right to the protection of property, and to security and privacy.[50] The issue of land ownership and the problem of illegal land claims is one of the most pressing issues in Myanmar.[51] Under Thein Sein, a Commission on Land was established to receive and determine disputes over land claims. However, there is no constitutional right to just compensation for state acquisition of private property. Grievances and hardships due to land grabs remains one of the most serious and pervasive problems in contemporary Myanmar.

The Constitution does contain some economic, social and cultural rights although the emphasis is largely on cultural claims. The Constitution refrains from the use of the term 'self-determination'. To appease persistent ethnic claims for self-determination, the Constitution does contain a group of rights expressly for national races. The Constitution provides for language rights, the opportunity to develop their literature and culture, and to practice their own religion and customs.[52] In the past, the socialist and military regime has been accused of attempting to force minorities to adopt Buddhism instead of allowing them to retain their own religion. It has also denied national races the right to publish in their own language or practice certain traditions and customs. The legislature

---

[48] Ibid, ss 350–352.

[49] Melissa Crouch, 'Promiscuity, Polygyny and the Power of Revenge: The Past and Future of Burmese Buddhist Law in Myanmar' (2016) 3(1) *Asian Journal of Law & Society* 85–104.

[50] 2008 Constitution, ss 356–57.

[51] Christina Fink, 'Re-envisioning Land Rights and Land Tenure', in David Steinburg (eds) *Myanmar: The Dynamics of an Evolving Polity* (Lynne Rienner Publishers, 2015) pp 243–266; see also Elliott Prasse-Freeman and Phyo Win Latt, 'Class and Inequality' in *The Routledge Handbook of Contemporary Myanmar* (Routledge, 2017).

[52] 2008 Constitution, s 354(d).

has enacted a law to protect the rights of national races.[53] There is also a right to education[54] and a right to health,[55] though the Constitution leaves these to regulation by the legislature. Overall, the Constitution mentions civil and political rights only to heavily qualify and contain them. Social and cultural rights are also mentioned but remain subject to the will of the legislature to determine their scope and realisation.

D. Persons' Rights

There are some rights that apply more broadly to 'persons', although it is necessary to keep in mind the restrictive reading of this term, as discussed above. There are two main rights, the right to life and rights in relation to criminal proceedings. The right to life is a fragile right in the Constitution, because it can be restricted by law.[56] While the right to life is an inviolable right internationally, the Constitution allows the legislature scope to qualify the right. One reason for this is to ensure that the death penalty remains constitutional. The state has a long history in Myanmar of using the death penalty against political opponents, including pro-democracy advocates, members of ethnic armed organisations or insurgencies, and students. The Constitution confers power on the president to grant a pardon or amnesty, based on the recommendations of the National Defence and Security Council.[57] In January 2014, president Thein Sein commuted all death sentences being served to life imprisonment, which since 1988 has reportedly been over 800 people. However, the death penalty has been handed down by both state and non-state courts since 2014. In terms of state court trials, in 2016–2017, there have been reports of the death penalty handed down against Rohingya men accused of being involved in the conflict in northern Rakhine State.[58] In terms of non-state trials, there is evidence that the death penalty has recently been issued or carried out in areas under the control of ethnic

---

[53] Law No 8/2015 on Protection of the Rights of National Races.

[54] 2008 Constitution, ss 366, 368.

[55] Ibid, s 367.

[56] Ibid, s 353.

[57] Section 54 of the Penal Code provides that the President may commute the offender's sentence to any other punishment provided by the Code.

[58] *The Irrawaddy*, 'Death sentence for Maungdaw attacker raises questions about state executions in Myanmar', 14 February 2017, www.irrawaddy.com/news/burma/death-sentence-maungdaw-attacker-raises-questions-state-executions-burma.html.

armed organisations including in Karen State,[59] by tribunals of the Kachin Independence Organisation,[60] and in the Wa Region. In 2019, the death penalty was handed down to two of the accused in the case of the political assassination of Ko Ni, the lawyer affiliated with the NLD.

Other rights open to persons concern protections if convicted of a crime. A person can only be convicted for a crime under an existing law. A penalty cannot be imposed unless it is specified in the law.[61] A person cannot be retried for a crime of which they have been acquitted, unless a superior court annuls the original judgment and orders a retrial.[62] There is a right to defence for the accused and a Legal Aid Law has been introduced.[63] All these rights are subject to law, meaning that the rights can and are limited by legislation. A person cannot be detained in custody without a warrant from a judge for more than 24 hours,[64] although there continue to be instances where this occurs. The only mechanism for enforceability for breach of rights is the writs proceedings in the Supreme Court, although these remedies are unavailable in a state of emergency. Many of these rights concerning the criminal process may involve the police or military and so either are not brought to court, or are often unsuccessful if challenged in court.

E. State Assistance, Obligations and Prohibitions

The Constitution contains a range of state obligations and specifies ways in which the state must assist citizens. Some provisions appear to be positive obligations on the state to enforce by legislation. It also contains a list of prohibitions or actions that the state cannot take. These state duties within Chapter VIII are unenforceable. For example, the state has an obligation to assist citizens in certain matters, such as supporting good students with their education, and facilitating access to technology for economic development of the country.[65] These provisions can be compared to the Basic Principles Chapter, which also requires the state to

---

[59] Brian McCartan and Kim Joliffe, *Ethnic Armed Associations and Justice in Myanmar* (Yangon, The Asia Foundation, 2016) p 127.

[60] Nan Lwin Hnin Pwint, 'KIO Sentences Poppy Grower to Death for Killing Anti-drug Activist' 15 June 2017, *Irrawaddy*, www.irrawaddy.com/news/burma/kio-sentences-poppy-grower-to-death-for-killing-anti-drug-activist.html.

[61] 2008 Constitution, s 373.

[62] Ibid, s 374.

[63] Ibid, s 375. Legal Aid Law No 10/2016.

[64] Ibid, s 376.

[65] Ibid, ss 368 and 371.

provide assistance on certain matters (see Chapter 1). Other provisions appear to create a negative state duty through prohibition. For example, there is a prohibition on trafficking in persons, and on forced labour, although even the latter is qualified to allow hard labour by prisoners.[66]

There is no obligation on the state to address and reconcile past crimes. There are provisions in the Constitution that potentially prevent a truth and reconciliation commission or prosecutions for past crimes.[67] In the past, there have been proposals for a truth and reconciliation commission, although there is currently no political space or support for such efforts.[68]

III. CONSTITUTIONAL WRITS IN THE SUPREME COURT

Only the Supreme Court has the authority to issue writs, including the writ of mandamus, prohibition, certiorari, quo warranto and habeas corpus. The Constitution makes multiple references to its power to issue writs in the Basic Principles,[69] in section 296 (in Chapter VI on The Judiciary), and in section 378 (Chapter VIII on the Fundamental Rights and Duties of Citizens). It is only the latter provision, section 378, that specifies that the power to issue a writ is for the protection and realisation of constitutional rights. In theory, other lower courts can also issue the writs although this is not current judicial or legal practice.[70] The opportunity to seek the writs is limited and centralised in the Supreme Court.

The renaissance of the writs as a procedure to review the legality of decisions is a remarkable feature of the 2008 Constitution.[71] Yet the constitutional writs fit uneasily in the Constitution. This is because the constitutional writs are usually associated with a liberal constitution that aims to protect fundamental rights. To understand the limitations on the writs as a remedy, it is first important to keep in mind my analysis of the scope of rights in the Constitution (above). The re-emergence of the writs in the Supreme Court raises many questions. The use of the writs is affected by the shift in the relationship between the branches of government, the Tatmadaw, and the absence of the separation of powers.

---

[66] Ibid, ss 358 and 359.
[67] Ibid, ss 445, 43.
[68] Federal Constitution Drafting and Coordinating Committee, Adopted 12 Feb 2008. (Chiang Mai, Thailand, NCUB).
[69] 2008 Constitution, s 18(c).
[70] Ibid, s 378(b).
[71] See generally Melissa Crouch, 'The Prerogative Writs as Constitutional Transfer' (2018) *Oxford Journal of Legal Studies* 1–23.

Between 2011 and 2018, several hundred writs applications were filed directly with the Supreme Court. This suggests that lawyers have tried to take advantage of this new mechanism of review for protection of rights, even though most of the cases are not articulated in terms of rights protection. Many applications are dismissed without a hearing. When a case is brought against the executive, particularly the police or Tatmadaw in habeas corpus applications,[72] it is likely to be dismissed. In fact, no claim for habeas corpus has been successful. Further, the court has not defined the scope and content of constitutional rights, in part because this is the jurisdiction of the Constitutional Tribunal.

The constitutional writs are most often used as a final form of appeal, after all other avenues have been exhausted. The majority of applicants are landowners, employers or managing directors, civil servants and the police. This suggests that most applicants are relatively powerful actors, although some cases are also filed by tenants and tenant farmers. Cases are filed against officers of the General Administration Department, the Yangon City Development Council, the Arbitration Council (under the Ministry of Labour, Employment and Social Security), the Land Record Department and Land Administration Board, the Ministry of Education, the police, the Myanmar Motion Pictures Association (Ministry of Information) and the Ministry of Construction. Many writs cases involve issues over land, such as disputes over property ownership or the use of land or buildings; disputes by tenants over decisions of the urban rent controller; disputes relating to farmland use; or inheritance or divorce disputes over land. This is not surprising, given that land disputes are among the biggest legal issues in Myanmar.

Most writs cases seek review of a decision of a lower court or tribunal, not of the executive. For example, in one case,[73] the Supreme Court held that it could not overturn a lower court decision unless it was beyond the jurisdiction of that court according to the law. Again in another case the Supreme Court insisted that it will not interfere in the judgment of a subordinate court if the judgment is passed within its power of jurisdiction.[74] In another early reported case,[75] the Supreme

---

[72] Nick Cheesman, 'The Incongruous Return of Habeas Corpus to Myanmar' in Nick Cheesman et al (eds) *Ruling Myanmar* (Singapore: ISEAS, 2010). pp 90–111.

[73] *Daw Than Than Hte & 2 others v Regional High Court Judge Magwe Regional High Court, Magwe City & 7 others* (2011) MLR (Civil Case) 127.

[74] *U Myin Than & 5 others v President of the Republic of the Union of Myanmar & 2 others* (2011) MLR (Criminal Case) 79.

[75] *Shin Nyana (aka) Shin Moe Pya v President of the Republic of the Union of Myanmar* (2011) MLR (Criminal Case) 126.

Court held that it could not hear writs applications in relation to its own judgments, only in relation to inferior courts if an inferior court has heard a case that is not within its jurisdiction, if it has exercised power beyond its jurisdiction, or if it has failed to exercise its jurisdiction appropriately. While this is a traditional articulation of the function of the common law writs, this approach suggests that one of the main roles of the Supreme Court is to supervise decisions of lower courts, rather than decisions of the executive.

Very few court decisions in writs cases have been published in the official Myanmar Law Reports. Of cases that have, most decisions focus on general procedural issues and do not clarify the principles that animate constitutional writ claims.[76] The most successful case that could operate as an important precedent has not been officially reported. This unreported case has potential to expand the constitutional writs as a means of rights protection. The case concerned an economics professor who had been 'forced to retire' from her position by the Minister of Education. She lodged a writ application with the Supreme Court to seek a writ of certiorari against the decision of the Minister.[77] All university staff are civil servants, and the University of Yangon Distance Education is under the Ministry of Education. Being 'forced to retire' is a common practice and is a euphemism to describe a process by which a person is told they should retire voluntarily to allow them to save face and avoid being fired.

The professor argued that the Minister acted beyond his power under the Civil Servant Law. The case was brought based on two constitutional rights claims: equal rights before the law, and equal opportunity in public employment. The law lists a wide range of punishments that can be given if a civil servant violates the regulations, such as a demotion or being fired, but the list does not include the power to force a civil servant to retire. The court held that the decision of the Minister to force her to retire was beyond his power and awarded the writ of certiorari. While the court did refer to past Myanmar case law, it did not refer to the meaning of these rights nor to any comparative contemporary jurisprudence. This is the first time the Supreme Court has declared the decision of a government minister to be unlawful and it sent ripples of excitement through the legal profession. This success, however, was tempered by

---

[76] *U Kyaw Myint v Daw Tin Hla* (2011) MLR (Civil Case) 1.
[77] See *Professor Daw Kyin Hte v Minister for Education* (2013) Union Supreme Court of Myanmar (unreported case number 290), dated 5 June 2014.

the fact that the Minister who had made the decision was deceased at the time the court decision was handed down, so the decision did not have any implications for the late Minister. This appears to have been an exceptional case.

The writs have opened a new avenue for action in the Supreme Court. The inclusion of the writs in the Constitution has had unintended consequences for the legislature, such as the insistence by the Supreme Court and Attorney General's Office that general clauses for judicial review of executive action cannot be included in draft Bills. For example, in the redrafting of the Company Act, it was suggested that the judicial review provision should be removed and replaced with a provision allowing for judicial review by way of the constitutional writs. Instead, the writs are emphasised as the only means of judicial review of executive action.

IV. THE NATIONAL HUMAN RIGHTS COMMISSION

The Myanmar National Human Rights Commission ('the Commission') has gone through two distinct phases that correspond with its shifting legal status. The Commission does not have constitutional endorsement, although it does have legal status. The first period was 2011 to 2014, when the Commission was established by presidential decree. The second period is March 2014 to the present, when the legislature passed a new law on the Commission.[78] The Commission has not shown strong leadership on human rights, and instead tends to wait for the government to act and then to endorse the position taken by the government on human rights issues.

In September 2011, the president formed the Commission by notification.[79] The Commission had the broad mandate to conduct inquiries and make recommendations on compliance with international human rights. In October 2011 the Commission began to accept complaints. From 2011 to the end of 2012, the Commission claimed to receive over 3,000 complaints.[80] From 2011–2013, the main source of public information on the Commission was the public statements in

---

[78] Myanmar National Human Rights Commission Law No 21/2014.
[79] Presidential Notification No 34/2011 creating the Myanmar National Human Rights Commission.
[80] Statement 8/2012 of the Myanmar National Human Rights Commission on the International Human Rights Day, 10 December 2012.

the government-run *New Light of Myanmar*. In this first period, the Commission was criticised for failing to comply with the Paris Principles, as a key requirement is that it be established by a national law.[81] The Commission relied significantly on its position as the newest national human rights institution in the ASEAN region for public justification at the international and regional level for its existence and activities.

The Commission made official visits and issued public statements on ethnic and social conflict, yet these statements have largely supported the current position of the civilian-military government on these issues. One example is the Commission's response to the conflict in Kachin State. Since 2011, there has been serious fighting between the government and the Kachin Independence Army (KIA), which led to the displacement of thousands of people in Kachin State.[82] The Commission conducted several short field trips to the area for investigation. In its media statements in the *New Light of Myanmar*, the government-run newspaper, it praised the quick response of the Kachin State Government to meet the needs of those who were displaced by the conflict, urged the army to help restore order, and highlighted the need to avoid the use of landmines.[83] Given the continuation of the conflict, the Commission conducted two follow-up investigations with similar statements.[84] These statements all supported the government's position in this conflict. The Commission did not attempt to address any of the allegations that violations of human rights had been conducted by the Tatmadaw.

Public statements by the Commission on other issues take a similar tone of supporting government action. One demand of many democracy advocates is the release of political prisoners. In 2011–2012, the Commission visited several prisons, which in the past have remained tightly closed to any demands for accountability through international inspections. The Commission issued several statements that called on the government to release all prisoners of conscience.[85] In May and October 2011, and January 2012, the government announced the

---

[81] Statement by the Myanmar National Human Rights Commission, 10 October 2011.
[82] ICG, *A Tentative Peace in Myanmar's Kachin State* (International Crisis Group, 2013).
[83] Statement by the Myanmar National Human Rights Commission, 13 December 2011.
[84] See Statement 5/2012 of the Myanmar National Human Rights Commission; Statement of the Myanmar National Human Rights Commission 1/2013.
[85] Statement by the Myanmar National Human Rights Commission, 12 November 2011; Statement by the Myanmar National Human Rights Commission 10 October 2011; Statement 1/2012 by the Myanmar National Human Rights Commission, 14 January 2012; Statement by the Myanmar National Human Rights Commission, 30 December 2011.

release of many political prisoners.[86] The sequence of events, with the government initiating the release of political prisoners even before the Commission was established, suggests that the calls from the Commission for the release of many prisoners simply reinforced what the government had already begun to do.

Members of the Commission are frequently appointed by the government to ad hoc investigation committees set up to investigate human rights abuses. For example, in 2012, a Commissioner was elected as the secretary of the Investigation Committee into the night attack by police on demonstrators at the Letpadaung Coppermine.[87] These appointments, however, were at the directive of the executive and were not an initiative of the Commission itself. The Commission did not establish its own independent investigation into the incident. By establishing an ad hoc committee in some cases of alleged human rights violations, the executive appears to be signalling that the Commission does not or should not investigate these incidents on its own.

Such incidents have led to a pattern in the response of the Commission to violations of human rights, in which the Commission waits for the government to act before it determines its own course of action. For example, although the Commission visited Rakhine State after the Buddhist-Muslim conflict in June 2012 and issued a statement that noted that all 'Rakhine nationals' (that is, only ethnic Rakhine citizens and not Rohingya) were being taken care of,[88] it failed to launch a thorough investigation into this incident after the conflict escalated further. The chairperson claimed that it would not investigate the violence because the government had decided to establish its own special committee.[89] In August 2012, the government formed the Rakhine Investigation Commission and one of the Commissioners was subsequently appointed as a member. In May 2013, the Rakhine Investigation Commission submitted its report to the government and the government made a public response in support of the Commission's findings that ranged from the need for increased security and immigration control, to the monitoring of religious leaders and birth control policies. Only after this did

---

[86] The power of the President to release prisoners is set out in s 401(1) of the Code of Criminal Procedure.

[87] See Presidents Office Notification No 92/2012 on the Formation of the Investigation Commission.

[88] Statement No 4/2012 of Myanmar National Human Rights Commission.

[89] On 10 June 2012, the President declared a state of emergency through Ordinance No 1/2012. On 6 June 2012, a local investigation commission was formed by Presidential Notification No 43/2012. Due to the ongoing nature of the violence, on 17 August 2012, a national investigation commission was formed.

the Commission issue a public statement in response to the report of the Rakhine Investigation Commission. Instead of providing a critical response to the report, such as the failure to identify who was responsible for the violence, the Commission quoted from the points raised by the president in his statement, and simply urged the implementation of the recommendations, rather than expressing an opinion on their relative merit.[90] This is another example of the way in which the Commission has worked at the direction of the executive.

The Commission has caught the attention of the legislature and its legal basis was brought into question. In March 2012, the legislature debated the submission by the Commission of its proposed budget.[91] Daw Nan Wah Nu of the Bill Committee in the Pyithu Hluttaw voiced her concerns that the Commission had not been established with the approval of the legislature. This was a significant assertion of the role of the legislature in approving the establishment and funding of independent accountability institutions. The subsequent refusal of the legislature to approve the budget of the Commission as a body not established by law sent a clear message to the executive about the need to follow legal procedures and to have its actions formally approved by the legislature. This incident was one of the catalysts for the drafting of a national law on the Commission.

The second phase of the Commission (2014-present) is marked by the introduction in 2014 of a law regulating and clarifying the role and powers of the Commission.[92] The Commission is required to have between 7 and 15 members. In terms of their status, the position of the Chairperson of the Commission is equivalent to that of a Union minister, and the other Commissioners as Deputy Ministers. The term of Commissioners is five years and they cannot serve more than two terms. The Commission is required to recommend to government treaties that it should enter; review laws for compliance with international human rights to which Myanmar is a party, and to prepare reports for the government concerning human rights. In undertaking these responsibilities, it has an obligation to consult relevant actors, and in investigating human rights abuses, it has power to question witnesses, compel the production of documents, visit the sites of alleged human rights violations, and inspect prisons. Individual complaints can be filed with the Commission, and both the president and the legislature can refer duties to the Commission.

---

[90] Statement 3/2013 of the Myanmar National Human Rights Commission.
[91] See PH2012-3:20.
[92] Law No 21/2014 on the Myanmar National Human Rights Commission.

The Commission has been the subject of fierce criticism. For example, in late 2016, a scandal erupted over the handling of an investigation into years of alleged torture, physical and psychological abuse, and withholding of pay to two underage maids. The four Commissioners handling the case did not recommend the police press criminal charges. Instead, when the Commissioners gave their press conference about the investigation, they emphasised a negotiation and conciliation approach, which is permitted according to section 34 of the Commission Law. The Commissioners suggested that the perpetrators pay out to the victims as a final settlement in the case. However, the media coverage of the investigation provoked strong outcry, criticising the Commissioners for failing to recommend criminal proceedings and even accusing the Commissioners of accepting a bribe.[93] While the President's Office was still seeking advice from the Union Attorney General's Office, the four Commissioners voluntarily resigned with the permission of the president, according to section 17 of the Commission Law. This incident had echoes of the voluntary resignation of the Constitutional Tribunal back in 2012, although under different circumstances. It is one indication that the impeachment of high-level officials will rarely be followed through, as often the official will resign before any final action or decision to impeach is taken. Activists argued that the president should not have accepted the Commissioners resignation and instead should have exercised his powers under the law to initiate impeachment proceedings for failing to do their duties under the law. It was emphasised that Commissioners are Union Level officials and so should be held to the standards that other Union Level officials are constitutionally required to uphold (see Chapter 5).

V. CONCLUSION

A top-down analysis of compliance with international human rights law has little purchase due to the dualist approach to international law in Myanmar's legal system. Chapter VIII of the Constitution was not modelled on international human rights conventions. Instead, the

---

[93] Shoon Naing, 'Four National Human Rights Commissioners resign over child domestic workers scandal', *The Myanmar Times*, 7 October 2016, www.mmtimes.com/national-news/yangon/22961-four-national-human-rights-commissioners-resign-over-child-domestic-workers-scandal.html.

constitutional mandate for citizens to abide by certain duties and responsibilities is designed to come conceptually prior to the granting of constitutional rights. This has resonance with the idea that citizens are perceived by the state as a threat and potential enemy, as Callahan has argued. These constitutional obligations are a precondition which must be met before rights may be exercised. These duties ensure that the three meta-principles of Myanmar's military-state are upheld. In this regard, the Constitution uses these duties to require obedience from citizens. The legislature has complete discretion to restrict rights as it chooses through its law-making function. The constitutional distinction between citizens and persons has hardened, and minority groups are aware of the dangers of being as a non-citizen.[94]

The extent of rights protection as articulated in legislation then acts as a limitation on the courts, which are rarely a forum for overt constitutional rights litigation or protection. This is evident from the kinds of cases brought to the Supreme Court under its writs jurisdiction. The writs are used as another form of appeal and are often not specifically connected to the protection of constitutional rights. When applicants do make rights claims, such as in cases of habeas corpus, the fact that the case is against the police or Tatmadaw means that these cases are likely to be dismissed. While a National Human Rights Commission has been created by statute, it has failed to show strong leadership for the protection of human rights, and instead reinforces the common perception that such agencies lack independence from the executive.

FURTHER READING

Nick Cheesman, 'The Incongruous Return of Habeas Corpus to Myanmar' in Nick Cheesman et al (eds) *Ruling Myanmar: From Cyclone Nargis to General Elections* (Singapore: ISEAS, 2010).

Melissa Crouch (ed) *The Business of Transition: Law Reform, Development and Economics in Myanmar* (CUP, 2017).

Melissa Crouch, 'The Common Law and the Constitutional Writs in Myanmar' in Melissa Crouch and Tim Lindsey (eds) *Law, Society and Transition in Myanmar* (Hart Publishing, 2014). pp 141–158.

---

[94] Roberts has noted this awareness of the dangers of being considered a non-citizen among the Chinese of Myanmar, see Jayde Lin Roberts (2016) *Mapping Chinese Rangoon: Place and Nation among the Sino-Burmese*. University of Washington Press, p 16.

Morten Pederson, *Promoting Human Rights in Myanmar* (Lanham: Rowman & Littlefield Publishers, 2008).

Ardeth Maung Thawnghmung, *Everyday Economic Survival in Myanmar* (University of Wisconsin Press, 2019).

David Kinley and Trevor Wilson 'Engaging a Pariah: Human Rights Training in Burma/Myanmar' (2007) 29 *Human Rights Quarterly* 368.

10

The Peace Process and Constitutional Change

Peace Process – National Ceasefire Agreement – Formal Constitutional Amendment – Proposals for Constitutional Change – Federalism

THE CONSTITUTION HAS been unable to address two major policy goals: the end to decades of armed conflict and the creation of a durable nationwide peace agreement; and a governance system that the people see as legitimately democratic and federal. Despite the ceasefire agreements of the 1990s and new constitutional arrangements to recognise select national races, conflict has re-emerged. Democratic, though not necessarily liberal, groups such as the National League for Democracy (NLD), continue to take a strong pro-reform stance to the 2008 Constitution. The twin tensions of peace and constitutional reform have led to two separate processes.

The first process is a national ceasefire process that commenced in 2012. There are questions about how this process fits with the current constitutional order, the legal source of its power, and the potential constitutional outcomes. The National Ceasefire Agreement is a remarkable text that for the first time commits signatories to disarmament and federalism. In contrast, the 37 Principles of the 2017 Peace Accord rolls back this progress by reverting to disciplined democracy and the coercive centralism of the current Constitution. While the 21-Panglong Peace Conference is a group of mostly unelected representatives, it functions as a quasi-Constituent Assembly. The main achievement of the peace process is that it has normalised discussions of federalism that were previously taboo, even if there is a question mark over the meaning of federalism.

The second process is formal constitutional amendment. The amendment process is an example of a constitutional rule that gives a direct structural advantage to the Tatmadaw. There has been an overemphasis on the structural advantages of the Tatmadaw and a lack of attention to the Tatmadaw's indirect advantages. It is critical that local perspectives on constitutional amendment are appreciated and taken seriously. For example, proponents of the Constitution argue that the formal amendment procedure only allows for 'amendment' of the Constitution, and not 'addition', 'suspension' or 'removal' of clauses. This is one reason why politicians are strategic in the proposals they advocated for and so the debate did not feature many of the more radical constitutional reforms that have been proposed.

I. THE PEACE PROCESS: NORMALISING DEBATES ON FEDERALISM

At the start of the transition in 2011, it was clear that the Constitution had been unable to resolve the grievances of ethnic armed organisations and a new peace process was necessary. Although the peace process was initiated by the president through an exercise of executive power, the peace negotiation process has been led by the Tatmadaw and non-state actors. The peace process has had two unexpected outcomes. The first development is that the peace process has normalised debate and discussion of federalism, which in the past was a prohibited topic due to its perceived links to secession. The second development is that the 21-Panglong Conference under the NLD Government is acting like a quasi-Constituent Assembly, formulating 37 Principles that could form the basis of a revised Chapter I of the Constitution. This raises questions about public participation and the legitimacy of the process.

The peace process was initiated in August 2011 when president Thein Sein began to reach out to ethnic armed organisations (EAOs) with the explicit aim of negotiating and concluding a nationwide ceasefire.[1] Initiating talks with EAOs was significant because up until this time most of these organisations were classified as unlawful associations. Beginning this process of negotiation was an implicit recognition of the existence and claims of EAOs. This process was undertaken at the initiative of the executive and without explicit legislative approval. On 18 November 2011, the government initiated the peace process at the State/Region level, and then through the Union Level Peace Dialogue. By May 2012, the peace process was formalised by the establishment of two organisations: the Union Peace Central Committee and the Union Peace Working Committee.[2] After some initial issues over which of

---

[1] Presidential Announcement No 1/2011.
[2] Decree 12/2012 of the Union Level Peace Team.

these bodies was leading the process, in November 2012, the Myanmar Peace Centre was officially launched with backing from the European Union and other international donors.[3] This is the first time that a technical institute was established as part of a peace process in Myanmar, and the first time that the government has received outside assistance and funding as part of a peace process. Three kinds of dialogue were initiated. The first was dialogue with specific ethnic groups, such as the Kachin and Pa-O. The second dialogue was sub-national, and the third level of dialogue was on thematic issues at the Union level, such as with civil society.[4]

From 2011–2014, as a result of these peace dialogues, the Thein Sein Government signed bilateral ceasefires with 14 armed groups, including the United Wa State Army (UWSA), the National Democratic Alliance Army (NDAA-ESS), Democratic Kayin Benevolent Army-5 (DKBA-5), Restoration Council of Shan State (RCSS/SSA), the Chin National Front (CNF), Karen National Union (KNU), the Shan State Progress Party (SSPP/SSA), New Mon State Party (NMSP), the Karen National Liberation Army (KNLA), Karenni National Progressive Party (KNPP), Arakan Liberation Party (ALP), the Naga (NSCN-K), the Pa-O National Liberation Organisation (PNLO) and the All-Burma Students Democratic Front (ABSDF). By August 2014, the relevant parties to the peace negotiations had agreed to work towards a federal system. Given that the 2008 Constitution avoids the language of federalism (see Chapter 7), the inclusion of federalism as a key objective of the peace process is significant.

The peace process has been led by actors appointed by the executive and the Tatmadaw, but from time to time matters concerning the peace process have been discussed in the legislature. For example, on 13 October 2014, the Pyidaungsu Hluttaw discussed funding that had been received from the international community.[5] The rush by the Thein Sein Government to sign the National Ceasefire Agreement before the 2015 elections (when the USDP lost votes to the NLD) meant that only eight of 15 armed groups were willing to sign. On 15 October 2015, eight ethnic armed organisations, the government and the Tatmadaw gathered in the capital to sign the National Ceasefire Agreement. The signatories included the ABSDF, the ALP, the CNF, the Karen National Union

---

[3] Presidential Notification No 38/2012 establishing the Myanmar Peace Centre.

[4] Su Mon Thazin Aung, 'The Politics of Policymaking in Transitional Government', in Nick Cheesman and Nicholas Farrelly (eds) *Conflict in Myanmar: War, Politics, Religion* (Singapore: ISEAS, 2016) pp 25–47.

[5] See PDH2014-11:13.

(KNU), the Democratic Kayin Benevolent Army (DKBA-5), the KNLA, the RCSS, and the PNLA. In 2018, the NLD added two more signatories though of relatively small armies: the Lahu Democratic Union and the NMSP. Several of the most powerful armed ethnic groups have not signed the NCA, including the KNPP; the SSPP/SSA-North; the Kachin Independence Organisation (KIO); the United Wa State Party (UWSP); the National Democratic Alliance Army (NDAA, 'Mongla group'); the Shan State Progress Party (SSPP/SSA-North); the Ta'ang National Liberation Army (TNLA); the Myanmar National Democratic Alliance Army (MNDAA, 'Kokang group'); and the Arakan Army (AA). Of these, it is the Wa that is the largest ethnic armed group in Myanmar and a key determinant of whether the ceasefire process will be truly nationwide.

Following the signing of the National Ceasefire Agreement, from 12–16 January 2016, the outgoing government held the First Union Peace Conference. Over 700 participants were invited, including non-signatories to the NCA, who had observer status. One of the main differences between the peace process pre and post-2016 is that under Thein Sein's administration, the peace process was enabled and coordinated by the President's Office. Under the NLD Government, the peace process has been under the authority and guidance of the State Counsellor's Office (see Chapter 6). The peace process is a key example of the pronounced shift in the exercise of executive power. Under the NLD, the conference was rebadged as the 'Union Peace Conference – 21st Century Panglong' (or 21-Panglong), to draw on the symbolic legitimacy of the first Panglong Agreement of 1947 (see Chapter 2).[6] On 28 June 2016, the Union Peace Dialogue Joint Committee was reconstituted as the central negotiation body, led by State Counsellor Aung San Suu Kyi. From 31 August to September 2017, the First 21-Panglong Conference was held in Naypyidaw and was attended by UN Secretary General Ban Ki-Moon. The 21-Panglong Conference is part of the political roadmap for the peace process.[7] After the signing of the NCA, the seven-step roadmap for the peace process includes drafting a Framework for Political Dialogue and then holding the dialogue; holding a Union Peace Process and signing a Union Peace Accord to then submit to the legislature; and then implementation of the Union Peace Accord.

In terms of the process of the peace negotiations, there has been significant controversy over who is included or excluded from the process.

---

[6] Some have disputed this renaming of the process, arguing that the National Ceasefire Agreement does not use these terms.

[7] National Ceasefire Agreement, s 20.

Due to ongoing fighting with the Tatmadaw, three groups were initially excluded from peace talks, including the MNDAA, the TNLA and the Arakan Army.[8] Despite fighting between the Tatmadaw and the Arakan Rohingya Solidarity Association (ARSA) since 2016, ARSA is not invited to the peace process because they are classified as a terrorist organisation.

II. THE NATIONAL CEASEFIRE AGREEMENT:
PEACE IN THE MILITARY-STATE

The National Ceasefire Agreement is a departure from the Constitution, although the precise nature of its relationship to the Constitution remains ambiguous. The Ceasefire Agreement is a written agreement without precedent in Myanmar. On 8 December 2015, a motion concerning approval of the National Ceasefire Agreement ('Ceasefire Agreement') was put to the Pyidaungsu Hluttaw and approved with unanimous agreement from legislators.[9] This is an example of an issue of national significance being dealt with by the Pyidaungsu Hluttaw, rather than the two houses sitting separately (see Chapter 5). My primary focus here is on the legal and constitutional status of the Ceasefire Agreement, which has received insufficient attention. The Ceasefire Agreement itself reveals the way in which existing principles – such as non-disintegration and the concept of the Union – are part of the implicit basic structure of the Constitution and remain untouched by the Ceasefire Agreement.[10]

The Ceasefire Agreement draws on the 2008 Constitution implicitly. Chapter 1 of the Ceasefire Agreement contains Basic Principles that echoes some of the Basic Principles of the Constitution. This includes the three meta-principles of the military-state: non-disintegration of Union, non-disintegration of national solidarity and perpetuation of national sovereignty. The Ceasefire Agreement supports and affirms these principles and depicts the peace process as fitting within this framework. It does not challenge or seek to dislodge these principles.

In other ways, the Ceasefire Agreement goes beyond the limits of the Constitution. The Ceasefire Agreement refers to 'democracy', rather than the more qualified term of 'disciplined democracy' in

---

[8] *Frontier*, 'The National Ceasefire Agreement and National Reconciliation', 27 October 2017, https://frontiermyanmar.net/en/the-national-ceasefire-agreement-and-national-reconciliation.

[9] See PDH2015-12:3.

[10] Ardeth Maung Thawnghmung, 'Signs of Life in Myanmar's Nationwide Ceasefire Agreement?' (2017) 49:3 *Critical Asian Studies* 379.

the Constitution. This is unusual and constitutes a departure from the text of the Constitution. The debate over genuine democracy has been a key fault line in constitutional debates. The Ceasefire Agreement also refers explicitly to the idea of a federal system, which again is not included in the Constitution. The overt reference to federalism is striking, given the Tatmadaw's preference for the term 'Union' in the Constitution. This is one indication of the distinct shift and willingness among government negotiators at the time the Ceasefire Agreement was drafted to include this term. Related to the concept of federalism, the National Ceasefire Agreement also mentions the 'Spirit of Panglong'. This is a reference to the historic agreement signed between General Aung San and several ethnic groups in 1947 (see Chapter 2). Evoking the legacy of this important agreement is a strategic move and one designed to generate legitimacy for the terms of the Ceasefire Agreement. Again, the approach is contrary to the Constitution, which avoids mention of Panglong.

The Ceasefire Agreement specifies the right to self-determination based on liberty, equality and justice. This is yet another significant departure from the status quo, because the Constitution deliberately avoids the use of the term 'self-determination'. While the government has ratified the ICESCR, it submitted a reservation on the provision on self-determination (see Chapter 8). It is remarkable that the Ceasefire Agreement uses the language of self-determination, given the past association of this idea with autonomy and secession.

On religion, the Ceasefire Agreement offers a completely new vision of the relationship between religion and state. The Ceasefire Agreement refers to the establishment of a secular state,[11] which is contrary to the Constitution's special recognition of Buddhism (Chapter 8). Nowhere does the Ceasefire Agreement privilege Buddhism or any other religion. Religious freedom has long been a demand of religious minorities and many attribute General Aung San as a proponent of a secular state. On other rights, the Ceasefire Agreement does refer to some of the same protections the Constitution offers, such as cultural rights, education, health, freedom of movement and protection of property.

Of immediate benefit to EAOs, the Ceasefire Agreement declares that all EAO signatories will be removed from the government's Unlawful Associations list, and anyone who had been detained for being part of an EAO shall be released from jail.[12] EAOs have long been branded illegal

---

[11] National Ceasefire Agreement, s 1(e).
[12] Ibid, s 24.

organisations under the Unlawful Associations Act 1908, and people who were suspected to be associated with an ethnic armed group are detained or prosecuted under this law.[13] The Ceasefire Agreement has real and important legal consequences for EAOs that sign on to its terms.

The critical provision of the Ceasefire Agreement in terms of implementation and its connection to constitutional reform is section 22(d), which holds that any decision agreed upon at the Union Peace Conference should be the basis to amend, repeal or add provisions to the Constitution, or to relevant laws. The Ceasefire Agreement specifies that it must be submitted to the legislature for ratification.[14]

One issue that has emerged is the relationship between the sub-national dialogues and the Union dialogue. The Union-level dialogue has been postponed on several occasions due to lack of progress with the sub-national dialogues, particularly in Shan State and Rakhine State. But this has meant that the timeline for dialogue meetings has not been met, and the Ceasefire Agreement does not provide for an extension of the timeline. Another reason for the delay is the opposition to the terms of the Ceasefire Agreement itself, which raises questions about the constitutionality of the agreement and whether it can be amended before more groups sign on. The initial source of opposition was from the United Nationalities Federal Council (UNFC) as the main coalition of non-signatory groups. Since 2017, the UNFC has been overtaken and replaced by the Federal Peace Negotiation Central Committee (FPNCC). Convened by the Wa and including seven north-eastern armed groups, in early 2017 the FPNCC met and publicly announced its rejection of the Ceasefire Agreement. The FPNCC proposed specific ways in which the Ceasefire Agreement should be amended. But the Ceasefire Agreement itself does not anticipate the possibility of amendment, and neither the Tatmadaw nor the NLD Government is willing to consider amendment of the Ceasefire Agreement.

Some have questioned how the 21-Panglong conference and the Ceasefire Agreement relate to the 1947 Panglong Agreement. Others argue that the Panglong Agreement is still valid, while others suggest that the Ceasefire Agreement effectively nullifies the 1947 Panglong Agreement. There have been breaches of the Ceasefire Agreement by many parties though the consequences of breaching the agreement are unlikely.

---

[13] AHRC and ALRC, *Cases under the Unlawful Associations Act 1908* (Hong Kong: Asian Human Rights Commission, 2013).

[14] National Ceasefire Agreement, s 26.

While my focus is on the origins and terms of the Ceasefire Agreement, at the time of writing the peace process stalled after the Karen and Shan suspended their involvement in the process. A disconnect has emerged between the terms and ideas in the Ceasefire Agreement, and the more conservative position as expressed in the 37 Principles, as I show next.

III. THE 37 PRINCIPLES AS CONSTITUTIONAL FOUNDATION

Compared to the Ceasefire Agreement, the 37 Principles are a more modest proposal and largely reflect the status quo. From 24 to 29 May 2017, the Second 21-Panglong Conference was held. This time the Kokang, Palaung and Arakan armies were permitted to join as observers, despite previously being excluded. At the 21-Panglong, the representatives discussed 41 principles. The aim was to have all ethnic armed organisations sign on to these 41 principles, however only 37 Principles of the Union Peace Accord ('the Accord') were approved.[15] These principles are divided into political, economic, social and environmental matters. The Preamble to the Accord upholds the three meta-principles of the military-state in the Constitution. The Accord also references key principles of democracy, federalism, national equality and self-determination. The affirmation of federalism and self-determination is like the Ceasefire Agreement and marks a departure from the 2008 Constitution.

Some provisions of the Accord are the same as the 2008 Constitution. For example, the Accord acknowledges that sovereign power is derived from citizens, as set out in section 4 of the Constitution. The Accord also includes the same provision on the separation of powers. The Accord also refers to the principles of a multi-party system, maintaining the commitment to elections and a semi-competitive political system.

Other aspects of the Accord appear to be variations of principles in the 2008 Constitution or potentially new principles. The Accord introduces the concept of a '*federal* economy', whereas the current Constitution only refers to a 'market economy'. The Accord does not clarify the meaning of a federal economy, though this can be taken to mean greater control of natural resources by ethnic minorities or greater distribution of the benefits of natural resources. The Ceasefire Agreement also contains an economic principle on the prevention of the monopoly

---

[15] 37 Principles of the Union Peace Accord, signed 29 May 2017.

of the economy by any one person or organisation, which is also found in the Constitution. This is an implicit rejection of the Tatmadaw as the dominant actor in the economy. A range of new economic principles are added: to reduce poverty and increase living standards, to promote sustainable development, to ensure equal opportunity for economic growth in the states and regions; to provide for the fair allocation of the national budget; sharing responsibility for the management of the economy between the Union and sub-national governments; and managing the economy according to principles of transparency, accountability and responsibility. These economic principles are to be combined with a Regional Comprehensive Development Plan to enhance both domestic and foreign investment. The emphasis on economic principles underscores the financial and socio-economic concerns inherent in calls for federalism.

In terms of the social principles, the Accord identifies the need for a solution to address internal displacement due to natural or man-made disasters and conflict. Unusually, the Accord agrees that solutions must be based on international human rights norms (contra Chapter 9). The Accord emphasises the resettlement of internally displaced communities as a core priority. In 2018, there were approximately 240,000 displaced people across Kayin State, Kachin State, Shan State, and Rakhine State.[16] The Accord also identifies the need for protective and empowering measures for three particularly vulnerable groups – the elderly, the disabled, women and children, although this provision mirrors the existing Constitution. Finally, the Accord singles out the drug trade as a severe social ill that must be fought against. The Accord does not clarify how the illegal drug trade is to be addressed. The cultivation and trade in drugs is prevalent in areas controlled by EAOs in Myanmar. This principle in the Accord recognises that any effort to reduce or contain the illegal drug trade and its harmful social effects would require cooperation between the government, Tatmadaw and EAOs.

The land and natural environment section of the Accord consists of ten principles. It mandates a country-wide land policy, and specifies that the land policy be just, align with human rights and democracy, and promote decentralisation and federalism. The land policy must be clear and transparent, take into consideration the interests of farmers and local people, and promote the right to own and manage land, for both men and women. The land policy must aim to protect the

---

[16] Relief Web, Myanmar Humanitarian Needs 2018.

natural environment. If there is a failure to use land, then the right granted can be withdrawn (presumably to prevent stockpiling of land for use at a later point in time). Land grievances due to land confiscation, particularly due to illegal appropriation over the past 30 years, will remain the biggest issue for ordinary people in Myanmar and remains a formidable task for any future government to tackle.

Finally, and most importantly, there is disagreement on several of the principles such as the non-secession clause and the proposal for a Union army. Ethnic signatories argue that they have already agreed to non-disintegration as a principle, so a secession clause should be permitted. Their remains disagreement over the proposal by ethnic armed organisations for a federal army that would diversify the Tatmadaw by ensuring some form of ethnic representation or inclusion of ethnic armed organisations as part of a federal army.

IV. THE PROCESS AND PROCEDURE OF CONSTITUTIONAL AMENDMENT

The political opening has created space for previously unheard-of discussions, debates and advocacy on constitutional law and the prospects of reform.[17] It has been frequently observed that the Constitution is a 'rigid' constitution because of its constitutional amendment provision. The constitutional amendment rule is a key example of a rule that gives a structural advantage to the Tatmadaw. However, it is more than just the formal amendment rule that contributes to the rigidity of amendment. It is the Tatmadaw's combination of direct and indirect advantages that reinforce its leading and coercive role in the political system. Even if the threshold for constitutional amendment was reduced, this would not necessarily lead to amendment of core aspects of the Constitution. This is because the Constitution has been used to create and maintain a military-state. It is the combination of explicit and implicit advantages that constitute the real reasons for the rigidity of the Constitution.

The formal constitutional amendment provision – section 436 – is perceived to be the only way to amend the Constitution. There is debate in Myanmar over the meaning of the word 'amendment' (ပြင်ဆင်ခြင်း). This debate highlights the importance of taking local interpretations of

---

[17] The process of constitutional amendment followed in 2013–2015 is described in detail in Melissa Crouch and Tom Ginsburg (2016) 'Between Endurance and Change in Southeast Asia: The Military and Constitutional Reform in Myanmar and Thailand', in *Annual Review of Constitution Building*. Stockholm: International IDEA. pp 1–16.

constitutional language seriously, and points to the dangers of reliance on English translations. Some pro-Tatmadaw stakeholders in Myanmar argue that the provisions in the Constitution can only be 'amended' and provisions cannot be 'added' or 'replaced'. While this is a literal interpretation, it is one that has been fiercely defended by some in Myanmar. This debate has its origins in the 1947 Constitution, which specifically provided provisions could be repealed, varied or added to. Supporters of the 2008 Constitution argue that the omission of this full range of terms is significant and deliberate. This is one reason why the legislative debate in 2015 was so narrow in its focus on simply 'amending' existing provisions, rather than 'adding' entirely new provisions.

A proposal to amend the Constitution must be submitted in the form of a Bill exclusively concerning amendment. The proposed Bill must be supported by at least 20 per cent of all members of the Pyidaungsu Hluttaw, which means 133 of the 664 members. The Constitution sets out two different levels of amendment, depending on the provision concerned. Both tiers require more than 75 per cent approval in the Pyidaungsu Hluttaw, and this is another example of the important role the third and dominant house of the legislature plays. Any constitutional amendment would require negotiation and agreement across a range of parties.

The procedure for these two tiers of amendment varies slightly. The first tier requires approval in the legislature and at a referendum. Tier 1 is the higher threshold: it requires more than 75 per cent approval in the legislature plus a nationwide referendum with the votes of more than half of those who are eligible to vote (not merely half of those who *cast* a vote). Again, the wording of the Burmese version of the provision is crucial, and the reference to 'more than 75 per cent' (not 'only 75 per cent'). This approval process applies to most of the provisions on the powers of the government and the Tatmadaw: Chapter I on Basic Principles, Chapter II on State Structures; the qualifications for president and vice president; the formation of all houses of the legislature at the Union and State/Region levels, which ensures protection of the unelected Tatmadaw seats in the legislature; the formation of the Union Government, the National Defence and Security Council, and the president's powers over the States/Regions and self-administered zones; the hierarchy of the court system; emergency powers; and the amendment provision itself. As I have explained, 25 per cent of all legislators are non-elected Tatmadaw members. This means that while the process of initiating a Bill can begin with non-Tatmadaw legislators, the ultimate approval requires the support of all democratically elected representatives plus at least some support from Tatmadaw members. Therefore, many in Myanmar argue that the Constitution is practically unamendable.

The second tier for constitutional amendment only requires legislative approval. This tier requires more than 75 per cent of approval of legislators in the Pyidaungsu Hluttaw. This requirement covers all sections of the Constitution other than those specifically mentioned in the first tier, such as the appointment and impeachment of MPs, the process of passing legislation, the process of forming legislative committees, the rights of citizens and remedies for protecting these rights, and elections. The inference that can be drawn from this two-tier structure of constitutional amendment is that the powers of the Tatmadaw and the founding principles of the Constitution should not be subject to change, while individual rights are subject to change by the legislature and the Tatmadaw (without a referendum of the people).

This formal constitutional amendment process has been activated twice. The first campaign for reform took place from 2013 to 2015. Two Bills were finally submitted to the Pyidaungsu Hluttaw, however only very minor amendments were approved, such as to the schedule of legislative power. This did not satisfy the long list of demands from pro-democratic actors, civil society or ethnic groups. In 2019 the National League for Democracy, the main party advocating for reform, has initiated another formal process of constitutional amendment that remains ongoing. This will not happen through formal amendment unless some Tatmadaw members agree to any proposal submitted.

There remain ongoing restrictions on the NLD Government in terms of how it refers to the past that indicate the coercive nature of the military-state. For example, in 2017 a major debate erupted in the legislature over whether the term 'dictatorship' was an appropriate description of the regime prior to 2011. This debate arose on 22 August 2017 in the context of a speech made by one NLD member, who suggested that the crisis in Rakhine State was a direct legacy of the past dictatorship.[18] This then provoked a response from Tatmadaw legislators, who demanded to know what she meant by the term 'dictator' (အာဏာရှင်). The Tatmadaw MP rejected the use of the label 'dictatorship' to describe past regimes and forcefully requested that the comments of the NLD member be officially deleted from the records of the legislature. The legislature

---

[18] See AH2017-5:47, which is where this debate was presumably initially recorded and then deleted before publication of these records.

complied with this request to retract the words, demonstrating just how sensitive the NLD is to the Tatmadaw, despite holding most seats in the legislature.

V. PROPOSALS FOR CONSTITUTIONAL REFORM

There have been a diverse range of contemporary proposals for consti-tutional reform, although many proposals have historical antecedents. These proposals have been raised during the legislative constitutional amendment process and the parallel peace process. Some of the most frequent concerns relate to democracy and the role of the Tatmadaw; the idea of federalism and ethnic aspirations; and limits on executive and legislative power. The 2008 Constitution remains the starting point for all discussions, due to the refusal of the Tatmadaw to entertain discus-sion of drafting an entirely new constitution.

A. Democracy and the Role of the Tatmadaw

Proposals to enhance democracy are connected to the role of the Tatmadaw in Myanmar. The 2015 constitutional amendment process suggests that a range of core constitutional issues are out of bounds due to the explicit and implicit limits on constitutional change. Certain provisions constitute the unofficial basic structure of the 2008 Consti-tution or amount to a set of informal eternity clauses such as the three meta-principles of the military-state; the Tatmadaw seats in the legislature; the Tatmadaw's power to appoint three key ministers; the Tatmadaw's veto on constitutional amendment; the presidential system, including the separation between the legislature and executive; the president's power to appoint key executive positions, including Chief Ministers; the term of Supreme Court judges; the existence, role and function of the Constitutional Tribunal; the composition of the National Defence and Security Council, and the one per cent threshold for the right to recall of legislators. All of these elements of the Constitution are perceived by pro-democratic actors to be a limitation on democracy.

There are concerns about the qualified nature of democracy as expressed in the Constitution. For example, in its proposal to the Constitutional Committee in 2013, the NLD sought to reinforce the prin-ciple of democracy by removing the word 'disciplined' which currently qualifies democracy.[19] Building on this, the NLD proposed to remove the role of the Tatmadaw from politics and remove its influence over any political appointments. This proposal included abolishing seats for the Tatmadaw in the legislature and removing the Tatmadaw's power to appoint a vice-president and other ministerial positions. These proposals remain highly controversial, although the NLD submission admits these reforms may need to be done gradually. The NLD also suggested reforms to separate the Tatmadaw from the police. None of these proposals were included in the amendment Bills voted on in the legislature in 2015.

The NLD did propose further radical changes to the Tatmadaw's structural advantages. The NLD wanted to change the constitutional amendment provision so that proposals could be approved by a two-thirds vote of civilian legislators in the Pyidaungsu Hluttaw. This proposal would have excluded Tatmadaw members from the vote. The NLD wanted to delete section 59f that prohibits a presidential candidate from owing allegiance to a foreign nation and amend section 59d so that a presidential candidate did not have to have military experience. This was aimed at ensuring Aung San Suu Kyi could be appointed as president. The constitutional amendment Bill did propose changes to section 59(d) to emphasise knowledge of affairs related to the 'military' with the word 'defence',[20] as a subtle image make-over for the Tatmadaw, although the matter was never put to a referendum to complete the amendment process

The NLD also proposed abolishing one of two vice presidents so that the Tatmadaw would no longer have a vice-president as one of its key appointees. Further the NLD wanted to shift the balance of power in the National Defence and Security Council, by adding the Speakers of the Pyithu Hluttaw and Amyotha Hluttaw as members.[21] In terms of Chapter I on the Basic Principles, the NLD proposed to make the provisions in this chapter enforceable. On one hand, this was a concern to ensure greater protection for the cultural rights in the chapter. However, this appears to overlook the military principles in the Basic Chapter and the way that this change could potentially strengthen the power of the Tatmadaw in governance.

There are a range of issues concerning the Basic Principles of the Constitution on which there have not been proposals for reform.

---

[19] NLD submission on 2008 Constitution, December 2013.

[20] This is the distinction between စစ်ရေး (military affairs) and ကာကွယ်ရေး (defence affairs).

[21] 2008 Constitution, s 201.

The Tatmadaw has an extensive network of bases that stretch right across the country. It has an active intelligence apparatus in the Special Branch, although they are formally under the Ministry of Home Affairs. Even relatively benign seminars on constitutional law that are held in the capital Naypyidaw or in Yangon are attended by Special Branch officers, who make a note of attendees, and the organising institution. The Special Branch has also been involved in political trials, such as in 2017, when two journalists reporting on mass killings in Rakhine State were taken to the Aung Tha Pyay interrogation centre of the Special Branch. The Tatmadaw retains a significant share of the national budget, which in 2016, was 14 per cent.[22] The Tatmadaw has not given up its commercial interests, although its two major entities, Union of Myanmar Economic Holdings Ltd and Myanmar Economic Corporation have reportedly begun paying taxes.[23] The Tatmadaw still remains the most well-equipped force in the country, with an estimated combined force of 400,000 across the army, navy and air force.

The removal of the Tatmadaw from direct involvement in the legislature is not currently a proposal that is being entertained. Even if the Tatmadaw does agree to withdraw from the institutions of government and become subordinate to the executive at a later stage, second generation reforms, such as reducing the military's business interests, will likely prove to be particularly difficult. Aside from proposals for greater democratic reform, another core constitutional proposal has been the idea of federalism, considered in detail next.

B. Federalism and Ethnic Claims

There is debate over the meaning of federalism and whether the 2008 Constitution is federal or not. The 2008 Constitution does not use the language of federalism and, for many years, federalism was taboo. In a calculated move, some Tatmadaw officers claim that the 2008 Constitution is in fact a federal system.[24] This is contested by ethnic armed organisations. The broader debate is over whether the most appropriate

---

[22] Andrew Selth (2018) 'All Going According to Plan? The Armed Forces and Government in Myanmar' 40(1) *Contemporary Southeast Asia* p 10.

[23] Ibid p 11.

[24] Maung Aung Myoe (2018) 'Partnership in Politics: The Tatmadaw and the NLD in Politics in Myanmar in 2016', in Gerald McCarthy, Justine Chambers, Nicholas Farrelly and Chit Win (eds) *Myanmar Transformed? People, Places, Politics*. ISEAS, p 212.

system for Myanmar is a federal democratic Union, as ethnic armed organisations suggest, or a democratic federal Union, as the NLD suggest. Federalism remains paramount to both the peace process and constitutional reform. Proposals in favour of federalism include greater recognition of cultural claims such as language and education; redesigning the sub-national structure or at the least enhancing the legislative and executive powers of the States/Regions; reaching an agreement on the secession issue; granting greater control or at least a greater share of revenue of natural resources to States/Regions; and appeasing demands for State/Region constitutions. These demands for federalism were not part of the 2015 amendment bills.

A key example of federal demands for enhanced cultural rights is language recognition and education.[25] Burmese is the language recognised by the state. However, many languages and dialects are spoken across Myanmar. These languages span different linguistic families, with Burmese part of the Sino-Tibetan languages; Mon part of the Austro-Asiatic languages (which includes Khmer and Vietnamese), and Shan which is part of the Tai family of languages (like Thai and Laotian).[26] In the period of parliamentary democracy (1947–1962), proposals were put forward to allow English to be spoken in Parliament. This proposal was rejected by the majority who insisted on the use of Burmese, even though it was parliamentary representatives from ethnic minority groups who were often fluent in English (as well as their own languages), but who were not fluent in Burmese. After the 1962 coup, the regime began to explicitly crackdown on non-Burmese language education.[27] There have been proposals put forward in some State/Region Hluttaw regarding local languages. For example, in December 2017, Chin State Hluttaw considered a proposal to unify the Chin language. The Lai dialect is the main dialect in Chin State, although there are at least eight main dialects and even in the main towns of Falam and Hakha people speak different versions of this dialect. The Speaker of the Chin State Hluttaw (of the NLD) dismissed the proposal, citing a shortage of teachers.[28]

---

[25] Ashley South and Marie Lall, 'Language, Education and the Peace Process in Myanmar' (2016) 38(1) *Contemporary Southeast Asia* 128.

[26] David Bradley, 'Languages', in Ian Holliday et al (eds) *Routledge Handbook on Contemporary Myanmar* (London, Routledge, 2018).

[27] Mary P Callahan, 'Language Policy in Modern Burma', in Michael E Brown and Sumit Ganguly (eds) *Fighting Words; Language Policy and Ethnic Relations in Asia* (MIT Press, 2003).

[28] Salai Gei, 'Chin State Hluttaw passes proposal for a common Chin language' 6 December 2017, *Chin World*, www.bnionline.net/en/news/chin-state-hluttaw-passes-proposal-common-chin-language.

Proposals in favour of a federal Union range from minor to more radical and contested. Among the contested proposals is the 'Eight state solution'. This idea is advocated by ethnic groups that seek to realise the promise in the Panglong Agreement concerning an 'equal union' between Burmans and other ethnic groups. Proponents of this view argue that the current designation of 14 States and Regions gives disproportionate power to the Burmans through the seven Regions. They propose that the seven Regions are merged and governed as one Burman Region, but that the seven States be retained, and their powers of autonomy enhanced in comparison to the one Burman Region. The ethnic States would have the right to self-determination, including the right to secession. At its extreme, this proposal has often had a distinctly anti-democratic edge, with additional proposals to remove Burmans from ethnic areas, deny them citizenship in that state or redraw the boundaries of the state to exclude Burmans. This proposal has no traction among the Tatmadaw or the NLD.

In terms of milder proposals, there have been demands to change the names of some States and Regions; to readjust the borders of some States and Regions; to change the distribution of Ministers of National Races Affairs to reflect current census data; to expand the boundaries and powers of Self-Administered Areas or create new Areas (see Chapter 7). Some groups dispute the name of their State and seek to rename it. For example, the KNPP has placed emphasis on the term 'Karenni' State instead of the currently used 'Kayah' State. They claim that the military regime deliberately chose the term 'Kayah' in order to avoid agreeing with the KNPP's version of colonial history and its political aspirations for autonomy.[29] The Basic Principles of the Constitution do anticipate and allow for a State/Region to change its name. In order to change the name of a State/Region, the Chief Minister of that State/Region must make a recommendation to the president and then the president can decide whether to act.[30] This is a relatively low threshold if a president was sympathetic to the cause of an ethnic group that wished to change the name of their State/Region. Naming controversies are not uncommon in Myanmar, with the most controversial being the Tatmadaw's 1989 decision to rename the country from 'Burma' to 'Myanmar', as well as rename many towns and regions. Some ethnic

---

[29] Peacebuilding, 'Burma's Ethnic Problem over Two Names and the Path to Resolution', http://peacebuilding.asia/burmas-ethnic-problem-over-two-names-and-the-path-to-resolution/.

[30] 2008 Constitution, ss 9(c), 54.

activists dispute this change as the term 'Myanmar' is perceived to refer to one ethnic group (Burmans), while the term 'Burma' is associated with a multi-national state.[31] Even newspapers have been asked to change the spelling, such as the English language edition of the newspaper the 'Irrawaddy' to 'Ayeyarwaddy' (the paper refused).

Other groups have disputed the territorial boundaries of the States/ Regions. The president does have the power to initiate the redrawing of boundaries, and then the legislature and the constituencies directly concerned must vote on any proposed changes.[32] Any changes to the boundary of a State/Region require the consent of eligible voters in the affected area. One example of such demands is the New Mon State Party who argue that the borders of Mon State should be redrawn to include Bago, which was once the former Mon capital but is now located in Bago Region.[33] Some States/Regions have stretched or exceeded the boundaries of their powers conferred under the Constitution. For example, in December 2016, the Shan State Hluttaw declared the 'Northern Alliance' a terrorist organisation. The vote in the Hluttaw was supported by an alliance of Tatmadaw legislators and the USDP, although the Shan Nationalities League for Democracy disagreed.[34] The Northern Alliance is a coalition of four armies (KIA, AA, MNDAA, TNLA), none of which have signed the National Ceasefire Agreement (see Chapter 9). Although Myanmar does have an Anti-Terrorism Law,[35] the law does not empower State/Region Hluttaw to declare an organisation as a terrorism organisation. A motion by Shan State Hluttaw was passed after a failed attempt by a USDP member to propose a similar motion in the Pyithu Hluttaw at the national level. There has been no effort to challenge the constitutionality of this motion in the Constitutional Tribunal. This incident is also an example of the military-USDP influencing a State Hluttaw after having failed to have its way in the Union legislature.

One proposal that appears to have been accepted as part of the peace process is for States/Regions to have the opportunity to draft their own

---

[31] Lian Sakhong (2012) *The Dynamics of Sixty Years of Ethnic Armed Conflict in Burma*, Burma Centre for Ethnic Studies. Analysis Paper No 1 January 2012. file:///E:/BCES-AP-01-dynamics(en).pdf.

[32] 2008 Constitution, ss 50–54.

[33] See Ashley Smith, *Mon Nationalism and Civil War in Burma* (New York: Routledge, 2003).

[34] Lun Min Mang, 'Did Shan parliament exceed its constitutional boundaries?' 20 December 2016, *The Myanmar Times*, www.mmtimes.com/national-news/24295-did-shan-parliament-exceed-its-constitutional-boundaries.html.

[35] Anti-Terrorism Law No 23/2014.

constitutions.[36] The States/Regions currently do not have their own constitutions,[37] but this has been a key demand since the 1960s. This idea gained traction among ethnic elites in exile in the early 2000s, who drafted state constitutions at this time. If state constitutions are permitted in the future under the Constitution, there is very little that could be included given the high level of codification of the Constitution. A radical proposal that has traction among ethnic armed organisations is a constitutional right to bear arms as a way to avoid disarmament.

The primary suggestion to introduce federalism and ensure direct representation at the sub-national level is for the States/Regions to appoint their Chief Minister, rather than the Chief Minister being appointed by the President. This would have enhanced the independence of the States/Regions and reduced the tendency for the States/Regions to be seen as simply assisting the Union Government. This was proposed by the NLD in the 2013–2015 debates on constitutional amendment but failed. In 2019, a proposal to amend section 261 to allow for greater sub-national control over the appointment of the Chief Minister was suggested by the USDP in a bid to gain the support of ethnic minority groups.

There have been numerous constitutional proposals for reform of the Self-Administered Areas. There have been demands to expand the borders of the existing Areas to include more townships; demands to increase the powers of the Areas in relation to the Union and sub-national governments and demands for new Areas by groups that are not currently recognised.[38]

One of the reasons that federalism is such an important issue in Myanmar is because of the relative poverty of ethnic States, contrasted with the wealth of natural resources. Discussions on federalism find their origins in the 1940s and 1960s. When General Aung San was deliberating with ethnic groups at Panglong in 1947, he reportedly said that 'If Burma receives one kyat, you will get one kyat' (see Chapter 2). This was a reference to the perceived economic dominance of the Burmans and was understood by ethnic groups as a promise that regional ethnic

---

[36] Chao Tzang Yawnghwe and Lian H Sakhong (eds) *Federalism, State Constitutions and Self-Determination in Burma* (Chiang Mai, UNLD Press, 2003).

[37] David C Williams, 'Changing Burma From Without' (2012) 19(1) *Indiana Journal of Global Legal Studies* 121; 'Constitutionalism Before Constitutions: Burma's Struggle to Build a New Order' (2008) 87 *Texas Law Review* 1657.

[38] Sai Wansai, 'Wa angered by government's statement on its NCA stance', *Panglong*, 20 March 2018, http://english.panglong.org/2018/03/20/wa-angered-by-governments-statement-on-its-nca-stance/.

areas would receive a significant share of fiscal resources. Myanmar's natural resources are significant, and include natural gas, oil and gem stones. Myanmar is a major exporter of natural gas in the Asian market, its exports comprising up to 50 per cent of exports in the region.[39] Myanmar provides 10 per cent of the global supply of metal and meets a third of China's demand.[40] Tin production has increased exponentially in recent years.[41] The tin reserves are found in the Wa region, controlled by the UWSA, although there is uncertainty over the sustainability of this source. Myanmar has gained a global reputation for its wealth of gemstones, ranging from high-quality rubies, sapphires and particularly jade.[42] An estimated 90 per cent of the global market for rubies originates from Myanmar.[43] In 2015, Global Witness found that the jade industry is worth up to US$31 billion, ranking higher than oil and gas. The jade industry is one indication of the enormous resources available, yet there are challenges to ensure that profits go through official markets and that wealth is distributed across Myanmar for the benefit of all people. Further, at the turn of the twentieth century, Myanmar was known as the rice bowl of Asia, a reference to its booming rice industry. While there are strong prospects for rice production and export in the future, there remain significant challenges in terms of poor quality and productivity.[44] Finally, Myanmar also has an abundance of water, and 18.2 million ha of arable land,[45] which has a ready market due to the water and resource demands of India and China's growing populations.

There is as yet no clear proposal as to how natural resources are to be managed or the benefits distributed in a federal Myanmar. To genuinely address this issue, any effort to address this sector through constitutional means would need to tackle the vested interests of the Tatmadaw, cronies and ethnic warlords.

---

[39] World Bank Group, 'Myanmar Economic Monitor' (Washington, World Bank, 2016), p 126.

[40] Michael Peel and Henry Sanderson, 'Mystery Myanmar mines shake up world tin market' *The Financial Times*, 29 August 2016 www.ft.com/content/808c277a-6b53-11e6-a0b1-d87a9fea034f?mhq5j=e7.

[41] ITRI, 'Report on Global Tin Resources & Reserves' (London, 2016), p 12.

[42] Emma Irwin, 'Gemstone Sector Review' (Extractive Industries Transparency Initiative, July 2016) p 14.

[43] Andrew Bauer et al, *Sharing the Wealth: Distributing Myanmar's Natural Resource Revenues* (Natural Resource Governance Institute, 2016).

[44] World Bank, 'Myanmar: Capitalising on Rice Export Opportunities' (World Bank, 2014) p xv.

[45] ADB, *Myanmar: Agriculture, Natural Resources and Environment Initial Sector Assessment Strategy,* (Manila, Asian Development Bank, 2013).

C. Limiting Executive and Judicial Power

The relationship between the Tatmadaw and the USDP remains important to the future of constitutional reform. In 2014, Shwe Mann supported a proposal to change the Constitution so that the positions of president, vice-presidents and ministers are drawn only from elected members (rather than unelected members). This was an effort to reposition the USDP as controlling the Tatmadaw, rather than the Tatmadaw controlling the USDP. The effect of this would have been to require any senior Tatmadaw officer who aspired to be elected to these positions to resign from the Tatmadaw and join the USDP led by Shwe Mann. One reason this was not successful is because the Commander-in-Chief himself has presidential ambitions, and yet would prefer to be elected by the presidential electoral college without having run in a general election for a seat in the legislature. The proposal failed though it is one indication of how tensions between the military and USDP affect the possibilities for constitutional change.

There is broader agreement that the formal separation between the executive and the legislature and political parties is unworkable, although the Tatmadaw remain committed to this idea. In 2015, the amendment Bill proposed that ministers should not be required to resign from the legislature and can remain as an active member of a political party. They also proposed that only Hluttaw members (and not unelected members) can be appointed as Ministers. This would have brought the executive and legislative branch closer together, removed the prohibition on the president, vice-president and ministers being active in their political party, and introduced a more representative appointment process for Ministers. The NLD also supported this motion, although the proposal failed to obtain sufficient support in the legislature.

The NLD have suggested a range of proposals that would add further limits on executive power. They suggest that the term of office of the president and vice-presidents should be limited to one term. Rather than leave many decisions in the sole power of the president, the NLD suggested balancing many decisions by requiring the president to make decisions together with the Speakers of the Amyotha Hluttaw and Pyithu Hluttaw. They also seek to change the balance of power in the National Defence and Security Council by adding the Deputy Speakers of the Amyotha Hluttaw and Pyithu Hluttaw as members, which would mean that the government of the day, rather than the Tatmadaw, would have a majority on the Defence Council. The NLD seek to change the balance of power and reporting lines slightly at the sub-national level. Instead of the Ministers of State/Region Hluttaw being responsible to the president, they suggested that the Ministers be responsible to the Chief Minister. None of these suggestions were adopted, but it shows a concern to limit executive power, at least while the NLD was still in opposition.

The constitutional amendment process has featured minor debates on aspects of the Constitutional Tribunal's powers but has also included proposals that would reduce the independence of the judiciary. In terms of appointments, the NLD proposed to change the centralised judicial appointment processes of High Court judges so that the Chief Justice of the Supreme Court, together with Chief Ministers of the States/Regions, made these appointed instead of the president alone. The NLD also proposed that the Supreme Court be the highest court and by implication the courts martial must be subordinate to it. Following on from this, the NLD proposed to abolish the Constitutional Tribunal and give these powers to the Supreme Court. The full proposal of the NLD was not adopted in the 2015 constitutional amendment Bill, although some partial changes were suggested. It was proposed that the Speakers of the Pyithu Hluttaw and Amyotha Hluttaw, along with the president, would appoint the Deputy Chief Justice, and that the Pyidaungsu Hluttaw would vote on which judge would be Chief Justice via the same appointment methods as for the president. None of these proposals received enough support.

Proposals for constitutional amendment also addressed the issue of who can appoint judges to the Supreme Court and on what criteria. The proposal included amending sections 300 and 301 of the Constitution to allow either the Speaker of the Pyithu Hluttaw or the Amyotha Hluttaw to appoint Supreme Court judges, including appointment on the ground of 'eminent jurist'. This was part of a broader package of reforms to balance and dilute the power of the president with that of the legislature. Proposed amendments to section 302 would have given the Speakers of the legislature a role to play in the impeachment of the Chief Justice, rather than leaving it to the executive. Finally, there was also a proposal to tie the term of the Supreme Court and High Court judges to the term of the government, that is, to restrict them to serving five-year terms.[46] This would have meant a large portion of the leadership of the judiciary being tied to the term of the government of the day.

---

[46] 2008 Constitution, ss 303, 312.

The 2015 Bills sought to retain the Constitutional Tribunal but made some minor proposals. It was proposed that the appointment of the chairperson be by agreement among the Speaker of the Pyithu Hluttaw, the Amyotha Hluttaw and the president, rather than the president alone.[47] While decisions of the Tribunal would still be regarded as final and conclusive, there was a proposed insertion to allow revision or appeal cases to be heard by the Tribunal on matters of national importance.[48] Like the appointments to the Supreme Court, it was also proposed that appointments to the Constitutional Tribunal be by agreement between the president, Speaker of the Pyithu Hluttaw and Amyotha Hluttaw. In 2015, the military clearly opposed any changes to the judiciary and the related constitutional provisions.[49] The Tatmadaw argued that the changes would simply substitute executive control with legislative control of the judiciary. Some USDP members argued against the Tatmadaw and in favour of these proposals. Overall, the proposals for constitutional amendment in 2015 demonstrate that leaving the process of constitutional amendment to the legislature will see the process influenced primarily by its own interests and those of the Tatmadaw. In this instance, several years of confrontation with the executive led the legislature to suggest proposals to the Constitution that would enhance its powers and dilute the power of the president, particularly in relation to appointments and impeachments.

VI. CONCLUSION

A much wider range of demands and proposed options for constitutional reform continue to be discussed and debated. The NLD Government formed a committee for constitutional amendment in early 2019, although this was strongly opposed by the military. Debates on constitutional amendment will continue in the future. There are several key constitutional issues raised by the status of the National Ceasefire Agreement, the process of peace negotiations and the possibility of amendment. The main difference with the peace process since 2016 has been the shift from the President's Office to the State Counsellor's Office. This is a key

---

[47] Ibid, s 321.
[48] Ibid, s 324.
[49] Htoo Thant, 'Military MPs oppose changes to judicial provisions in Constitution', *The Myanmar Times*, 3 July 2015, www.mmtimes.com/national-news/15328-military-mps-oppose-changes-to-judicial-provisions-in-constitution.html.

indication of where power in the civilian government lies under the NLD. The main contribution of the peace process to date is that it has helped to normalise or at least destigmatise discussions of federalism, and for the first time propose concrete steps on disarmament.

The Ceasefire Agreement contains commitments to federalism, democracy and self-determination which are distinct from the text of the Constitution. The precise relationship between the Ceasefire Agreement and the Constitution is unclear, and this could be a source of dispute in the future. The Ceasefire Agreement does anticipate ratification by the Pyidaungsu Hluttaw at some point, which may then lead to a process of constitutional amendment. It does not anticipate a role for the Constitutional Tribunal. The agreement on the 37 Principles at the Second Panglong Conference is less important that the principles that were the subject of disagreement and shows there are still differing approaches to the issue of secession.

Control over the formal amendment procedure is a formidable structural advantage that the Tatmadaw has under the Constitution. The restrictive Burmese interpretation of 'amend' has limited the proposals for reform of the Constitution. The combination of formal and informal advantages that the Tatmadaw enjoys is the main reason for the difficulty of achieving future constitutional reform. Even if the threshold rule is lowered, there would not necessarily be radical change to the Constitution. Proposals for constitutional reform broadly suggest discontent with the military-state, particularly the idea of disciplined democracy and the Union (rather than a federal system). The principle of coercive centralism – including the powers of the president and Union Government over the State/Region governments – has also been challenged. Debates on constitutional reform, and efforts to introduce constitutional amendments, are likely to continue for many years to come.

FURTHER READING

Mary P Callahan, 'Language Policy in Modern Burma', in Michael E Brown and Sumit Ganguly (eds) *Fighting Words; Language Policy and Ethnic Relations in Asia* (MIT Press, 2003).

Ardeth Maung Thawnghmung, 'Signs of Life in Myanmar's Nationwide Ceasefire Agreement?' (2017) 49:3 *Critical Asian Studies* 379.

David Williams, 'Asymmetrical Federalism in Burma', in Susan Williams (eds) *Social Difference and Constitutionalism in Pan-Asia* (CUP, 2014).

Chao Tzang Yawnghwe and Lian H Sakhong (eds) *Federalism, State Constitutions and Self-Determination in Burma* (Chiang Mai, UNLD Press, 2003).

11

Conclusion

The Military-state – Ideological Commitments – Coercive Centralism –
Disciplined Democracy – The Union

MYANMAR'S TRANSITION FROM direct military rule is not only
a story of personalities and powerholders. It is also a story
of principles and legal structures. This does not mean the
Constitution is followed, enforced or is relevant all the time. My aim
in this book has been to identify where and how constitutional principles are at work. Myanmar's political system operates with reference
to the framework of the 2008 Constitution. This is the form in which
the country has returned to constitutional rule. This legal system is
disproportionately influenced by one institution more than any other,
the Tatmadaw. Through the Constitution, the Tatmadaw lays claim to
political authority.

Central to my concerns in this book has been to explain how people
in Myanmar understand, use, interpret or ignore the 2008 Constitution.
Much of constitutional discourse and practice comes back to key debates
over federalism, democracy and constitutional change. Questions are
constantly raised about whether the Constitution is federal, the extent to
which it is democratic, and whether it can be changed. Broadly speaking,
many people in Myanmar see the Constitution neither as truly federal
nor as fully democratic, and most acknowledge the almost impossibil-
ity of formal constitutional change. Even if the threshold for the formal
constitutional amendment provision is lowered, the Constitution has
an implicit basic structure that will remain difficult to change without
political willingness from the Tatmadaw.

The Constitution was an ambitious project of the former military
regime and is part of the monumental resurrection of constitutional life
in Myanmar. Within this constitutional arrangement, the Tatmadaw
exists as a check on democratic power and as a regulator of democracy.
In this concluding chapter I reiterate the centrality of the Constitution to

the formation and maintenance of the military-state, and then consider the implications for comparative constitutional law inquiry.

I. THE CENTRALITY OF THE CONSTITUTION TO THE MILITARY-STATE

In this book I have identified the foundations of the military-state as articulated in sections 6–8 of the Constitution. The Constitution is central to how we understand Myanmar's military-state, how power is divided and where ultimate control lies. I have built this concept of the military-state from three key elements of the Constitution: the political leadership of the military, its ideological commitments to military slogans, and an organisational arrangement based on coercive centralism. This amounts to an informal 'basic structure' of the Constitution.

A. The Endorsement of the Military's Leading Role in Governance

The first element of the military-state is the leading role of the Tatmadaw in governance. The Constitution is painstaking in its level of detail about the legal and political governance of the country, which includes institutional autonomy for the Tatmadaw. The Constitution ensures that civilian rule operates within a framework devised by and under the watch of the Tatmadaw. In its formal role, the military is the fourth branch of government. In its informal role, the military retains an omnipresent influence across all branches of government. The status of the Tatmadaw compounds the difficulty of analysing civilian-military relations. The militarisation of governance has involved the direct and indirect influence of Tatmadaw personnel, institutions, and practices of legality on civilian governance. The militarisation of governance means the control and influence of the Tatmadaw over matters that are usually considered to be under civilian control. There is no easy or clear divide between civilian and military interests in Myanmar's military-state. The militarisation of governance is one of the biggest issues for the future of Myanmar.

Militarisation has occurred explicitly through constitutional structures that give the Tatmadaw an entrenched advantage. Examples include the Tatmadaw legislators who function as watchmen, surveying the civilian political system; appointments of minsters to key ministries; and the military's veto power over constitutional amendment. The debate over the constitutional amendment rule has focused on the rigidity of this rule and so has misconstrued the real issue. Even if the amendment threshold were lowered, this would not necessarily result in amendment of the most controversial provisions of the Constitution. This is because the indirect influence of the Tatmadaw is powerful and pervasive, and it has not yet indicated that it would be willing to agree on changes that compromise the informal basic structure of the Constitution.

This process of militarisation has occurred by stealth in terms of informal and indirect influences in the executive, legislature and judiciary. The Tatmadaw's indirect forms of influence include the Union Solidarity Development Party and its members who are mostly (though not always) perceived to be Tatmadaw loyalists, exchanging their Tatmadaw uniforms for the civilian longyi. In recent years, Tatmadaw transfers into the administration have been a regular occurrence particularly at the highest levels, such as the Supreme Court, permanent secretaries and director generals, but also at the bottom, from officers in the Ministry of Health to staff of the Constitutional Tribunal. The indirect influence of the Tatmadaw is facilitated by geography and territorial design. The Tatmadaw has an extensive network of outposts throughout the country that is stronger than the reach of the government administration in some areas. It is possible that the indirect influence of the Tatmadaw may change or weaken over time. For example, the loyalties of former Tatmadaw personnel to the Tatmadaw are not fixed, and divisions within the USDP demonstrate that these loyalties can shift. USDP members have shown that they do not necessarily side with the Tatmadaw. For now, there remains little by way of public challenge to the Tatmadaw's leading role in the military-state.

B. The Ideological Commitments of the Constitution

The Constitution is used as a form of ideological endorsement of the military-state. There is myriad of ways in which the Tatmadaw insists on faithfulness to the Constitution and to these three principles, which are a precondition though not a guarantee for qualified democracy and rights. Also known as 'Our Three Main National Causes', the three meta principles of the military-state are the leitmotif of the Constitution. This is the essence of the militarisation of governance in Myanmar. Non-disintegration, or territorial integrity, invokes the need to protect against secessionist demands. National solidarity creates a peculiar conception of the people, one which is based on a constructed ideal of ethnicity and that excludes certain others. National sovereignty is about the power and unity of the country as a nation, rather than a reference to sovereignty residing in the people. In its short form – territorial integrity, national sovereignty, national unity – these principles may suggest comparative analogy with the sentiments of other governments around the world. I have emphasised that these principles are not benign statements of a conservative liberal government, but rather have had a long affiliation with the Tatmadaw and with the history of unconstitutional rule in Myanmar. They fit with my revisionist periodisation of constitutional history. These principles emerged in the 1990s as an ideological tool of the Tatmadaw to maintain control of the country during direct military rule and were reinforced publicly and by force. Maintaining and strengthening these principles lies at the core of Myanmar's military-state. These limits on democracy, its very nature as 'disciplined', is designed to subordinate and subdue the people and their demands to the Tatmadaw.

Throughout the book I have explored ways in which people and institutions have reinforced, or contested, the three meta-principles of the military-state. For example, in 2015, the principle of non-disintegration was clearly articulated and reinforced by the government's reservation to the principle of self-determination in the ICESCR (Chapter 9). Ongoing conflicts throughout the country, but particularly in Shan State, Kachin State, Rakhine State and Chin State, are testimony to the unresolved claims of ethnic groups. Demands for a right to secession clause in the Constitution linger. The concept of national solidarity has been reinforced by Ministers of National Races Affairs who have sought to realise the constitutional promises of cultural and traditional rights (Chapter 7). The ethno-nationalism and exclusivism inherent in the concept of national races and national solidarity has been hardened with the removal of the right to vote for white card holders through the concerted actions of the legislature and the Tribunal (Chapter 4). The three meta-principles are being contested in limited ways, such as the dispute over the classification of national races and demands for re-categorisation.

C. The Organisation of the State: Coercive Centralism

The third idea that animates the informal basic structure of the Constitution is coercive centralism. Coercive centralism describes the relationship both between and within the branches of government, and between Union level branches and State/Region level branches. Power is concentrated at the Union level. Coercive centralism is more than just collaboration or cooperation among the branches and levels of government and carries negative connotations. The system is designed to reduce and disincentivise competition or contestation among the branches of government – judiciary, executive, legislature, Tatmadaw – and between the Union Government and sub-national authorities (State/Region, Self-Administered Areas and Union Territories). The Tatmadaw is the fourth branch of this system of coercive centralism. By controlling the terms of 'national politics', the Tatmadaw lies at the centre of the Union. Coercive centralism requires compliance with the military apparatus and its informal influence across a range of institutions

The qualification of democracy as 'disciplined' is a part of coercive centralism and the efforts to prevent indulgence in the perceived excesses of democracy. The electoral system neutralises political ambition where it would rival Tatmadaw pre-eminence. The military remains as the final check and balance over the political system. Disciplined democracy has been challenged but gone unmoved. The Tatmadaw has co-opted the ideals of democracy for its own cause, claiming to institute 'genuine' democracy while at the same time insisting on democracy's disciplined nature.

Those in positions of state power in Myanmar act in ways that are consistent with the demands of their superiors to whom they remain accountable. In a range of appointment processes, the Union executive has significant authority while the legislature has a token role of approving a chosen candidate, without powers to reject a nominee. The legislature has a minimal role in judicial appointments, with a 'no right to refuse' rule limiting its role to checking that the proposed candidate meets the relevant criteria, and only being able to refuse the candidate if they do not meet the criteria. It is common for high level officials to exercise their 'right to resign', as in the case of the Constitutional Tribunal members, rather than lose face in formal impeachment proceedings. Coercive centralism is also evident in the informal lines of accountability and sense of deference, loyalty and respect show by former Tatmadaw officers within the civilian system to retired or active officers in the Tatmadaw.

The use of the term 'Union' was a deliberate choice by constitution-makers who sought to exclude and deny federalist demands. However, the Union has been challenged in a more fundamental way by demands for federalism as embodied in the peace process. The National Cease-fire Agreement 2015 is a document that departs from the system of coercive centralism. Yet the 37 Principles that followed have retreated from the position set out in the National Ceasefire Agreement, and it appears that if any shift from 'Union' to 'federal' is to take place, it may be one of semantics in the same way that the 'genuine democracy' of the 2008 Constitution is in fact also 'disciplined'.

The constitution-drafters created a range of loopholes designed only for use by the Tatmadaw or USDP. This has led to risks for the NLD as it seeks to use these loopholes to enhance its power to govern, such as the conferral of executive power on the Office of the State Counsellor. The Pyidaungsu Hluttaw, the two houses sitting jointly, dominates and presides over the Amyotha Hluttaw and Pyithu Hluttaw. The frequent joint sittings of the two houses distinguishes Myanmar from other bicameral legislatures, where joint sittings are rarely held and only on extraordinary issues. The Pyidaungsu Hluttaw is the peak legislative forum for collective decisions. It presents a united front and show of force to outside institutions such as the Constitutional Tribunal and the Presidents' Office. The legislature is best understood as a tricameral system, with the Pyidaungsu Hluttaw operating as the dominant legislative body. It is a symmetrical tricameral system because all three houses are at stake in elections every five years. The State/Region Hluttaw are subordinate to the Union executive and legislature.

The legislature acts as a check on the executive, and on the judiciary. This latter role reverses the standard assumptions of the separation of powers because the judiciary cannot act as a check on the power of the administration or the legislature. Rather than the legislature simply acting as a check in relation to judicial appointment and removal procedures, the legislature's actions often border on interference with the day-to-day function of the courts. The role of the legislature as a check on the courts is seen as a normative good. The courts are subordinate and accountable to the legislature. The legislature treats the courts like another administrative department and in fact the Supreme Court is a Union Level Organisation. The court is the part of government that is most subject to the daily influence of the police and the General Administration Department, and by implication the Ministry of Home Affairs and the Tatmadaw. The courts are a subordinate ally of the military-state. This indirect influence amounts to Tatmadaw capture of judicial institutions. The structural rules enable the executive and legislature to exercise authority over the courts. This leaves little room for interpretation of the law and constitutes a challenge for future reform. The courts do not have interpretive authority. Courts do not yet play a role in sustaining constitutional democracy. Constitutional provisions are not self-executing but generally require execution by the legislature in the form of an enabling law. Rather than being an evolving text that requires interpretation by the courts, constitutional provisions remain dependent on the legislature to give them meaning.

In the Union, there is little need for an authoritative body to determine the meaning of the Constitution, as the system presumes there will be no major disagreement. The meaning of the Constitution has primarily been determined by the Hluttaw. This is not to dismiss the role and function of the Constitutional Tribunal, whose decisions I have discussed throughout this book. The Tribunal's decisions should be approached with caution because it may not be considered binding and authoritative for other state institutions. The legislature has been quite open in its refusal to follow Constitutional Tribunal decisions at times.

Finally, the emphasis in the legal and political system is on collaboration between the branches of government, rather than checks and balances. The Tatmadaw is the main check and balance on the other branches of government. The legislature also plays an oversight role of the executive and the courts. These checks and balances invert common assumptions about the role of courts in a democratic system. There is significant overlap between 'institutions' and 'powers' with some institutions exercising multiple types of power, such as executive institutions exercising judicial power, judicial institutions exercising legislative power, and the Tatmadaw exercising executive, legislative and judicial power. There is also overlap in implementation, with the General Administration Department (both a Union and State/Region body) having responsibility for implementing most State/Region legislation. In this way, the principle of coercive centralism is a principle of *anti*-separation of powers.

II. IMPLICATIONS FOR COMPARATIVE CONSTITUTIONAL INQUIRY

In this book I have prioritised key issues in local constitutional debates in Myanmar: can the Constitution be changed and, if so, how given that the Tatmadaw retains veto power? Does the decentralisation of power under the Constitution go far enough, and if not, what kind of federalism is the answer to ethnic grievances to ensure future peace? How democratic is the Constitution and what should the role of the Tatmadaw be in the future of Myanmar? How is power divided in Myanmar and which branches act as a check on power? How can a Constitution governing a territory that is rich in natural resources ensure the fair and equitable distribution of resources for the benefit of the people? To what extent will constitutional reform feature in the peace process, and can the National Ceasefire Agreement itself be amended? These questions are just some of the complex constitutional debates that are relevant to comparative constitutional inquiry.

The case of Myanmar requires a deeper appreciation of the military and its complex role in governance. We need to study the processes by which a state becomes militarised and the extent to which law and the constitution may be a key part of this. The case of Myanmar offers a prime example of the consequences when a constitution is structured around the military. How does the militarisation of the Constitution occur? Through what processes? What key historical events, conditions and decisions set in motion and facilitate military involvement in politics? The Constitution has not broken with the military past but rather builds on it. The militarisation of governance is an important aspect of the nature of constitutional law in Myanmar, and a significant impediment to any future prospects for transitional justice.

Another implication of this book is the importance of the choice of comparison in comparative constitutional law. This book has captured the renaissance of constitutional law in Myanmar. I have gone beyond common concepts in comparative constitutional law, partly because the Constitution in Myanmar stretches conventional understandings of constitutional law. This requires us to reflect on whether these concepts are conventional or not. Globalised concepts in constitutional law are inevitably challenged as we expand our geography of comparative constitutionalism. For example, the concept of the military-state offers a means of understanding authoritarian rule in Myanmar as sanctioned by the constitution. There are three key influences that can be discerned from Myanmar's past: colonial legality, socialist legality and military legality. For example, Myanmar's affinities with socialist legality and communist regimes suggest that the state and its constitution in Myanmar may have more in common with present-day China, Laos, Vietnam, Cuba and North Korea, or the former socialist regimes of eastern and central Europe. More specifically, discussions of federalism in Myanmar may have more in common with conceptions of federalism in the former Yugoslavia, the Soviet Union and Czechoslovakia, or the territorialised administrative divisions for certain ethnic groups in the present-day communist regime of China, than it does with the liberal federal states of Germany, the US or Canada.

An additional area for comparative constitutional inquiry is the way in which the periodisation of constitutional law affects how we understand the meaning of the Constitution. Many of the core principles, as well as ideas about key structures and institutions of governance, emerged in the early 1990s, over 25 years ago. The implications of this new periodisation of constitutional law in Myanmar requires further consideration and rethinking conventional periodisations of constitutional law in other contexts could open new lines of inquiry. Time will of course remain important to the development and consolidation, or disruption and replacement, of the 2008 Constitution.

Finally, our understanding of the codification of constitutional law requires further exploration. To what extent do Constitutions exhibit features of codification? What are the implications of constitutional law by codification? Myanmar's Constitution is one example of the codification of constitutional law and this is likely to have implications for the extent of continuity and change in the constitutional system. Many more questions remain to be explored, but I offer this book as a foundation and starting point for future discussion and debate.

Glossary

Amyotha Hluttaw	Upper House/House of Nationalities
Pyithu Hluttaw	Lower House/House of Representatives
Pyidaungsu Hluttaw	Union legislature, both houses sitting jointly
Region	This is one of seven sub-national units in Myanmar. Prior to 2011 these units were known as 'divisions'
State	This is one of seven sub-national units in Myanmar that are based on the dominant ethnic minority group in that area
Tatmadaw	Defence Services

Index

Please note that specific constitutions are filed under the appropriate year

www.ingramcontent.com/pod-product-compliance
Ingram Content Group UK Ltd.
Pitfield, Milton Keynes, MK11 3LW, UK
UKHW031249020325
455689UK00008B/149